AMAZING
Cartier

Nadine Coleno
Translated by Deke Dusinberre

AMAZING
Cartier
Jewelry Design since 1937

Flammarion

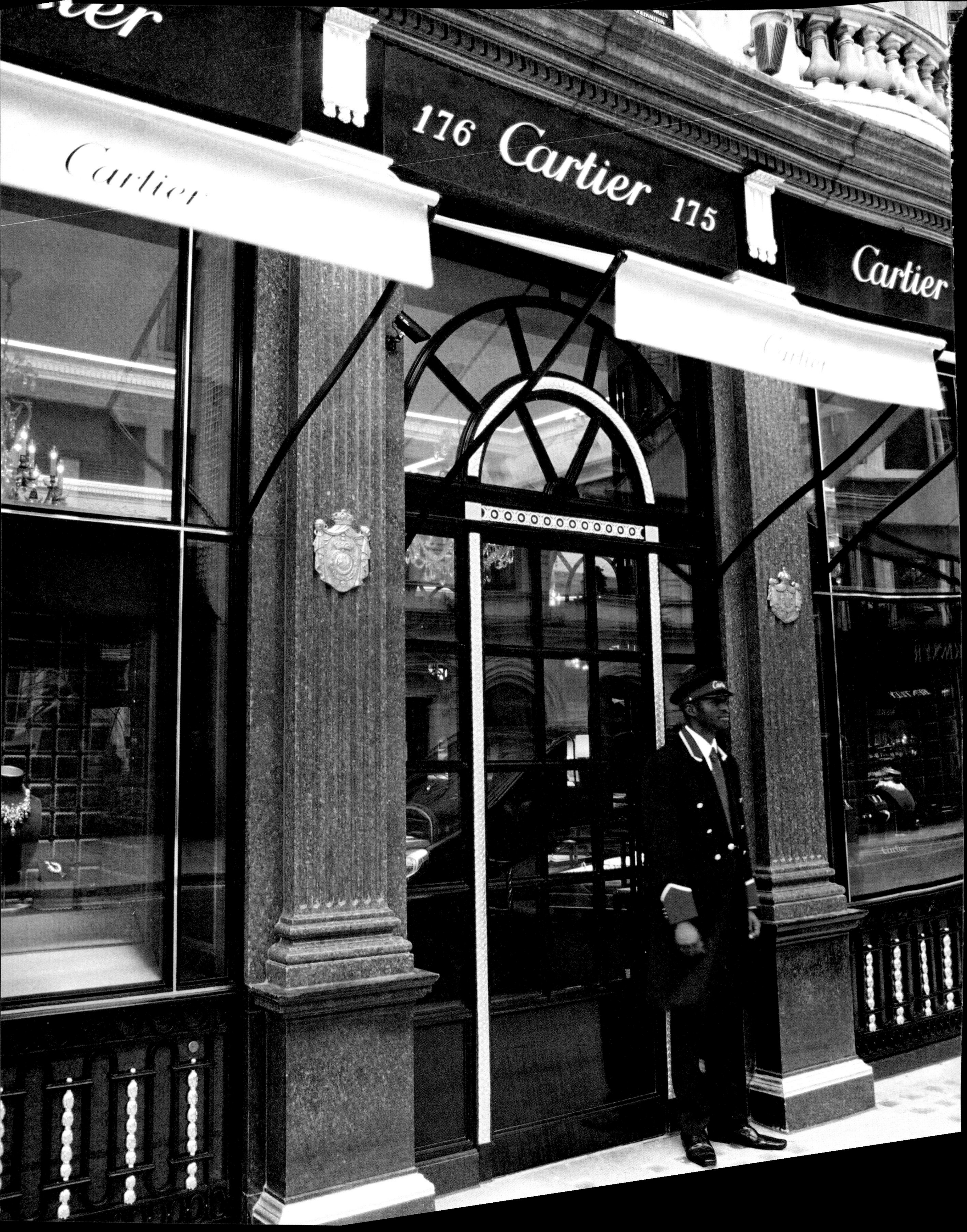
176 Cartier 175
Cartier
Cartier

CONTENTS

HISTORY
7

FIGURATIVE JEWELRY
22

ABSTRACT JEWELRY
128

COLOR
194

Bibliography
Photographic Credits
Acknowledgments
250

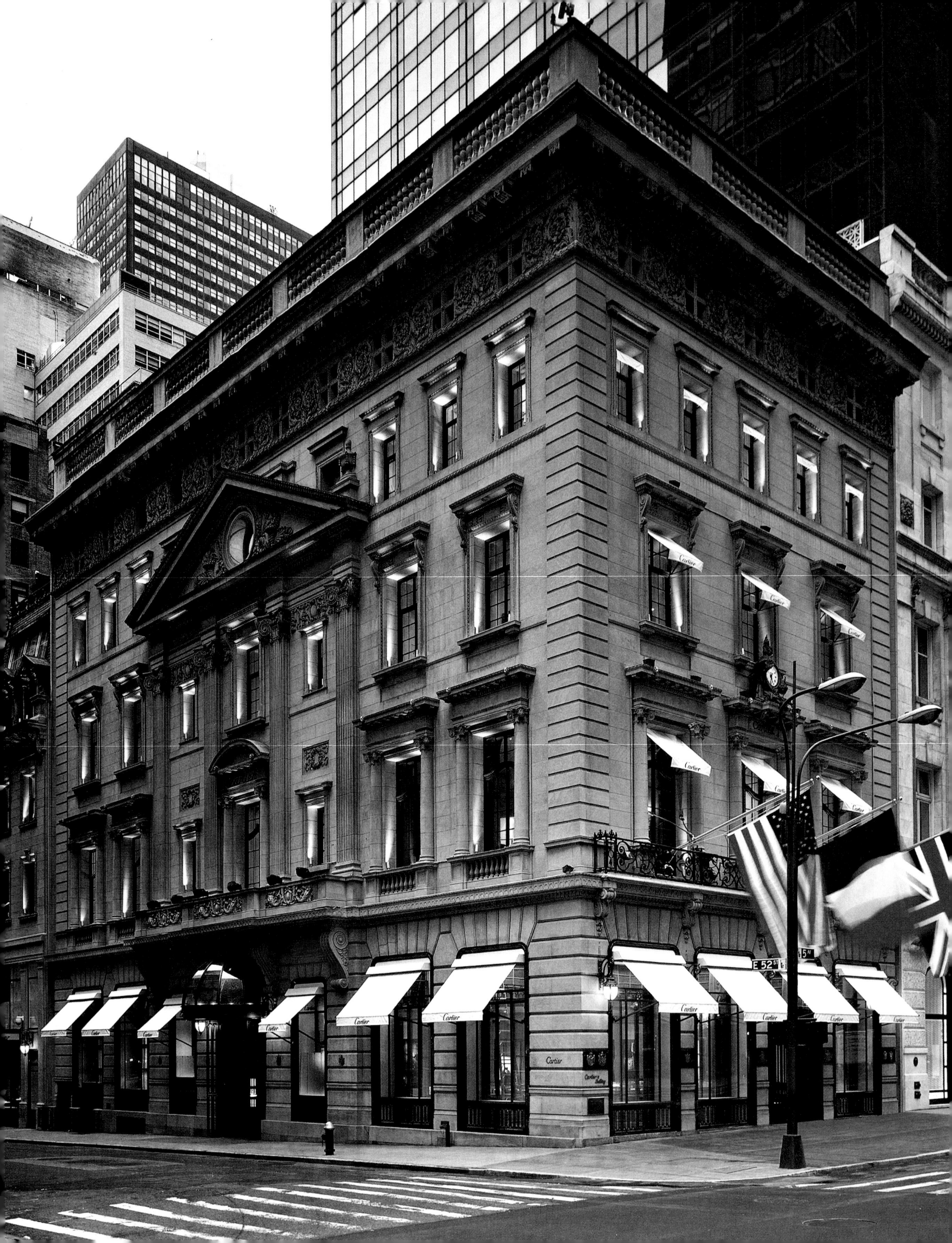
Cartier

HISTORY

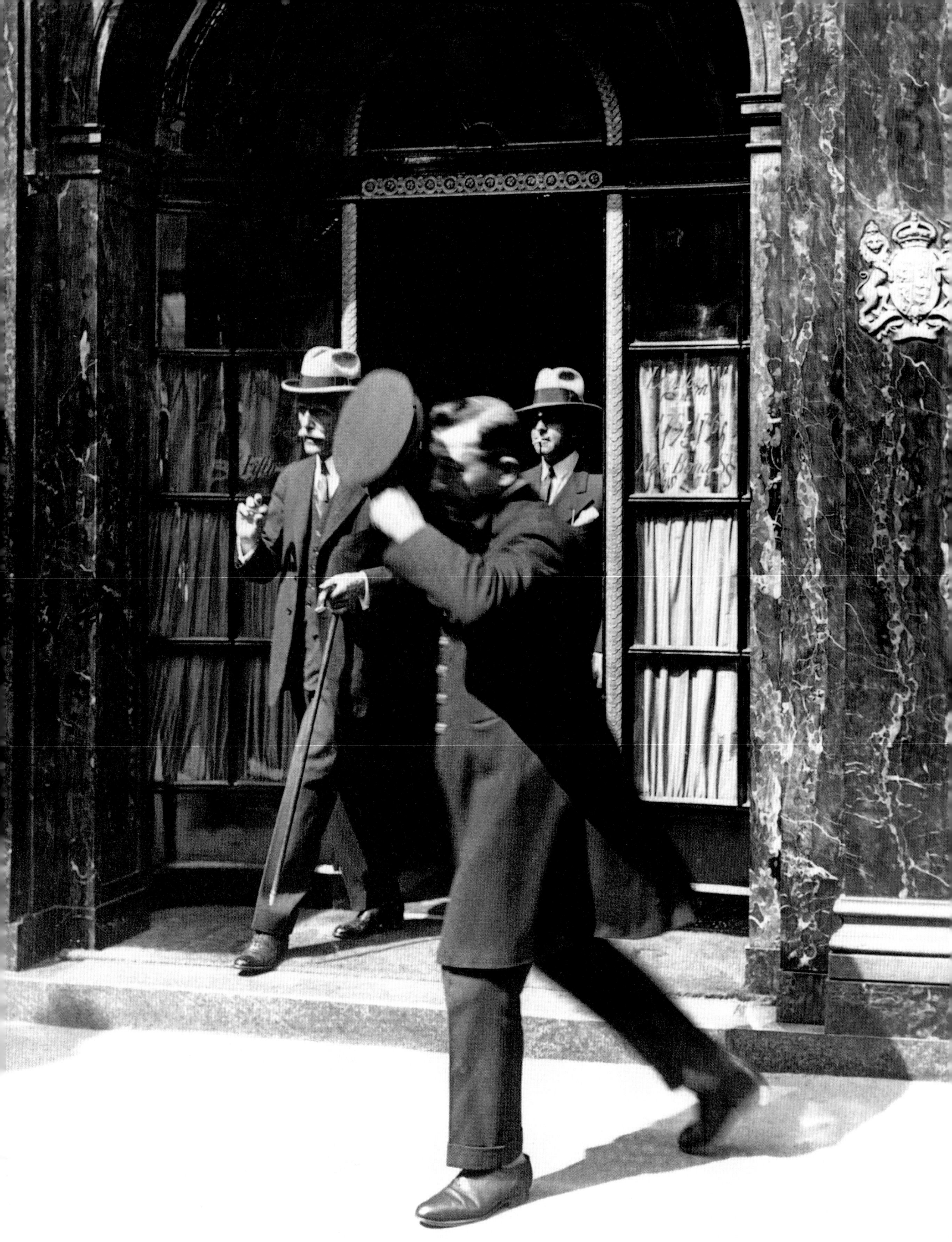

THE HOUSE OF CARTIER

A FAMILY, A HERITAGE

The lifetime of an artist is made up of periods of inspiration, pause, and feverish discovery; the history of a house such as Cartier follows a similar trajectory. Cartier is an entity composed of multiple talents, some of whom forged a house style and, when it came to excellence, turned the name of a dynasty of jewelers into a universal gold standard.

Louis-François Cartier launched this saga in 1847. Son of Pierre Cartier, a maker of powder horns, and grandson of Louis-François Cartier, a metal turner who worked for the royal household, he took over the Paris jewelry workshop of his employer, Adolphe Picard, when the latter moved from rue Montorgueil to rue de Richelieu. Picard helped the young man to strike out for himself six years later. Cartier opted for premises on rue Neuve-des-Petits-Champs, near the palatial residence of the Orléans family, and he was soon noticed by Princess Mathilde (niece of Napoleon I) and then by Empress Eugénie. When the empress ordered a silver tea service from Cartier in 1859, his ambitions were transformed from dreams into reality.

New premises on boulevard des Italiens reflected the migration of Parisian high society, which was steadily leaving the Palais-Royal quarter to be nearer to the grand cafés such as La Maison Dorée, Café Tortoni, and Café Riche, where the likes of Flaubert, Balzac, Dumas, and even the Prince of Wales might be seen. "Boulevard des Italiens! That's the center of the world."[1] Meanwhile, Louis-François Alfred Cartier was born in 1841, and when he reached the age of thirty-one his father made him a partner. And still another generation was soon coming into the world, one that would guide the firm toward its glorious future: Louis-Joseph (called Louis) was born in 1875, Pierre-Camille (Pierre) in 1878, and Jacques-Théodule (Jacques) six years later, followed by the only girl, Suzanne. The family's lifestyle already gave them daily access to the culture and refinement that was reflected in their trade, and their social rise could be measured by their cosmopolitan clientele of aristocrats and financiers, the fortunes of the latter being every bit as handsome as the those of the former.

As the nineteenth century drew to a close, another move became imperative. In 1899, rue de la Paix embodied French-style chic, and would remain a universal symbol of elegance for many decades to come. Mellerio, Vever,

Facing page: Doorman greeting clients at the boutique at 13 rue de la Paix, Paris.

Page 2: Cartier Boutique, 13 rue de la Paix, Paris.

Page 4: Cartier Boutique, 175–176 New Bond Street, London.

Page 6: Cartier Boutique, 653 Fifth Avenue, New York.

1. Louis Ernault, 1856, quoted in Gérard-Georges Lemaire, *Les Cafés littéraires* (Paris: Éditions de la Différence, 1997).

Queen Mary of England.
Easter egg for Czar
Nicholas II.
Louis Cartier (1875–1942).
Grand Duchess Maria
Pavlovna at the Boyards'
Ball, 1903.
Jacques Cartier (1884–1941).
Corsage ornament, 1906.

Aucoc, Jacta, and Fontana all opened shops on rue de la Paix, while firms such as Boucheron and Lalique had to content themselves with the square at the end, namely Place Vendôme—where, with perfect timing, César Ritz had just opened his famous hotel in 1898. Everyone who had anything to do with fashion wanted to be there, from perfumers to fashion designers via glovemakers, shoemakers, and hatters. Cartier thus moved into number 13 rue de la Paix. Number 7 was occupied by Worth, the most famous fashion house of the day; the two sons of celebrated designer Charles Frederick Worth were just then consolidating its future, for Gaston, the elder, was a shrewd businessman while Jean-Philippe was a talented stylist. The friendship that sprang up between the two families was cemented not only by an ever greater attention to the harmony between jewelry and dress, but also by two marriages: Louis to Andrée Caroline, daughter of Jean-Philippe, and Suzanne to Jacques, son of Gaston.

The clientele of Cartier was international—every elegant lady had to visit rue de la Paix twice a year to renew her wardrobe and replenish her jewelry case. England was prospering, and the United States was breeding Rockefellers, Morgans, and Vanderbilts. In 1902 Cartier opened a London branch at 4 New Burlington Street, headed by Pierre. In 1906 Pierre moved back into partnership with Louis, and Jacques took over the London operation, which he transferred to 175–176 New Bond Street in 1909, at which point Pierre opened a New York branch at 712 Fifth Avenue. Only in 1917 did the New York location of the firm become permanent, when Morton F. Plant, whose young wife was crazy about jewelry, offered to trade his private mansion at 653 Fifth Avenue, built by Robert W. Gibson in 1905, for one hundred dollars and a necklace composed of two strands of fifty-five and seventy-three pearls, respectively, worth one million dollars. The deal was a very good one, masterfully negotiated by Pierre, who nevertheless hardly dreamed that the value of pearls would fluctuate so much—forty years later, when placed on auction at Parke-Bernet, the necklace sold for just 151,000 dollars. The mansion was listed as a

Pierre Cartier (1878–1965).
Brooch, 1907.
Consuelo Vanderbilt,
Duchess of Marlborough.
Corsage ornament, 1910.
Grand Duchess Olga
of Russia.
Following pages: The
Cartier Boutique at 13 rue
de la Paix in Paris, c. 1915.

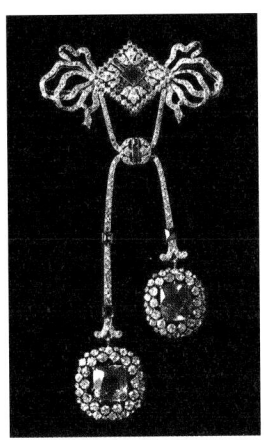

Landmark of the City of New York in 1970, and in 2002 New York paid tribute to the firm by naming the intersection of 52nd Street and Fifth Avenue "Place de Cartier."

Louis was cultivated, curious, inventive, and shrewd. With remarkable deftness he drew out people's talents, exploited their skills, and combined an artistry—whose constant innovation evolved into a classicism underpinned by timeless stylishness—with technical sophistication born of a fin-de-siècle interest in science and technology. Pierre, meanwhile, shone as a businessman, and in New York he naturally crafted a vision that accorded with the new world's entrepreneurs, who, like leading politicians and Hollywood stars, were soon embodying the dreams that the general public had invested in queens and princesses up till then. Finally, Jacques's knowledge of pearls, whose Oriental origins so fascinated poets, was as faultless as his judgment of other gems was precious. His London base opened the doors of India to him. The "three Cartiers"—as Raymond Hains wittily titled a show of his artworks at the Cartier Foundation in 1994, punning on the chic Trois Quartiers department store—ultimately went independent for reasons dictated by the economic policies of their respective countries, but signed a pact of solidarity that linked them all so that the firm would remain within the family.

By the time his brothers were contemplating marriage, Louis was already in divorce proceedings with Andrée-Caroline, who had borne him a daughter, Anne-Marie. Pierre married Elma Rumsey, whose father was a rich industrialist from Missouri; Jacques married Nellie Harjes, who came from a family of bankers linked to J. P. Morgan. Pierre's only child would be a daughter, Marion, who would marry another Pierre, namely the son of family friend and French author Paul Claudel, who served as ambassador to the United States from 1927 to 1933. Gems and jewels inspired the publication of Claudel's *Mystique des pierres précieuses*.[2] Jacques would have four children, Jacqueline, Alice, Jean-Jacques, and Harjes. Louis went on to marry a young Hungarian widow, Countess Almassy, who would give birth to a son, Claude.

A2. Paul Claudel, *La Mystique des pierres précieuses* (Paris: Cartier, limited edition, 1936).

11

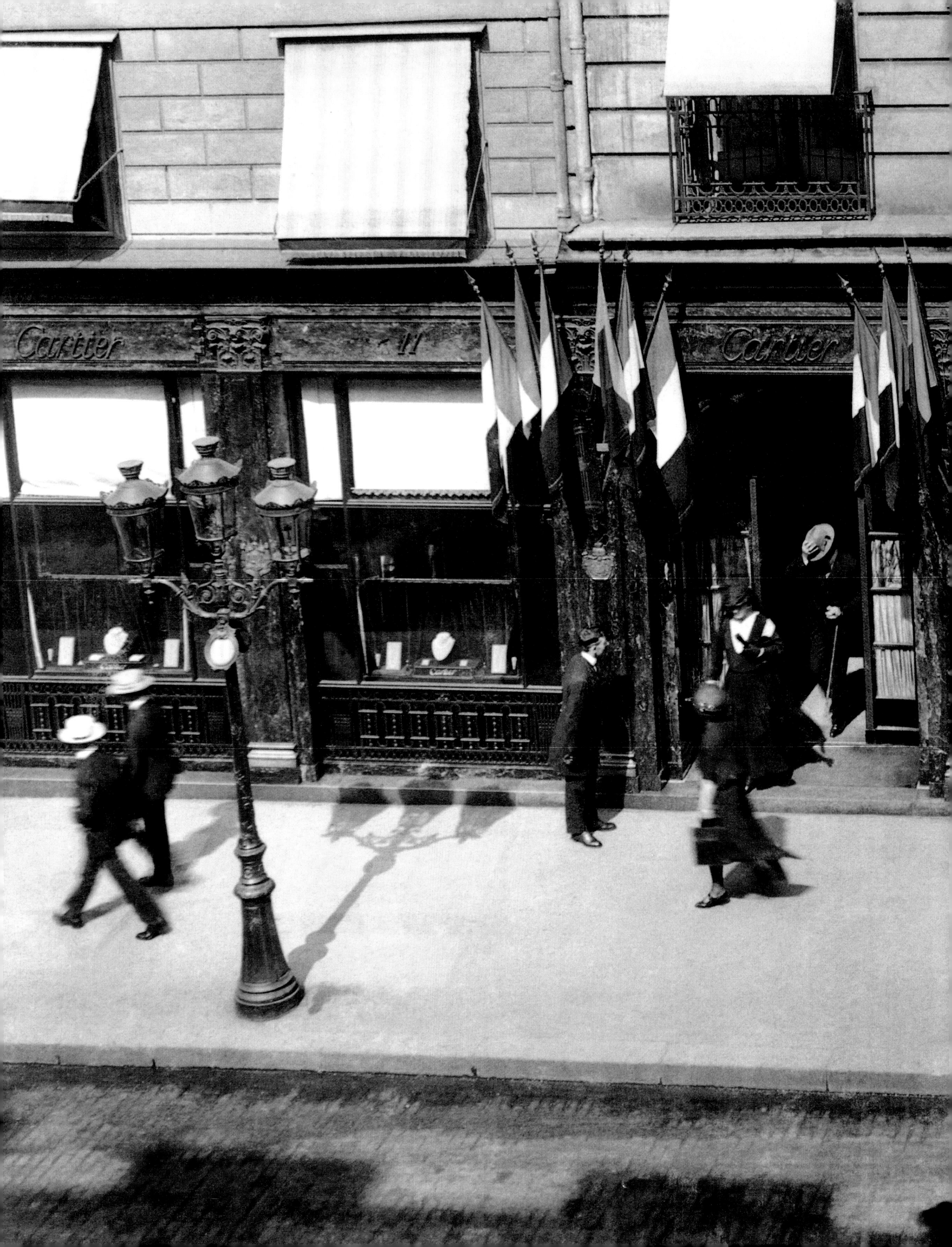
Cartier
Cartier

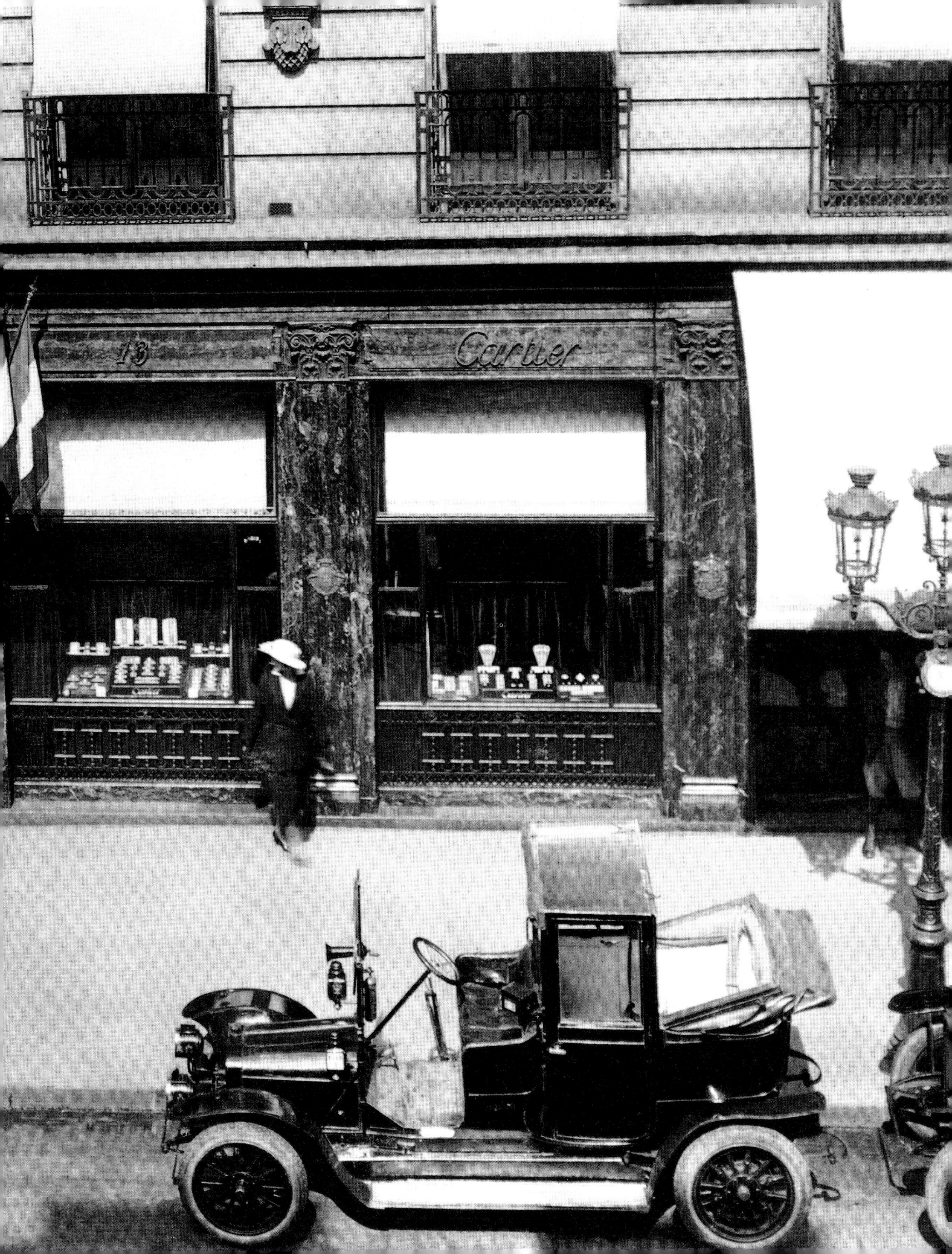
13
Cartier

Edwardian **bib necklace** of pearls and diamonds, 1910.
Elephant **mystery clock**, 1928.
Jeanne Toussaint (1887–1978).
Andrée Carron, Her Highness the Begum Aga Khan III.

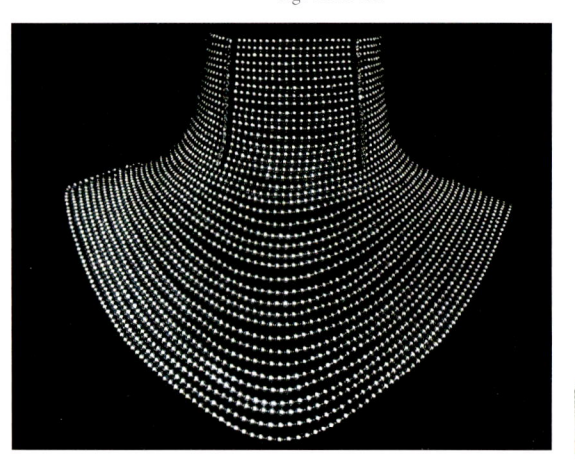

Commissions as royal suppliers arrived one after another, initiated by King Edward VII of Britain in 1904 and imitated by, among others, Alphonso XIII of Spain, Charles of Portugal, the king of Siam, Czar Nicholas II, George I of Greece, Prince Albert of Monaco, and Queen Mary of Romania. Other clients included the Aga Khan, the maharaja of Patiala, the nawab of Rampur, the gaekwar of Baroda, and the nizam of Hyderabad. Fantastic stones also passed through the house of Cartier, such as the Hope diamond, the Jubilee diamond, the Star of the East, and the North Star diamonds.

When Louis met Jeanne Toussaint, she was designing tapestry evening bags. She was a Cartier client, she liked Romanesque and Gothic art, and one of her closest friends was Gabrielle "Coco" Chanel. Louis then introduced Toussaint to the art forms that particularly inspired and appealed to him, ranging from eighteenth-century art to the arts of Islam and the Far East. An intellectual compatibility was soon established between the two. Toussaint headed Cartier's "S" (for Silver) department, which was set up in 1922 to produce more affordable yet still refined accessories. After earning her stripes there, Toussaint was named head of fine jewelry in 1933.

The economic outlook was no longer favorable, however, and the family went through a difficult period. Jacques's health declined, and he moved to Saint-Moritz. He and his wife founded Jacnel (Jacques and Nelly), a company that distributed S department items in Switzerland. Louis, meanwhile, suffered a heart attack and was forced to retire. Pierre, without leaving the firm, turned the presidency over to Jules Glaezner, a long-time colleague, while the vice presidency went to his son-in-law. But the outbreak of the Second World War, followed by the successive deaths of Jacques in December 1941 and Louis in July 1942, left the firm in deep disarray. True, Jean-Jacques and Harjes were in London, and in 1939 Louis had clearly conferred daily operating authority to Toussaint, but the German occupation made the transfer of ownership very complicated. In 1945 Pierre headed Cartier International

Queen Mary of Romania.
Maharaja Sir Yadavindra
Singh of Patiala.
Elephant **powder compact
and lipstick holder**, 1925.
Shoulder ornament
(the Bérénice necklace),
tiara, ear pendants,
and brooch, 1925.
Tutti Frutti **necklace**, 1936.

while Jean-Jacques ran the London firm. Louis's daughter, Anne-Marie, was a widow and a depressive; her half-brother Claude moved into their father's office, while Marion and Pierre Claudel remained in New York. More upheavals followed at the close of the decade when Claude, who had divided his childhood between Hungary, Switzerland, and the United States, decided he could not get used to France or to his role of successor to a father whose mark was indelible. He therefore offered to "swap" Paris for New York, and his uncle agreed. In 1962 Claude sold his stake to Edward Goldstein, who headed the Black, Starr & Frost corporation. Two years later Pierre Cartier, the last survivor of the three dynamic brothers, who had retired to Geneva, passed away. In 1968 his daughter Marion brought in Anglo-American investors. The dynasty died out for lack of warriors.

Throughout all those years, Toussaint remained present and vigilant, applying the lessons she had learned from her "boss." Louis had seen in her the qualities she would demonstrate throughout her career: a sharp eye, solid judgment, and boldness. To those qualities she added, over the years, a broad vision of art history that would inspire an artistry in tune with its times without being a slave to fashion. When Toussaint expressed a desire to learn to draw, Louis dissuaded her. She should not be tied to any technique, but should follow her intuition, and impose respect for it. As the Second World War dragged on, both labor and materials became scarcer, and Toussaint was forced to dip into the firm's endless repertoire, thereby slowly developing and enriching a style all her own. She and designer Peter Lemarchand formed a team similar to the one Louis had forged earlier with Cartier designer Charles Jacqueau, and they both found animal shapes appealing. Nicknamed "the panther" for her fondness for the beast as well as for her own powerful character, Toussaint particularly liked yellow gold—perhaps inspired by her taste for Indian jewelry—and was as interested in semiprecious stones as in gems. She understood the relationship between garment and jewelry, and she wanted the latter to exist boldly. Cartier's

Cartier Boutique,
New York.
François Kollar,
Lady Mendl, 1939.
Chimera **mystery clock**, 1926.
Cecil Beaton, *Barbara Hutton*.

leading clients, notably the Duke and Duchess of Windsor, swore by her jewelry. Christian Bérard called her a great colorist, while Violette Leduc, Princess Bibesco, and Cecil Beaton praised not only her skill as a jeweler but also her temperament as reflected in her clothes, her home, everything around her: "In the course of the last three decades this birdlike little woman, with a beak of a nose, an exquisitely pretty mouth that hints of her sensitivity, and with chinchilla-colored hair worn in the bobbed wisps of the twenties, has designed jewelry for the firm of Cartier. Her influence has encompassed the earth. She might have been an architect or a sculptor, an actress or a wonderful cook, but she has brought her original gifts to the handling of jewels."[3] Despite herself, Toussaint became heir to the artistic destiny of an empire, which she anchored to modernity once and for all. A 1967 portrait testifies to a youthful temperament that age could not alter—people who knew the woman who remained "Mademoiselle Toussaint" even after she became Baroness Hély d'Oissel, recall her somewhat gravelly voice, her highly personal manner of appreciating everyone's work, and her undying enthusiasm for her craft. Toussaint willingly received colleagues in her library; her sure judgment and confidence in the reliability of her decisions made her receptive to suggestions from others. Whenever a new piece left the workshop, she needed only one glance and a simple gesture to assure herself of its lightness, suppleness, and fluidity—as taught by Louis Cartier.

In 1968 an oval-shaped cigarette lighter with retractable thumbpiece, notable for its sober lines and fine proportions, was designed by Cartier and placed on sale in a hundred upscale tobacconists. It was a true first: none of firm's creations had ever been marketed in this way. The lighter and the company formed to market it, Briquet Cartier, were the brainchild of Robert Hocq. One of Hocq's friends, Joseph Kanoui, assembled a group of investors who bought Cartier Paris in 1972 and Cartier London in 1974, and another group acquired Cartier New York in 1976. Three years later, the three branches were reunited, becoming Cartier Monde, just as Louis, Pierre, and Jacques would have wished.

3. Cecil Beaton,
The Glass of Fashion
(London: Weidenfeld &
Nicholson, 1954).

Bow-knot **brooch**, 1909.
Mrs. Carl Bendix, 1930.
Lipstick holder and powder compact brooch, 1925.
Horst P. Horst for *Vogue* magazine, 1936.
Brooch, c. 1933.

In 1973 the Must de Cartier concept was launched, inspired by Hocq's analysis of consumer trends and developed by Alain Dominique Perrin, who was named president of the new unit. When the two companies merged in 1981, Perrin became head of both. Twelve years later, Cartier became part of Richemont's Vendôme Luxury Group. In order to maintain the firm's reputation, war was declared against counterfeiters, involving numerous legal cases as well as publicity campaigns such as the one in which the sculptor César (Baldaccini), famous for his "compressions," was asked to compress thousands of fakes that had been seized. Meanwhile, in an effort to reconstitute the firm's past, in 1983 Eric Nussbaum began attending auctions the world over, in order to build the Cartier Collection. Finally, the company's interest in the future of art was signaled by the establishment of the Fondation Cartier pour l'Art Contemporain at Jouy-en-Josas, outside Paris, in 1984; ten years later the foundation moved to boulevard Raspail in Paris, in a building specially designed by the architect Jean Nouvel.

The Cartier Collection now constitutes a priceless record of the fertile creativity of the house of Cartier ever since it was founded. Many prestigious exhibitions of the collections have been hosted throughout the world, from the Tokyo Metropolitan Teien Art Museum to the Metropolitan in New York via the British Museum in London, the Hermitage in St. Petersburg, the Fondation de l'Hermitage in Lausanne, and the Petit Palais in Paris.

A STYLE

At a time when Art Nouveau favored organic swirls of flora and fauna, Cartier was a jeweler concerned with placing design at the service of the gem, rather than the reverse. There thus emerged the "garland style," named after the medieval headdress of braided flowers worn during festivities. A more immediate inspiration for the style, however, came from eighteenth-century anthologies of ornamentation, which Louis Cartier showed to his designers in

Brooch, 1933.
Horst P. Horst for
Vogue magazine, 1934.
Ear pendants, 1926.
Diamond necklace
for the Aga Khan, photo:
Vogue Studio, Paris.
The Cartier boutique
in London, 1909.
Fibula **brooch**, 1924.

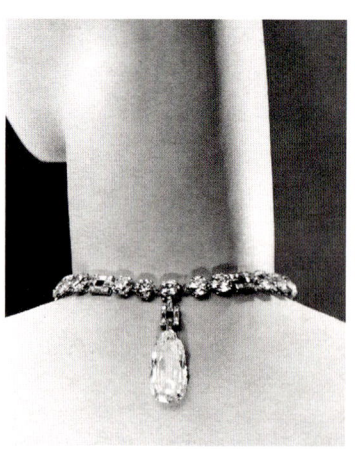

an effort to revive such artistry in the tiaras, chokers, and corsage ornaments made popular by the fashion of off-the-shoulder dresses. Floral motifs of great finesse owed their harmony and balance to calculated symmetry, sometimes tending toward a stylization that prefigured the later art deco movement. Such items were the delight of glamorous clients such as Mrs. Cornelius Vanderbilt, Princess Paley (the countess of Hohenfelsen), Princess Marie Bonaparte (soon much less interested in her princely title than in her role as psychoanalyst and spokesperson for Sigmund Freud in France), and Caroline "La Belle" Otéro (who fascinated men of a world to which she did not belong and who, toward the end of her days, acknowledged that the beautiful María Félix was worthy of portraying her in the film based on her life). The garland style's subtle, often lacelike designs encouraged Louis to pioneer the use of pliant, sturdy platinum, a metal whose whiteness underscored the sparkle of pearls and diamonds.

Still in the early twentieth century, other objects drew Louis's attention. The magnificent Easter eggs that made the fame of Peter-Karl Fabergé, official supplier to the court of Russia, were typical of the decorative objects in which Fabergé excelled, and which no refined interior could be without. His enameling was peerless. Soon Cartier was designing pots and vases of flowers to be executed by the best workshops in St. Petersburg and Paris. Their lifelikeness was rightly appreciated. In a supreme honor, a Cartier egg was even offered to Czar Nicholas II himself.

In 1904, Alberto Santos-Dumont, who was one of Louis's best friends and was known for his aeronautical exploits, complained that his pocket watch was difficult to read when he was at the controls of a primitive airplane. Louis thereupon designed the first true wristwatch for his friend. Although ladies had already been wearing watches on the wrist—on costly bracelets with expensive clasps—it is worth examining the design of Cartier's prototype (the Santos model would not be marketed publicly until 1911). It reflects the character of a man and a name whose output so skillfully conjugated an eighteenth-century spirit with an

Vase **brooch**, 1922.
Allegory of America,
1986—87, detail.
Marc Couturier, *Drawings of the Third Day*, 1996—97, Fondation Cartier pour l'Art Contemporain.
Caresse d'Orchidées **necklace**, Cartier Paris, 2005.

extremely modern approach. The special features of this watch included the direct incorporation of the lugs into the case, and the clear visibility of the screws on that case—a perfect marriage of form and function that would have been approved by Adolf Loos, whose essay on *Ornament and Crime* was published in France nine years later. Then the famous Tank watch—whose initial design, based on the treads of the British army's new weapon, dates back to 1916—once again incorporated the lugs for a strap into the case, thereby permanently establishing the concept of the modern wristwatch.

From the late nineteenth century onward, Western artists began borrowing from exotic arts, dramatically altering their handling of both perspective and color. Universal Expositions (also known as World's Fairs) enabled everyone to admire poorly known cultures; museums opened; antique dealers became specialized. Two different trends emerged at Cartier: one stemmed from a stylization that pointed toward abstraction; the other looked to the arts of China, Japan, Egypt, Persia, and India. Louis himself collected Egyptian antiquities and Persian miniatures; Cartier designer Charles Jacqueau was struck by the intense colors of Sergei Diaghilev's Ballets Russes, first performed in Paris in 1909; and in 1913, Cartier New York organized an exhibition of jewelry inspired by "Hindoo [*sic*], Persian, Arab, Russian, and Chinese" arts. Many magnificent objects would arise from this merger of pure abstraction, unusual color combinations (blue and green), and Japanese or Chinese ornamental motifs, such as Cartier's "mystery clocks" (first made in 1912), those admirably intriguing timepieces ingeniously devised by Maurice Couët (who had researched prestidigitator Jean Eugène Robert-Houdin's secret method of "suspending" clock hands in rock crystal). Then there emerged, in the mid-1920s, the Tutti Frutti style (as it was dubbed in the 1970s), based on carved rubies, emeralds, and sapphires; this style was followed by a return to basic white, which itself later gave way to color and figurative jewelry.

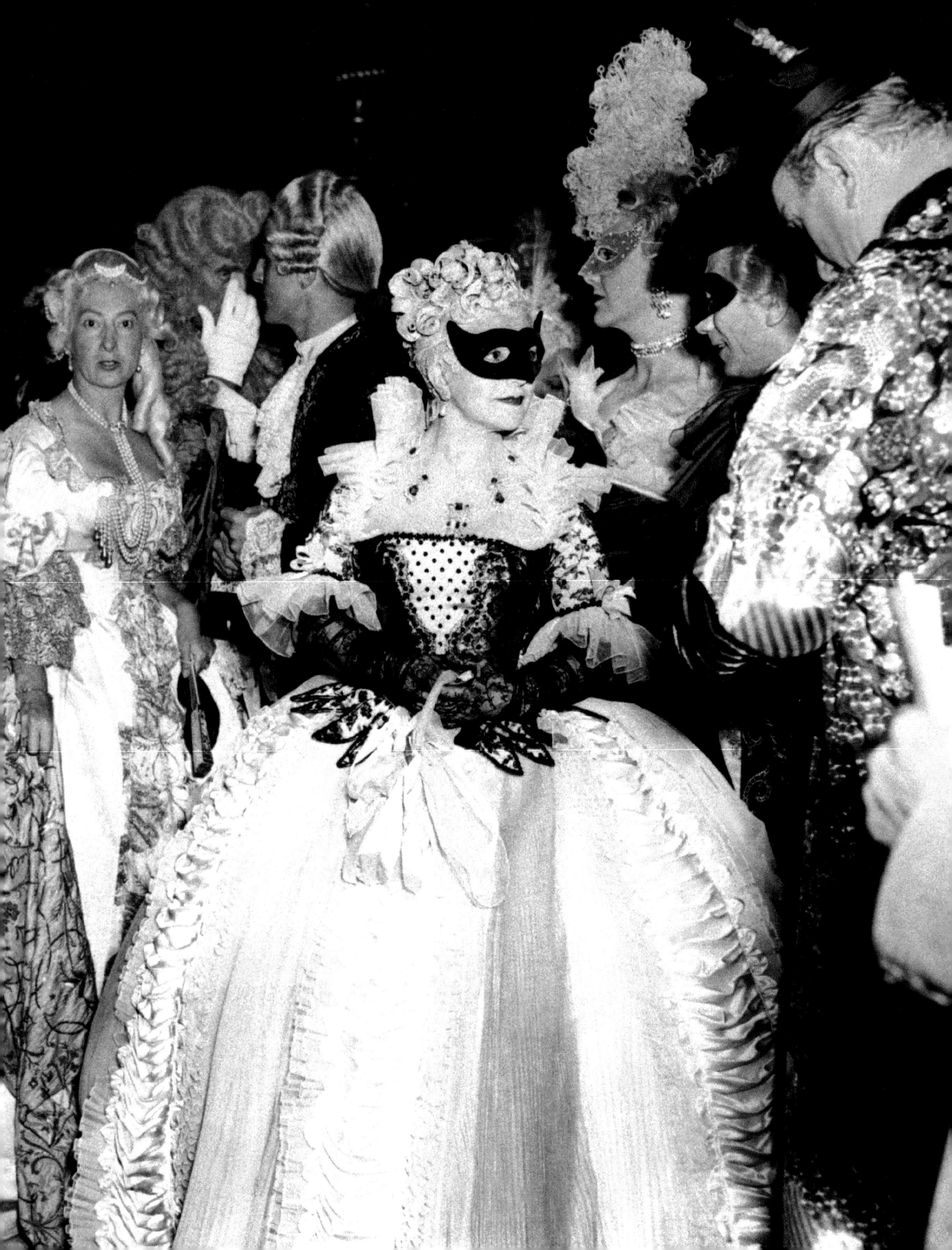

THE JEWELS

The day Wassily Kandinsky noticed one of his paintings inadvertently hung upside down, he realized that the spiritual values he wanted to impart to it were not dependent on the subject matter depicted. The year was 1910. Kandinsky soon painted the first abstract watercolor in history. That, at any rate, is how the birth of abstraction is usually recounted; the art world would henceforth be divided between abstraction and representation, various decades being dominated by one or the other as avant-garde movements arose. Representation of the world was transcended by original approaches that ranged from Mondrian's mathematical rigor to Kandinsky's gestural lyricism and Malevich's monochromatic integrity, even as Duchamp conferred the status of artwork on objects as banal as a bottle rack and a urinal merely by signing them, while his friend Brancusi sought the quintessence of the sculpted figure. The era tended to liberate ideas from all the moral and cultural dross clinging to them, a task soon enthusiastically adopted by the surrealists (on the heels of Dada), notably inspired by Freudian theories. Surrealist art favored representation, but one that was subject to an "inner model," hence open to as many forms as there are players.

The upheaval was considerable. In the space of twenty years, the foundations of society and its modes of expression, from the most superficial to the most profound, were transfigured. Even though they fulfilled requirements that differed from the ones assigned to the so-called "major" arts, the decorative arts—and jewelry in particular—faithfully reflected the changing times. Alternately dominated by purity or decorativeness, reality or chimera, they conveyed and magnified the spirit of the times and the aspirations of contemporary humans.

The liberating energy of the Roaring Twenties had been irrevocably dampened by economic depression by the time the Exposition Internationale des Arts et Techniques dans la Vie Moderne opened on June 5, 1937. The rise of fascism was embodied by Germany's Führer, Italy's Duce, and Spain's Caudillo—the approach of another world war seemed inexorable. The huge international exposition, in which fifty-two countries participated, painted a portrait of the world as it then was: colonies were still colonies, the strict lines of Albert Speer's German pavilion faced the Soviet building topped with Vera Mukhina's sculpture of a *Worker and Kolkhoz Woman*, while Picasso's *Guernica* decried Franco's massacres. Emphasis was placed on the alliance of art and technological progress: the highlights of the event included scientific discoveries exhibited at the Palais de la Découverte and the 500,000-watt circuit-breaker that accompanied the display of Raoul Dufy's notorious fresco, *La Fée Électricité* (Magic Electricity). A new pavilion designed by René Herbst featured ads and advertising professionals, prefiguring profound and lasting changes in consumer habits and production. When it came to art, representation got the better of its younger antagonist: bouquets, nudes, and rustic scenes earned the favors of a public in search of certainties and an accessible art whose reassuring obviousness seemed more appealing than novelty. The arts of finery brilliantly demonstrated French know-how, featuring the major players through magnificent pieces exhibited by Boucheron, Dusausoy, Van Cleef & Arpels, Chaumet, Marchak, Mauboussin, Boivin, Fouquet and, of course, Cartier. They almost gave the lie to the economic depression that had reigned since 1929. The lavish show indicated that one style was permanently on the way out: whereas the streamlining of the 1930s was eliminating sharp corners the better to cut through the air, art deco had become somewhat chubby as it aged and indulged in stylized representation, slowly losing its way. Another style was emerging, one that would last well beyond the coming war.

Facing page: Costume ball in Venice, 1951.

FI GU

RATIVE JEWELRY

24

Pages 22–23, left to right and top to bottom:
Blackamoor head **clip brooch**. Platinum, gold wire, and twisted gold, brilliant-cut diamonds, turquoise cabochons, carved black tortoiseshell. Cartier Paris, 1955.
Blackamoor head **clip brooch**. Gold, diamonds, carved onyx, and coral, c. 1950.
Blackamoor head **clip brooch**. Platinum, gold wire, brilliant-cut diamonds, pear-shaped sapphire, turquoise cabochons, and carved black tortoiseshell. Cartier London, 1958.
Blackamoor head **clip brooch**. Gold, diamonds, turquoise cabochons, and carved ebony. Cartier Paris, c. 1950.
Blackamoor head **clip brooch**. Platinum, gold wire, brilliant-cut diamonds, pear-shaped sapphire, turquoise cabochons, and carved black tortoiseshell. Cartier London, 1958.

aFacing page:
Oiseau libéré **clip brooch**. Platinum, gold, rose-cut diamonds, coral, lapis lazuli, and sapphire cabochon. Cartier Paris, 1944.
Bird's nest **brooch**. Platinum, plaited and chased gold, brilliant- and baguette-cut diamonds, emerald, sapphire, and ruby cabochons, and pearls. Cartier Paris, 1944.
Bird **brooch**. Gold, coral, emerald, and diamond cabochons. 1959.
Right:
Owl **brooch**. Gold, citrine, diamonds, and sapphire. Cartier London, 1956.

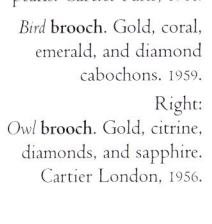

In the years when mankind was sinking into a kind of bestial state unknown even to the animal kingdom, nature was steadily asserting itself. The form taken by that assertion might be either absurd—when the collaborationist Vichy government advocated a rural, docile France in the face of German occupation—or subtle, when Jean-Michel Frank decorated his furniture with precious marquetry of straw, when André Arbus demonstrated the magisterial sobriety of long walnut tables, when Frank Lloyd Wright built his Fallingwater house in a rustic setting, when Louis Sognot bent rattan into distinctly modernist lines, and when the lapels of ladies' outfits sported appealing examples of flora and fauna.

During the war, the fashion industry had a hard time. Some workshops closed—notably at Chanel, Mainbocher, and Vionnet—and raw materials were scarce. The situation was hardly conducive to coquetry, although it couldn't kill it off. However frivolous fashion might seem, it still remained one of the last bastions that women defended with determination, employing countless ruses and ever-greater inventiveness. Dress was as warm as possible in winter and as practical as possible all year round, since a woman might have to crawl into a shelter during an air-raid alert, travel around on a bike, or wait endlessly in a line clutching ration coupons. Only accessories flaunted a whimsy that betrayed unflagging hope.

A ladylike suit—which Coco Chanel and Jean Patou, promoting a freer, more convenient look for women, had been featuring in their fashion shows since the 1920s, and which, during the war, was sometimes retailored from a man's suit—remained a key element of a woman's wardrobe throughout the 1950s. Its collar and lapel favored the wearing of brooches and pins, as did the deliberately square necklines of dresses, the fabrics used, and the sharply tailored lines of the female body. Such ornaments might be worn singly, or in symmetrical pairs, or on a shoulder, a hat, or near the waist. It was considered good taste to have matching bracelet, earrings, necklace, and clip brooch, these latter offering the advantage of multiple uses. Cartier excelled in this sphere, where clever mechanisms allowed the same piece of jewelry to be worn in several ways. Necklaces became bracelets, brooches became detachable motifs that could migrate from shoulder to choker,

The Duchess of Windsor wearing her *Flamingo* brooch, 1940.

Facing page:
Flamingo **brooch**.
Platinum, rubies, sapphires, emeralds, and citrines.
Cartier Paris, 1940.

from neck to arm. Flexible use was mirrored by flexible structure—wings fluttered at the least breeze and flowers and animals stirred at the slightest movement, thereby increasing one hundredfold the glittery, sparkling effect of light.

Animals have always found a home at Cartier, where they were given a lively interpretation with a freshness that exalted their precious materials. At the dawn of the twentieth century, quartz, agate, jade, and amethyst were fashioned into mice, dogs, diamond-eyed pigs, ruby-eyed penguins, and even a golden-clawed chick breaking its way out of an egg (a model chosen by the countess of Hohenfelsen in the year after the birth of her daughter, Nathalie Paley). In 1910 a little terrier was set with white and yellow diamonds, while one special order in 1913 yielded a highly realistic shrimp brooch with pavé-set diamonds. In 1925 a few brooches of brilliants and emeralds featured genre scenes with characters connected by a fine rod of platinum: a cat unraveling a ball of yarn, a dog chasing a rabbit, another dog confronting a frightened cat, two young elephants following their mother, a charming enamel crocodile basking on a cigarette case. The latter half of the 1910s gave rise to a series of highly colorful birds structured around a cabochon that was sometimes carved, sometimes as round as a ball or as perfect as an egg, in a harmonious overall geometry confirmed by the angle of wings, claws, and beak. A graceful pendant of 1920 featured diamond birds drinking from a fountain of moonstone, sapphire, and onyx; powder boxes and vanity cases were adorned with dogs, gazelles, or cats; the dial of a rock-crystal clock incorporated Chinese jade carp.

By the late 1930s, Cartier's animals had won the privileged status that they would always retain. Just like a portrait that captures the sitter's underlying personality, so the appearance and quality of these begemmed animals were magnified through plumage, fur, or shell that seemed so graceful, supple, and lively. Realism was not overdone; elegance called for evident simplicity and a certain distance that permitted every liberty except the liberty to betray the model. Charm vanquished triviality, mastery quelled bombast.

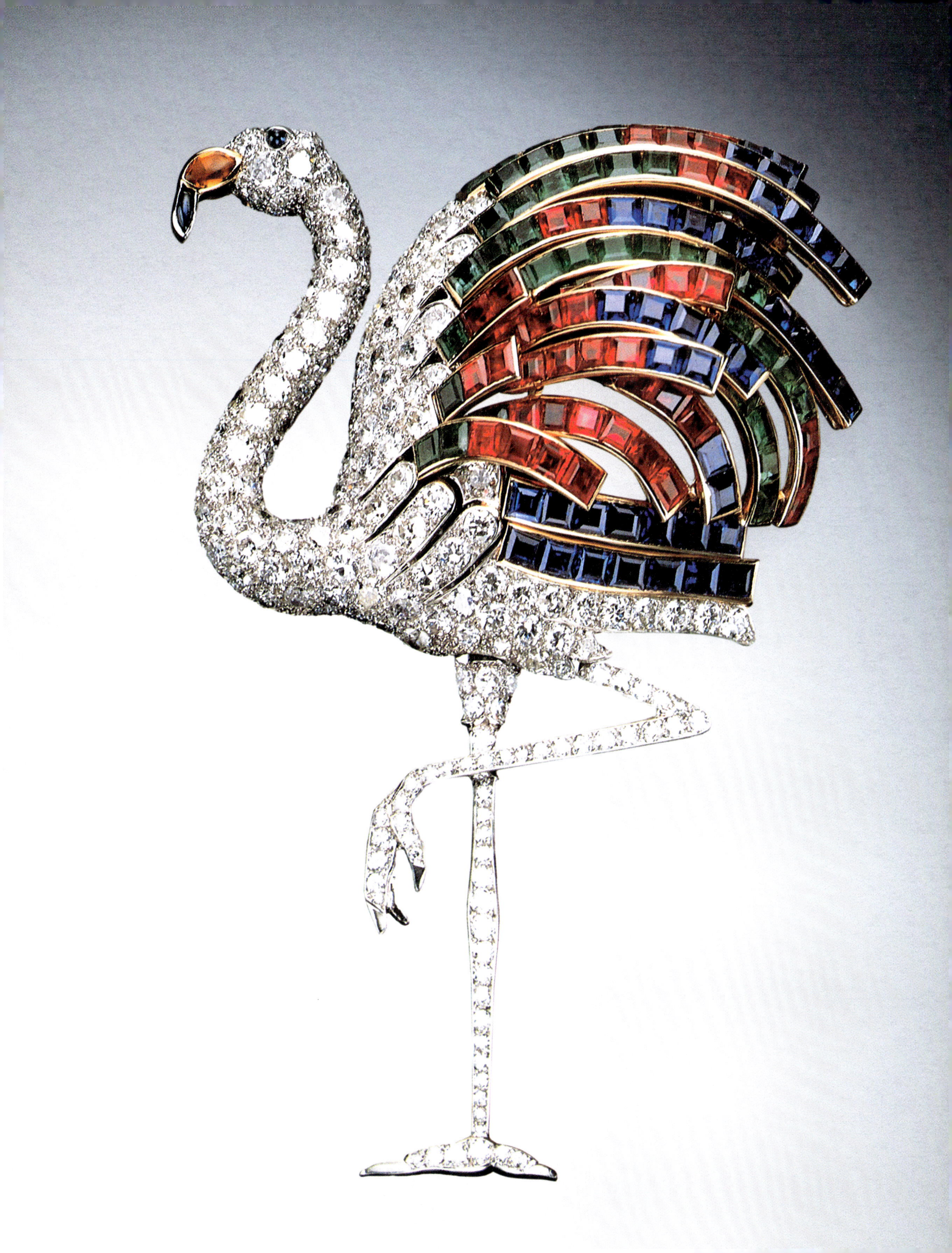

WINGED ANIMALS

aOwl **brooch**. Gold, amethyst, emeralds, and diamonds, c. 1960.

Owl **brooch**. Gold, diamonds, sapphires, topaz, and turquoises. Cartier London, 1956.

Kingfisher **brooch**. Opal, rubies, sapphires, and emeralds. Cartier London, c. 1960.

Owl **brooch**. Gold, oval and cabochon amethysts, turquoises, and diamonds. Cartier New York, 1951.

Owl **brooch**. Platinum, gold, sapphire, turquoise, and diamonds, c. 1950.

Facing page: Léonor Fini. Photo: André Ostier.

Owl brooch. Gold, cabochon emeralds, baguette-cut diamonds, 1968.

Given the pressing need to escape the unbearable reality of war, winged animals enjoyed especial favor. In many societies, birds serve as a link between humans and the heavens. In addition to their metaphorical qualities—as messenger from the heavens and symbol of the celestial world, of the elevation of the soul, of divine benevolence toward mankind, and of the power of life—birds also flaunt shimmering colors that gemstones can incarnate so well.

Cartier's range of birds was very broad, from duck to bird of paradise via owl and flamingo, each retaining its own character even as it conformed to the house style. They might fly, watch over the nest, or calmly perch on a branch, wings folded (often in twos or threes). Even when their exuberant plumage might be conducive to an affected naturalism, Cartier's birds never lost the equilibrium guaranteed by a perfect mastery of basic lines of force—which is true of all of the firm's animal jewelry.

This can be seen in the famous Flamingo brooch made for the Duchess of Windsor (from four bracelets supplied by the duke) and the Kingfisher brooch now in the Cartier Collection; both models are naturally stylized, thanks to their graphic silhouettes. Dating from 1940 and 1941, respectively, both have bodies of pavé-set diamonds, the regularity of their lines being enhanced through the use of caliber-cut stones. The flamingo is at rest, one leg lifted as appropriate, its profile forming a perfect, reverse S from the sapphire tip of its two-colored beak to the base of its neck; the feathers of emeralds, rubies, and caliber-cut sapphires create a clean yet full curve. The kingfisher, meanwhile, with its ruby eyes, gold beak, and carved-emerald wings, has been captured in mid-flight; its rectilinear body ends in a tail of caliber-cut sapphires, which also stud its diamond-tipped wings.

Cartier's most famous wartime bird was set in a cage. It cost Toussaint an interrogation by the German authorities, who with a certain insight realized that it was a symbol of occupied France. Exhibiting such brooches and pendants in the showcase on rue de la Paix seemed like a provocative statement at a time when Cartier London was housing General de Gaulle and was making the

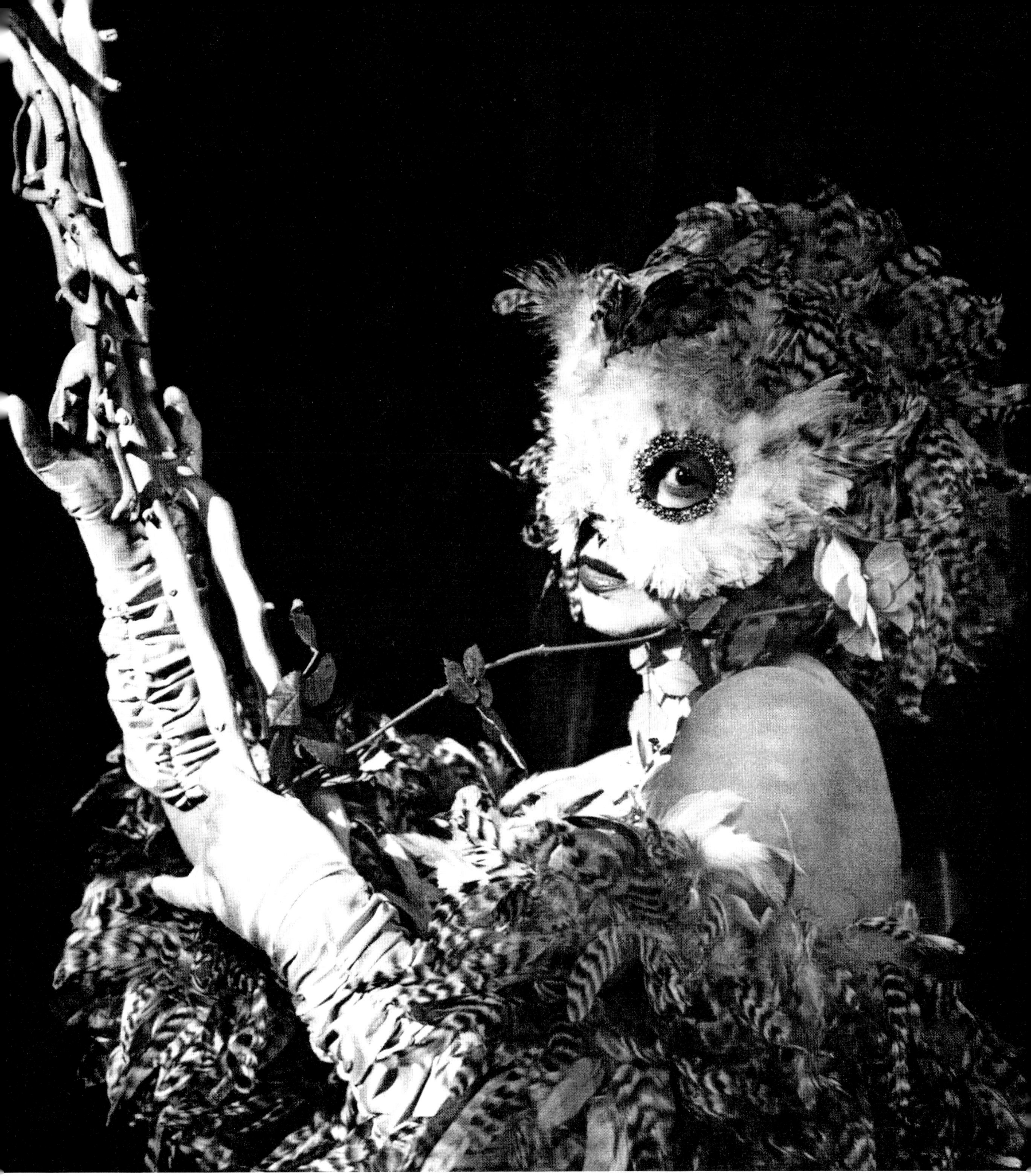

Bird brooch. Platinum, brilliants, rubies, and emerald. Cartier Paris, 1960.

Design for a Bird brooch of yellow gold, round diamonds, yellow sapphire, rubies, and turquoises. Cartier New York, 1957.

Design for a Kingfisher brooch of gold, emeralds, rubies, sapphires, and diamonds. Cartier Paris, 1941.

Design for a Parrot brooch of gold, emeralds, rubies, sapphires, and diamonds. Cartier Paris, 1943.

Design for a Bird brooch of yellow gold, diamonds, sapphires, rubies and turquoises. Cartier New York, 1956.

Design for a Bird in cage brooch of gold, platinum, emeralds, rubies, and diamonds. Cartier Paris, 1942.

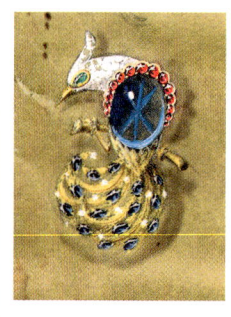

Design for a Crested Bird brooch of gold, topaz, sapphires, turquoises, and diamonds. Cartier Paris, 1943.

Design for a Bird brooch of yellow gold, diamonds, turquoise, and rubies. Cartier New York, 1957.

Design for a Bird brooch of platinum, gold, sapphires, emeralds, and diamonds. Cartier Paris, 1943.

Design for a Bird brooch of yellow gold, sapphire, rubies, and emerald. Cartier New York, 1958.

Design for a Tropical Bird brooch of yellow gold, diamonds, emeralds, and rubies. Cartier New York, 1956.

Design for a Flying Bird brooch of gold, emeralds, and diamonds. Cartier Paris, 1942.

Kingfisher **clip brooch.** Platinum, gold, two leaf-shaped carved emeralds weighing 17.66 carats in total, brilliant- and single-cut diamonds, faceted and caliber-cut sapphires, and ruby cabochons. Cartier Paris, 1941.

Flying bird **clip brooch.** Platinum, yellow gold, amethyst, turquoises, sapphires, and diamonds. Cartier Paris, 1965.

Bird **clip brooch.** Platinum, gold, four emerald cabochons weighing 14.42 carats in total, brilliant- and single-cut diamonds, oval faceted sapphires, and two navette-shaped ruby cabochons. The wings and tail are articulated. Cartier Paris, 1944.

Parrot **brooch.** Gold, brilliant-cut diamonds, rubies, yellow sapphires, emerald, crystal, onyx, and coral. Cartier Paris, c. 1995.

Parrot **brooch.** Pink briolette-cut sapphire, diamonds, rubies, sapphires, and emeralds. Cartier Paris, 1995.

Parrot **brooch.** Platinum, gray gold, oval ruby cabochon weighing 39.53 carats, diamonds, rubies, and baguette-cut emeralds, mother-of-pearl beak. Cartier Paris, 2003.

Parrot **clip brooch.** Platinum, gold, brilliant-cut fancy yellow diamonds, brilliant- and baguette-cut diamonds, oval faceted emerald, and carved coral. Cartier Paris, 1969.

Parrot **brooch.** Platinum, yellow gold, emeralds, rubies, and diamonds. Cartier Paris, 1951.

Bird **brooch.** Yellow gold, turquoise cabochon, lapis lazuli, sapphire, and diamonds. Cartier Paris, 1958.

Parrot **brooch.** Gold, brilliant-cut diamonds, rubies, sapphires, emeralds, and onyx. Cartier Paris, 1992.

Lorraine crosses that symbolized the French Resistance as well as parts for RAF aircraft. Meanwhile, a salesman at Cartier Paris, the American John F. Hasey, joined the Forces Françaises Libres (and would be one of the four Americans later awarded the title of Compagnon de la Libération). Toussaint, however, told the Germans that the model dated back to 1933, and had been a charm on a bracelet for Yvonne Printemps (perhaps a gift from Pierre Fresnay, with whom Mademoiselle Printemps would star the following year in *O Mistress Mine* by Cole Porter, another faithful Cartier client). She said she had chosen it at random, among other designs. A German officer verified the company's archives of drawings on the premises. No further action ensued. Some people concluded that Toussaint's friend Coco Chanel (who, like the singer and actress Arletty, did not put up much resistance) asked her lover of the moment, a German officer, to step in. No one now knows the truth, but everyone knows that when France was liberated the patriotic sparrow was seen again, jumping for joy, wings spread—outside the cage. Meanwhile another bird, whose profile was set against a ring of gold, exclaimed, "1946 will be better." Its body, represented by a simple coral

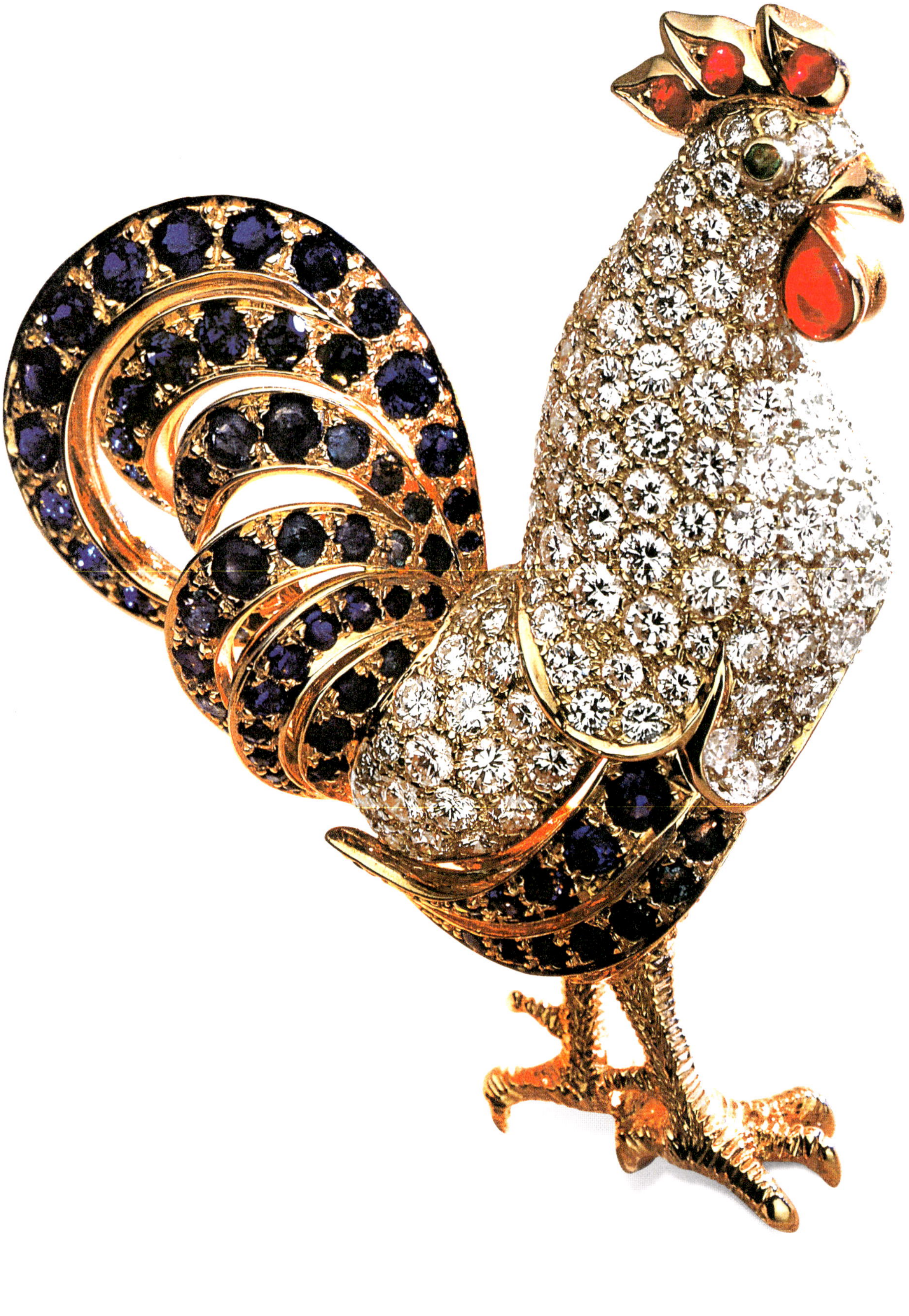

Rooster **brooch**.
Chased yellow gold,
diamonds, carved
rubies, and emerald.
Cartier Paris, c. 1948.

Rooster **clip brooch**.
Yellow gold, carved
emerald cabochon,
coral, brilliant- and
navette-cut diamonds.
Cartier Paris, c. 1950.

Rooster **clip brooch**.
Platinum, gold,
brilliant- and baguette-cut
diamonds, rubies,
and emerald.
Cartier Paris, 1959.

Facing page:
Francœur **brooch**.
Yellow gold, diamonds,
rubies, emeralds,
and sapphires.
Cartier Paris, 1988.

Cowboy Duck **brooch**. Yellow gold, white chalcedony, coral, and sapphire. Cartier New York, 1952.

Duck **brooch**. Yellow gold, tigereye, and lacquer. Cartier Paris, 1968.

Two Ducks **clip brooch**. Platinum, chased and polished gold, single-cut diamonds, carved coral, jade, lapis lazuli, and chalcedony cabochons. Cartier Paris, 1945.

Duck **clip brooch**. Platinum, gold, sapphire cabochon, and brilliant-cut diamonds. Formerly the collection of Princess Soraya. Cartier New York, 1948.

Three Ducks **clip brooch**. Platinum, chased and polished gold, single-cut diamonds, jade, lapis lazuli and chalcedony cabochons, and carved coral. Cartier Paris, 1945.

Duck Head **clip brooch**. Platinum, gold, blister pearl, brilliant-cut diamond, round faceted emeralds, oval faceted sapphire, and carved coral. Formerly the collection of the Duchess of Windsor. Cartier Paris, 1953.

Facing page:
Magpie goes to the Ball **clip brooch**. Carved and cabochon rubies, diamonds, and onyx. Cartier London, 1925.

Duck **clip brooch**. Gold, rubies, diamonds, and emerald cabochon. Cartier Paris, c. 1950.

cabochon, lent the bird a friendly, straightforward feel similar to the universal appeal of children's drawings: a circle for the body, a circle for the head, three lines for the wings. The same was true of a few mischievous ducks composed around an emerald or sapphire cabochon, whose heads, like the sparrow's, were set with diamonds and whose webbed feet seem to be tap-dancing. One of them, dated 1948, holding a ruby-studded floweret in its beak, had the good fortune to appeal to Soraya, the wife of the shah of Iran. Many birds were made along the same lines, the head sometimes formed by a smaller cabochon, like the 1928 models mentioned above, with wavy plumage that tempered the underlying geometric structure. Carved stones—emeralds, rubies, amethysts—might play this same central role, their shape and size governing the overall composition, as would baroque pearls (highly prized in the latter half of the Renaissance, when master goldsmiths used gold, enamel, and other gems to transform baroque pearls into "monster pendants" depicting tritons, mermaids, centaurs, lions, and butterflies). The Duchess of Windsor owned one such brooch, among her countless Cartier items: a blister pearl formed the head of a coral-beaked duck, dated 1953, whose head is crested with strands of gold that suggest a female duck; French people familiar with the friendship between the Windsors and Jeanne Toussaint will inevitably think of Georges Brassens singing, that very same year of 1953, "La Cane de Jeanne" (Jeanne's Duckling). Five years later, a handsome eagle of chased gold with onyx beak was composed around a triangular pearl that formed its cheek. (In a strange coincidence within the world of artforms, the following year Marcel Duchamp, that unreconstructed smasher of aesthetic codes, drew his own profile in pencil around a cheek made of a piece of white plaster, whose shape inevitably evokes this pearl.) In 1969, an eagle's pavé-set diamond claws would be shown clutching a cushion-shaped blue sapphire, while in 1975, for the one-hundredth anniversary of the birth of Louis Cartier, they clutched a magnificent yellow sapphire weighing eighty carats.

Given the ever-present danger, no farmyard would be complete without its sentinel, the rooster. The cock is not only a symbol of the sun, but also the emblem of courage and pride, and the mascot of France; in the late 1930s one of John Heartfield's famous photomontages showed a cock wearing the Phrygian cap that symbolized

Bird **brooch**.
Gold, diamonds, and
rubies, c. 1958.

Bird **brooch**. Brilliant-
and baguette-cut diamonds,
and emerald.
Cartier Paris, 1959.

Facing page:
Peacock **brooch**. Gold,
sapphires, emeralds, ruby
drops, and diamonds.
Cartier Paris, c. 1946.

the French Revolution; it turned its back to a Hitler-like butcher sharpening his knives and complacently said, in German, "Don't worry, he's a vegetarian!" Cartier's roosters always flaunt their panache, rising on the their spurs, in profile, head either held high or peering groundward to pick for food. Their ample plumage is sometimes topped by two proudly upright tail feathers. Some fine examples from the late 1940s and 1950s, boasting impressive crests of rubies, coral, or even sapphires, incorporate subtly worked yellow gold into the arrangement of gems.

Whereas Cartier's ducks may have a mocking air, its roosters a proud one, its owls reassuringly round bodies and heads with wide-open eyes, its lovebirds the graceful tilt of their attachment, and nest-watching couples their eggs of iridescent pearls, Cartier's flying birds always retain a remarkable elegance. Their lofty motion is soberly invoked by a slight bend in the neck and a subtle reverse curve of the tail, while their wings form two long, slightly feathery triangles attached to the top of the body. The Cartier Collection now holds one of the finest examples of such work: the body is formed of three emerald cabochons, the details are conveyed by brilliants underscored by yellow gold, and the articulated wings and tail are dotted with oval faceted sapphires.

The lavish plumage of parrots inspired all kinds of combinations of stones, pearls, and gold, without indulging in compositions that might display the affectation of exaggeratedly curved or irregular lines. Just as Cartier avoided extreme rigidity during its art deco period, so excessive sinuosity remained forever alien to the house style, as demonstrated by a few parrots depicted in profile, anchored to their perch, flapping their wings in the pose typical of those incorrigible chatterboxes. This early 1940s design, variously executed in diamonds, rubies, emeralds, and carved yellow gold, perhaps complemented by sapphires or black lacquer, is striking in its veracity. One example, like two of the cocks described above, displays a subtle modeling of gold feathers on neck, head, wings, and tail, all highlighted by diamonds and leaf-shaped carved stones in the Tutti Frutti style. This jewel is a veritable piece of animal sculpture, owing its perfection to realism as well as magic—the unsettling realism of its forms, the delightful magic of its materials.

39

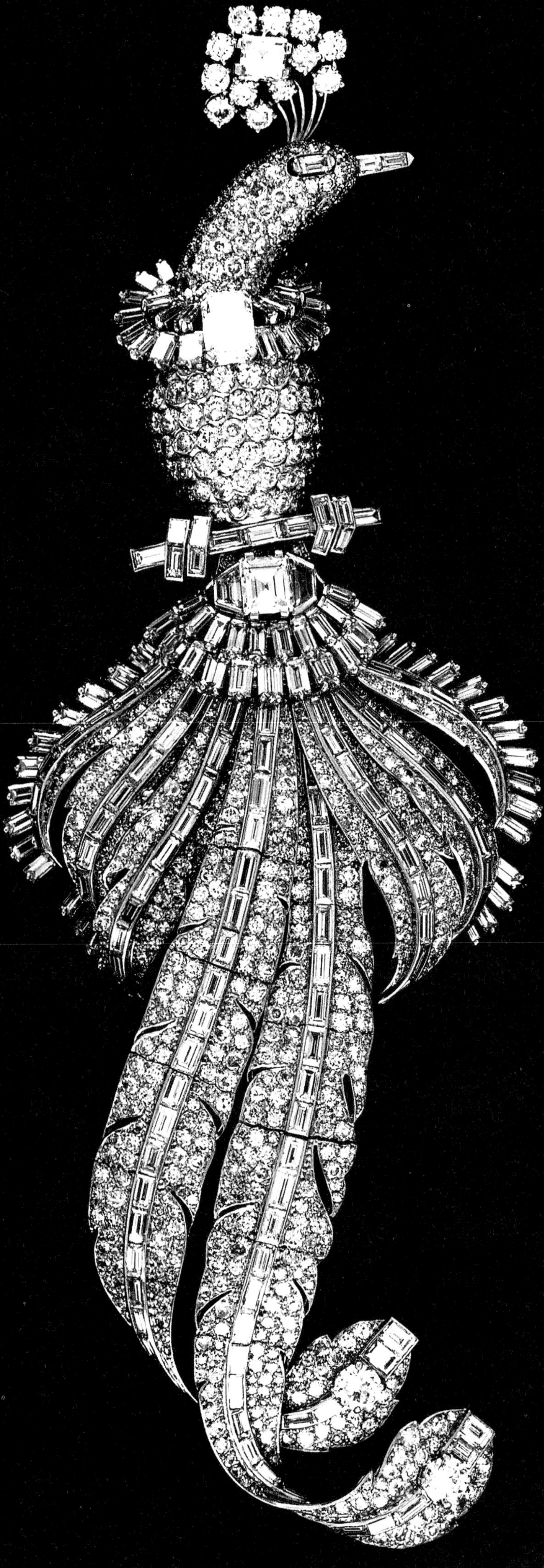

Peacock **brooch**. Platinum, yellow gold, brilliants, sapphires (round, pear-shaped, and one oval), and emeralds. Cartier Paris, 1988.

Peacock **brooch**. Yellow gold, sapphires, emeralds, and brilliants. Cartier Paris, 1989.

Facing page: *Bird of Paradise* **brooch**. Platinum and 894 diamonds weighing a total of 92 carats. 1948.

During those difficult wartime years, it was impossible not to fall for an animal whose name alone was a promise of eternal bliss: the bird of paradise. The first European examples of this species were found on the only ship to return from Magellan's early sixteenth-century expedition, unfortunately dead and missing their claws. It was thought they didn't have or need claws, remaining constantly in the air like the inhabitants of paradise; yet when the naturalist Buffon, two centuries later, claimed that the bird of paradise was "better known for its false, imagined qualities . . . than for its real and truly remarkable properties," he did not fail to evoke the beauty of its feathers, whose "colors shimmer, giving off different reflections according to the angle of the light." Would Buffon have described precious gems in any other terms? Although birds of paradise suffered because their finery was so prized, at least they might be grateful that a jeweler could capture them without making them suffer. Sometimes depicted from the back, sometimes from the front, crested head and pointed beak turned to one side, tail often ending in two long feathers (like certain roosters), Cartier's birds of paradise roost serenely on a perch. The Cartier Collection has a 1944 model all the more sober in that its chased gold tail dotted with emerald and ruby cabochons was removed three years later and replaced by a gold and diamond pattern similar to the one on its neck, recalling a peacock-feather motif. Its structure reflected Cartier's favored scheme—wings and body conveyed by a ruby cabochon (over forty-three carats), head by an emerald cabochon. A magnificent two-color (sapphire and diamond) bird of paradise of 1955 also featured a cabochon—this time a sapphire—

42

Ring. Gold, sapphire, and diamonds. Cartier Paris, 1969.

Facing page:
Bird of Paradise **brooch.** Chased gold, brilliant-cut diamonds, emeralds, and navette- and pear-shaped rubies. C. 1942.

Bird of Paradise **brooch.** Gold, diamonds, sapphire cabochons, and two emerald cabochons. Cartier Paris, 1949.

Bird of Paradise **brooch.** Platinum, sapphires, and diamonds. Cartier Paris, 1955.

similar to a model made nine years earlier for the Duchess of Windsor (one of the many pieces stolen from Ednam Lodge in England). At the base of the neck a ruff collar of caliber-cut sapphires ringed with baguette-cut diamonds adds majesty to the head crowned by a wonderfully flowerlike crest; the tail of two long, white, articulated feathers has turned-up tips that reveal a dark blue underside. One of these birds, a fabulous monochrome composed of 894 variously cut diamonds, is astonishing at first sight for its size. Pinned to the neckline of a black velvet gown by Piguet, as pictured in American *Vogue* in 1948 ("Mrs. Robert Lazard's peacock"), it seems as long as the bust; placed in the hair six years later, as presented in the *Daily Mirror*, it seems as high as the head. Its gentle profile, a lengthy, subtle S with countercurve at the end, is orchestrated by baguette-cut diamonds arranged in straight or angled lines, further multiplying the radiance of this gem-feathered creature.

By the late 1940s, however, another approach was adopted for birds of paradise, as for other animals in Cartier's bestiary. Where pavé-set stones had reigned, yellow gold began to triumph, highlighted with touches of gems; where full forms had been favored, voids emerged in linear compositions of gold wire on which gems were set in more or less regular patterns. This style, playing more on dispersion than compactness, evoked much contemporary creativity such as the geometric motifs employed by decorators and graphic designers (made of straight, intersecting lines dotted with patches of color) and the dangling colored shapes of Alexander Calder's mobiles. The press waxed enthusiastic about this new lightness in jewelry, which clearly reflected the feeling of relief felt by people once the war had truly ended.

Peacocks, as far as Cartier is concerned, don't strut their feathers. Perched on branches, they sometimes resemble birds of paradise, similarly crested and displaying a long train of feathers made of stones, pearls, or gold. An advertisement in a 1947 issue of *Femina* showed an aviary containing a variety of subjects including lovebirds, solitary sparrows, a couple tending a nest, and a bird of paradise with its long tail composed of palmettes. In the middle was a majestic peacock whose body was formed of geometric stones set in chased gold, while four curved feathers

Lovebird **earrings**. Gold, diamonds, and rubies. Cartier London, 1960.

Facing page:
Ladybird **brooch**. Gold with red and black enamel. Cartier London, 1956.

Ladybirds **brooch**. Gold with red and black enamel. 1940.

Ladybird **clip brooch**. Platinum, white gold, baguette- and brilliant-cut and half-moon-shaped diamonds, coral studded with collet-set diamonds, and black lacquer. Cartier Paris, 1969.

Ladybird **earrings**. Platinum, gray gold, single-cut diamonds, coral, and black lacquer. Cartier Paris, 1936.

of diamonds and eight long articulated secondary feathers of gold were adorned with round diamonds, with a ruby drop dangling from the end of each. Cartier's two styles, which existed side by side for many years, are perfectly illustrated by two Paris dragonflies. One dates from 1953; now in the Cartier Collection, it is similar, despite narrower wings, to a special order made in New York in 1948, entirely of diamonds except for sapphire eyes. The other, made in 1954, belonged to actress Jacqueline Delubac, a shrewd collector of modern art and a faithful Cartier client who succeeded Yvonne Printemps as Sacha Guitry's partner. Whereas gems dominate metal in the first dragonfly, the second is animated by twists and turns of yellow gold, which underscore every diamond and every ruby, evoking the Indian-style settings explored by Cartier as early as the 1920s. Pierced by a simple slit or by extensive openwork, their wings were given a "tremored" setting based on springs, which imparted a lifelike flutter.

It is impossible to mention wings without thinking of butterflies. In Japan, a butterfly is the symbol of a woman. Everyone is fascinated by a butterfly's lightness, and every civilization exploits its attributes (fluttery existence, metamorphosis, etc.) to specific ends, thereby appropriating the supernatural beauty of its apparel. For the duchess of Windsor in 1946, a butterfly might have had an emerald body and diamond wings, set on a coral cabochon ringed by emerald leaves; while for the actress Josette Day, a year earlier, it may have displayed admirable simplicity: here the brooch and two earrings (later turned into brooches, too) are clearly stylized, playing wonderfully on the original model and creating a remarkable visual impact. The two upper wings feature discreetly asymmetrical flamelike stripes of gold and black enamel over carved coral underwings adorned with emerald cabochons.

Wings—or rather, wing covers—also inspired Cartier creativity when it came to ladybugs, or ladybirds, who alighted here as early as 1935. The wing covers, once again of coral, were dotted with small diamonds and black lacquer; the ladybugs were all the more precious if head and feet were set with diamonds, as was the case with a fine 1969 example now in the Cartier Collection. Their popularity led to a wider variety of appearances, as ladybugs flitted from brooches and earrings to a candlesnuffer (bought by actor José Ferrer in 1947), to a leaf, to a rose of ivory, and even to a cigarette lighter (a superb 1949 item of perfect proportions, forming a compact monolith on which the little bug alights with charming ease).

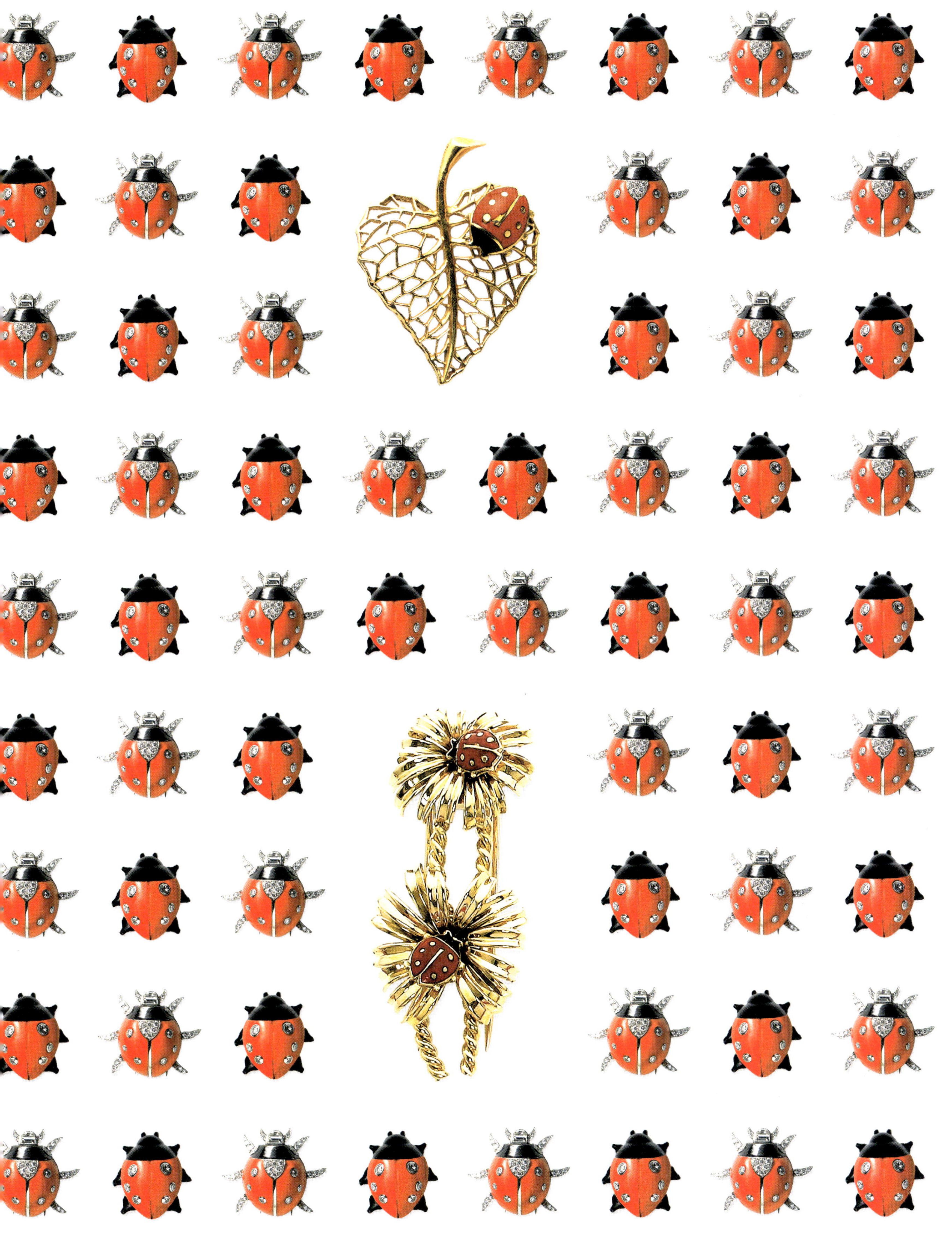

Butterfly **clip brooch**. Platinum, gold, carved coral, black enamel, single-cut diamonds, one emerald bead, and four emerald cabochons. Cartier Paris, 1945.

Butterfly **brooch**. Platinum, brilliant-cut diamonds, pink diamonds, sapphires, and emeralds, Cartier Paris 1998.

Dragonfly **clip brooch**. Yellow gold, platinum, coral, emeralds, and diamonds. Cartier Paris, 1955.

Dragonfly **clip brooch**. Platinum, gold, fancy-, emerald-, brilliant-, single-, baguette-, and rose-cut diamonds, one emerald cabochon, two round faceted rubies, and ten caliber-cut rubies. The openwork wings have a "tremored" setting, each attached to the body by a spring. Cartier Paris, 1953.

Facing page: Irving Penn, *Model with Dragonfly by Cartier on Her Face*, New York, 1966.

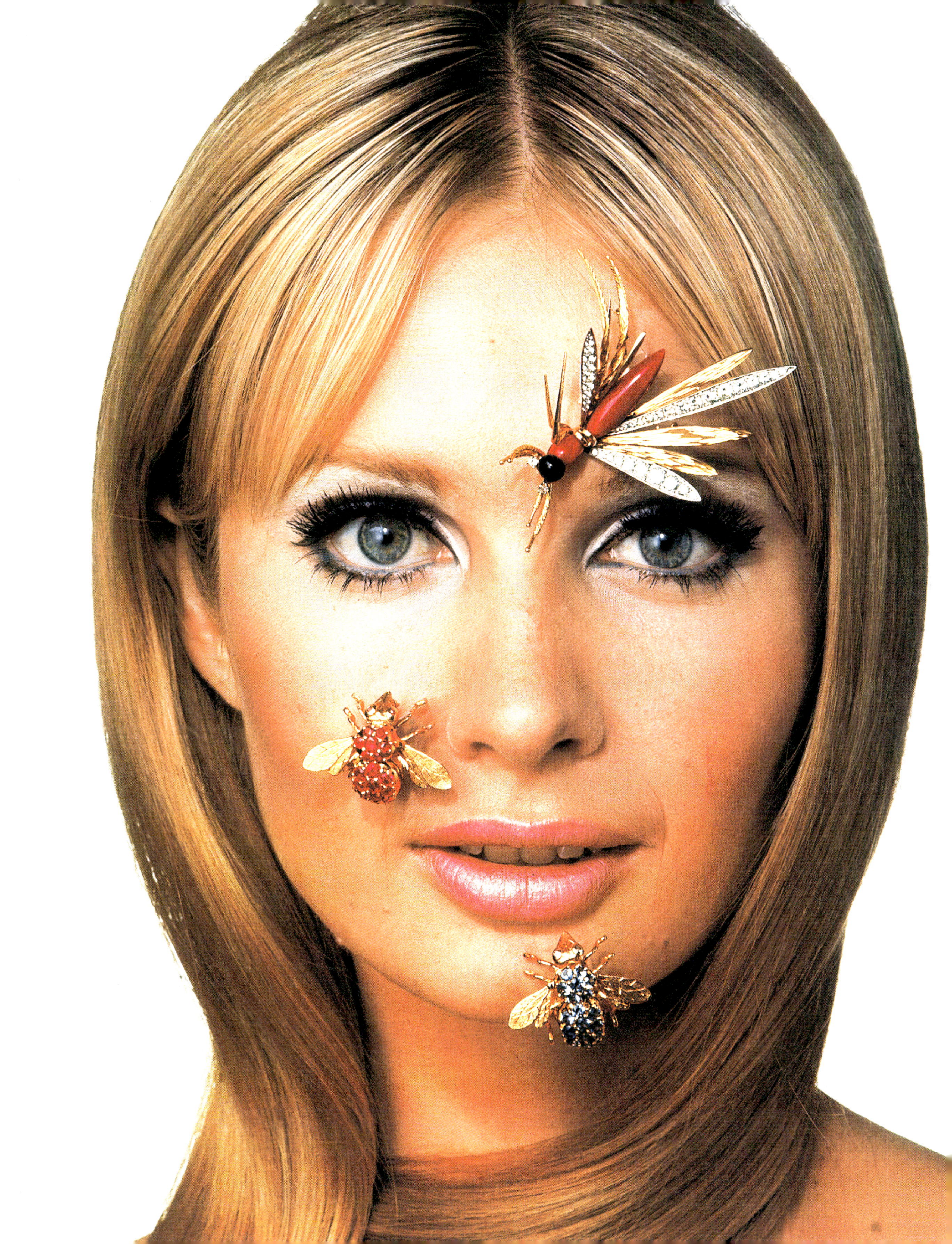

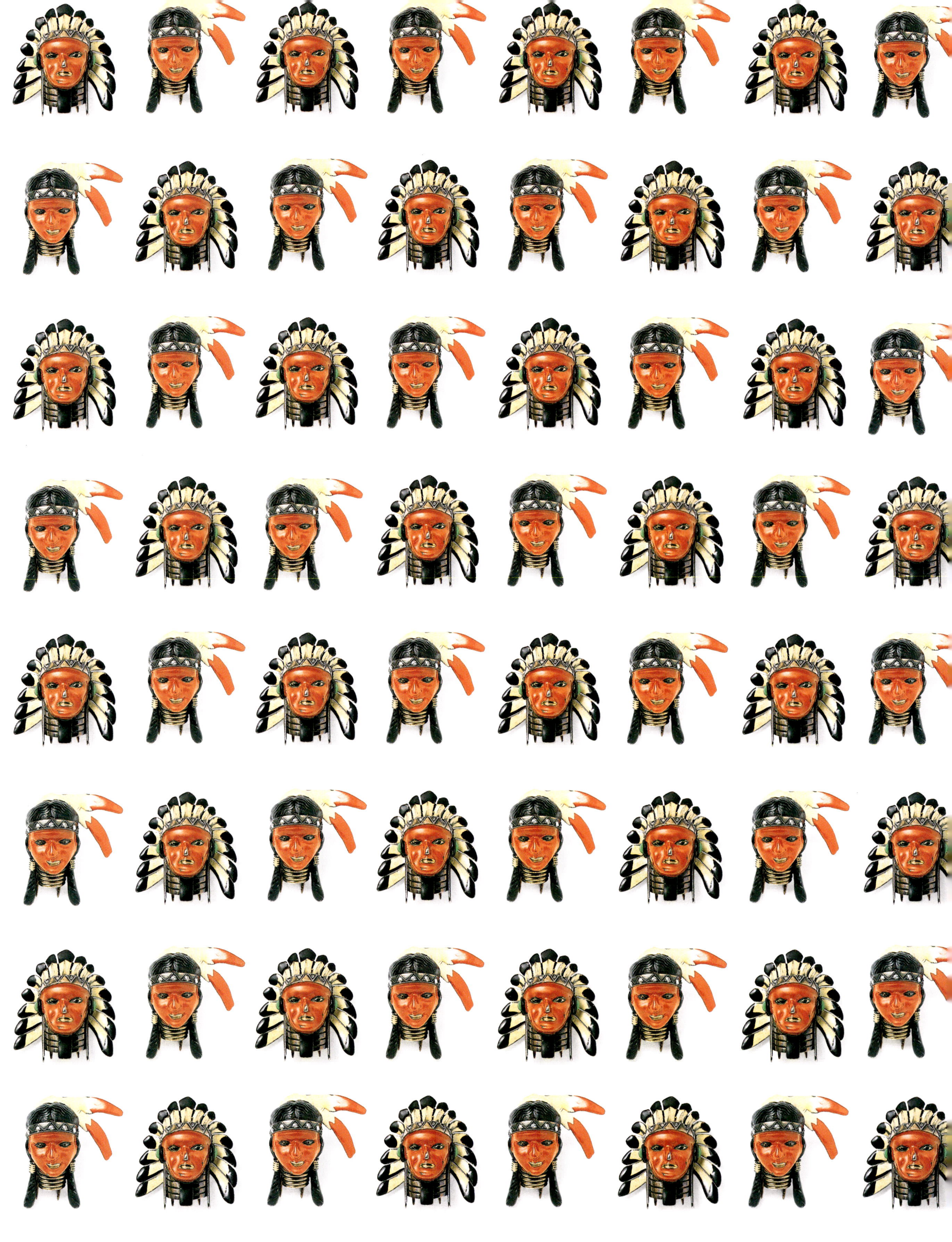

Talismans, Fetishes, Charms, and Swords

Pair of *King and Queen of Hearts* **clip brooches**. Yellow gold, enamel, and diamonds. Cartier Paris, 1938.

Charm **bracelet**. Platinum, gray gold, brilliant- and baguette-cut diamonds, rubies, and sapphires. Cartier Paris, 1931.

Facing page:
Sioux **clip brooch**. Gold, silver, rose-cut diamonds, turquoise cabochons, and red, ivory-colored, and black lacquer. Cartier Paris, 1938.

Squaw **clip brooch**. Gold, silver, rose-cut diamonds, and red, ivory-colored, and black lacquer. Cartier Paris, 1938.

Ladybugs, known as "the Good Lord's creatures" in medieval France because they protected roses and allegedly sheltered in winter at the foot of crucifixes, are often considered signs of good luck. Indeed, since the dawn of time the idea of the talisman or lucky charm has generated an infinite variety of amulets, whether living or dead, crude or precious, or animal, vegetable, or mineral.

By the mid-seventeenth century, commemorative jewels with an enamel back and a rock crystal front would contain a trace of a loved one; the jewel might come in the form of a ring, pendant, or sliding ring attached to ribbon and worn around neck or wrist, prefiguring the "charms" that dangled from a chain in the form of charm bracelets, which arrived en masse in the nineteenth century. Such charms were made with a small ring that could be attached to bracelet, necklace, or watch, thereby bringing magic power to the wearer. Charms went somewhat out of fashion in the 1960s, but are now resurfacing in a wide variety of forms that reflect Cartier's rich history.

In 1936 telephone-cum-lobster constituted a surrealist artwork by Salvador Dalí, who was still interested in telecommunications thirteen years later when he designed telephone earrings that were strangely organic in shape. But there is nothing surrealist about Cartier's little telephone, a perfect miniature device with pavé-set diamonds whose dial spins to reveal the words "I Love U" or "Hello." It is, of course, a charm, one of those precious, minuscule "trinkets" that could convey a personal, private message. Many of them date from the 1930s and were made by Cartier New York, where whimsical inventiveness was rampant: a book with a cover set with rubies, a hotel door with a "Do not disturb" sign, monuments of Paris hanging from a bracelet whose links spell out "Paris 37," an envelope, a playing card, a set of keys. The highly realistic handing of these items prefigured a style that would soon become classic.

In 1977 Cartier paid tribute to Charlie Brown's dog, Snoopy, that famous character from Charles Schulz's comic strip, *Peanuts*. Ever since the 1950s Snoopy had been observing, from his doghouse, the strange adventures of human beings. Another huge hit was Cartier's Golden Bar, a little gold ingot. Optical illusion, meanwhile, had been used to encode secret messages since the 1920s: half of the letters of "I love you" or "Te quiero" were written on each side of a gold disk, so that when it spins rapidly the entire message can be read. In 1948, simple gold medallions engraved with dedications framed the portraits of Marion and Pierre Claudel's six children. It was Cartier London, on the other hand, who in 1942–43 produced "gremlins" based on drawings by Bernard Dupérier, a member of the French air force who knew that gremlins were responsible for the blunders attributed to himself and his RAF companions. "Some gremlins loosened bolts, others scrambled radio messages, while Filfinella, the lady gremlin, drove her victims to distraction!" London also made numerous crosses of Lorraine, as well as items ordered by General de Gaulle, such as a paper knife marked with that emblem of the French Resistance. Likewise, the First World War had inspired charms based on tanks, airplanes, and national symbols made charming by their diminutive size and decorative gemstones.

Some objects acquire the status of fetish as they worm their way into the collective unconscious. Like the ladybug described above, three motifs on three clip brooches of 1936–37 functioned that way for many years: a hand in black lacquer wearing two bracelets and holding a rose with a diamond in its center; the head of a blackamoor with gold lips wearing an ivory lacquer turban adorned with a cabochon; and the head of a Sioux man or squaw in red lacquer, crowned with black and ivory feathers, sometimes sporting gold hoops around the neck. Although these exotic motifs were heavily inspired by the enthusiasm for the international Colonial Exposition held in France in 1931, their impact was certainly due to their perfect execution. The disembodied hand firmly clutches the flower, variously evoking Gérard de Nerval's *La Main Enchantée* (The Enchanted Hand) on which Maurice Tourneur based his film *La Main du Diable* (Carnival of Sinners), or else the hand in the castle of *La Belle et la Bête* (Beauty and the Beast), made into a film by Jean Cocteau nine years later, or else all those Mogul emperors portrayed with a flower in one hand (alluding to their legendary gardens). The heads, being separated from their

Facing page:
Tortoise **brooch**. Gold, diamonds, emeralds, and lapis lazuli. The head and limbs are articulated. Cartier New York, 1950.

Turtle **clip brooch**. Gold, brilliant-cut diamonds, turquoises, and sapphires. Cartier Paris, c. 1950.

Tortoise **brooch**. Chased gold, brilliants, and lapis lazuli. Cartier Paris, 1948.

Tortoise **clip brooch**. Chased and twisted gold, brilliant-cut fancy yellow diamonds, and sapphire cabochons. Cartier Paris, special order, 1969.

Tortoise **brooch**. Platinum, gold, oval faceted sapphire weighing 107.75 carats, cushion-shaped faceted sapphire weighing 2.48 carats, and round old-, brilliant-, and fancy-cut diamonds. Cartier Paris, 1951.

Tortoise **clip brooch**. Platinum, chased and twisted gold, brilliant-cut diamonds, sapphire cabochons. Model first designed in 1946. Cartier Paris for New York, 1956.

Tortoise **clip brooch**. Platinum, chased gold, one 93.14-carat star sapphire cabochon and one cushion-shaped sapphire, brilliant-cut diamonds, and turquoise cabochons. Cartier Paris, 1962.

bodies, suggest trophies; fashion columnists recommended wearing the Sioux heads in threes, diagonally, from shoulder to breast. The hand motif would be copied long and often, while Cartier's blackamoor (or "moor of Venice" from Shakespeare's *Othello*) appeared in a great number of variations, sometimes heavily ornamented. In 1985 *Beaux-Arts* magazine noted the extravagant price paid for a "Negro Head" [*sic*] with turquoise headdress when it came up for auction at Sotheby's in Saint-Moritz. Made by Cartier in 1937 for Her Highness the Begum Aga Khan, it sparked a bidding war between Stavros Niarchos and an anonymous American collector. Indeed, as the years went by the original blackamoor model was left far behind—in 1966, for example, the head of an African was given a leopard-skin headdress (thereby converging with Cartier's beloved panther theme).

Despite its rather unattractive physical appearance, a turtle or tortoise always inspires sympathy; in China and black Africa it is even viewed as a symbol of the universe, thanks to its rounded shell (heavenly dome) and flat body (earth). Its short but powerful feet, anchored to the ground, enable the tortoise to carry the world on its back. The Tikar people of Cameroon make stools in the shape of a turtle on which defendants have to sit, to prevent them from lying. The tortoise's slow-but-steady pace has inspired a famous fable, and children everywhere admire its ability to retreat from the world in a split second by pulling in head and feet. Hindus, meanwhile, feel that the turtle epitomizes the highly symbolic return to a primal state. In 1928 Cartier designed a handsome turtle of turquoise, sapphires, and brilliants, while in 1938 the head of a tortoiseshell-and-diamond version withdrew when the hind feet

Crucifix **pendant**. Crucifix: gold, silver, star and caliber-cut sapphire cabochons, rubies, rose-, single-, and round old-cut diamonds of various shapes, one opal and two imitation opals, button pearls, and topaz. Dove: gold, diamonds, sapphires, emerald, rubies, pearl, moonstone, and opal. Cartier London, 1934.

Hunting **pin**. Gold, rubies, and emerald. Cartier Paris, 1954.

Facing page:
Bodhisattva Head **clip brooch**. Platinum, yellow gold, coral, turquoises, seed pearls, rubies, and diamonds. Cartier New York, 1961.

Egyptian Head **clip brooch**. Gold, coral, and diamonds. Cartier Paris, 1966.

were pressed. Like Cartier's birds, many of these turtles were composed around a cabochon, the feet and head stylized in gold or diamonds. Numerous versions were created up to the 1970s; a shell of lapis lazuli or coral might be dotted with diamonds, composed of juxtaposed gemstones, or elaborated from a diamond-patterned gold net dotted with turquoise, ruby, or sapphire cabochons. In 1962, playing subtly on different blues—a 93.14-carat sapphire cabochon for the body, a cushion-shaped sapphire for the head, and turquoise cabochons for the feet—the tortoise adopted a less static pose, as its neck and feet were underscored by chased gold and studded with diamonds.

This shelled reptile, so appreciated by Jeanne Toussaint, inspired other Cartier objects. From 1927 to 1929, three semi-mystery (or magnetic) clocks devised by Maurice Couët entailed a little turtle (made of tortoiseshell) that swam around a silver bowl filled with water. In 1929 the silver bowl was replaced by an eighteenth-century Chinese jade bowl on which perched a chimera with emerald eyes and red enamel tongue, threatening the poor little turtle! In 1943 a piece of Chinese coral carved in the nineteenth century was used to present a crossbreed of the two animals—a turtle-chimera—which supported a vase topped by a clock dial. In the 1950s, it was said that one of Toussaint's employees regularly collected the shells of dead turtles from the pet shops along the Seine in Paris, which were then adorned with coral or lapis lazuli and transformed into table lighters that became an instant hit.

There where animals reign, humans hunt. Hunting-related jewelry, trophies, talismans, and insignia were certainly not a specialty reserved to Cartier, for other jewelers such as Mellerio (who launched its department in 1957) were equally attached to them. Yet it was Cartier who made the superb, diamond-studded stag head given by King Leopold II to the princess of Réthy on their silver wedding anniversary, and it was Cartier who made a pin in the 1940s on a hunting motif, featuring the head of a spaniel in gold, with a duck in its mouth. Cartier's output also included a few remarkable Latin crosses, from the simple to the highly baroque, such as a necklace of square emeralds and round diamonds holding an emerald cross of forty-five carats (Cartier London), or the charms worn by the Duchess of Windsor for her wedding

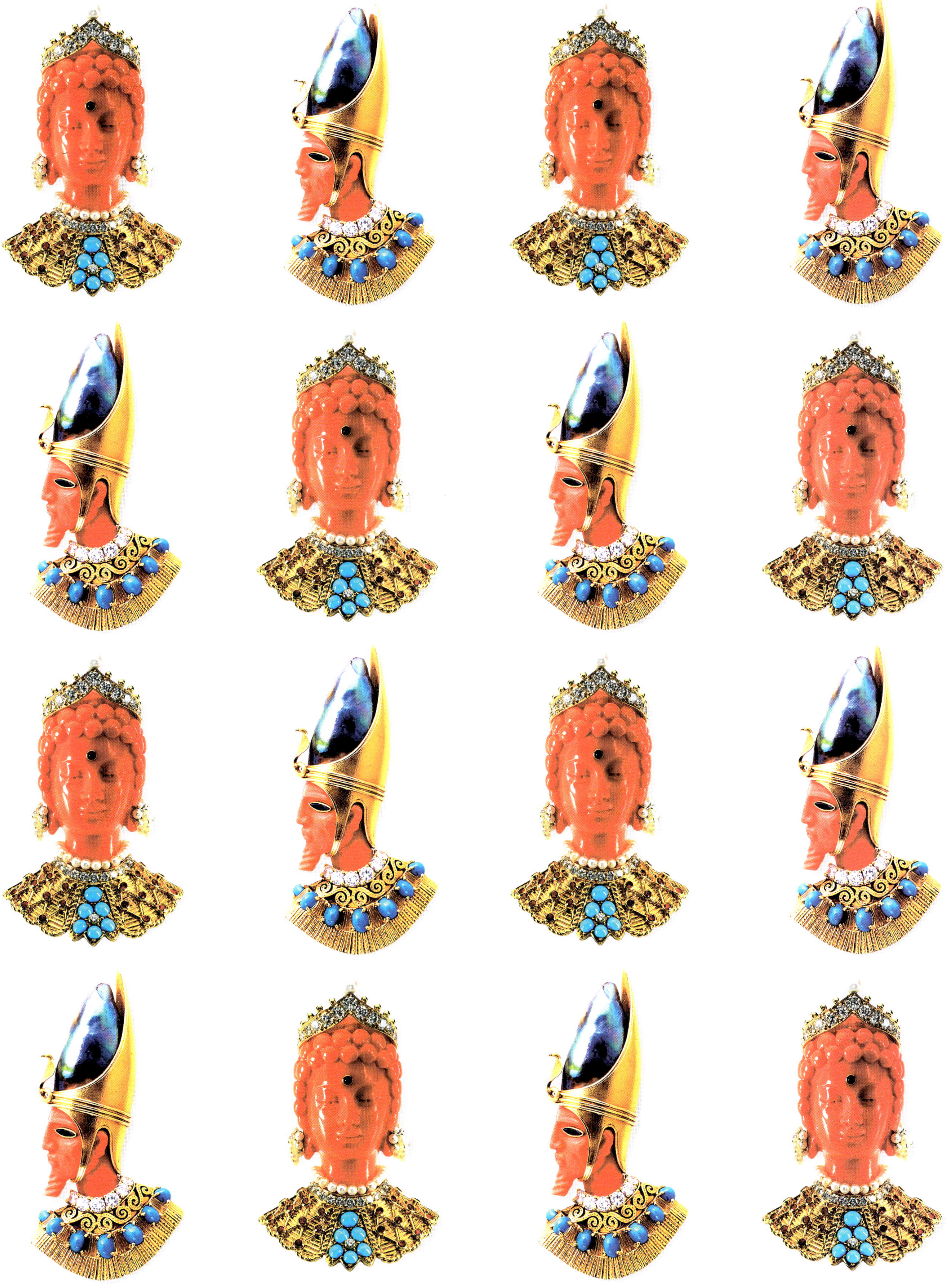

Hand Holding a Rose **clip brooch**. Platinum, yellow and pink gold, silver, round old- and rose-cut diamonds, and black and red lacquer. Cartier Paris, 1938.

Hand Holding a Rose **clip brooch**. Yellow gold, silver, lacquer, coral, and diamonds. Cartier London, 1937.

Hand Holding a Rose **clip brooch**. Platinum, yellow gold, coral, and diamonds, 1952.

Bouquet **clip brooch**. Platinum, pink and yellow gold, round old-cut diamonds, blue, red and white enamel. Made for a state visit of the British royal couple: the rose, thistle, daffodil, and clover symbolize England, Scotland, Wales, and Northern Ireland. Cartier Paris, 1938.

at the Château de Candé (two crossed rows of fine baguette-cut stones and plain platinum), or an unusual crucifix with a carved gold Christ plus sapphires, rubies, diamonds, pearls, topazes, and opals (from which a dove would be hung fifteen years later, in 1949). Around 1960, a very sober object of worship, now in the Fondation Pierre Cartier, took the form of a smooth gold ring topped by a tiny cross surrounded by ten beads of lapis lazuli set with diamonds.

Among these strictly commemorative pieces, two brooches were inspired by British state visits to France. The first, a bouquet bound in red, white, and blue enamel, combines the English rose, the Scottish thistle, the Welsh daffodil, and the Northern Irish clover (prefiguring the four-leaf clover charms, a lucky charm if ever there were one); it was made for the visit of the king and queen in 1938. The second, of black lacquer, chalcedony, and diamonds, depicts a beefeater at the Tower of London. "The English have gone mad over them!" exclaimed the press, and many were sold at the time of the coronation. All kinds of private events—even those that became public—were good excuses for original creations, such as a compact and a cigarette case made at the request of American aviator Jacqueline Cochran, engraved with gem-studded maps whose routes are traced in platinum; then there is a cigar case presented by Aristotle Onassis to Winston Churchill for his eighty-sixth birthday, on which is engraved the outline of Onassis's yacht *Christina* and the islands visited during its cruise, plus the inscription "Happy birthday from Ari 30th November 1960."

The ceremonial swords given to members of the Académie Française also number among these symbolic objects. Worn with an Academician's famous "green jacket," the sword sums up the life of a newly inducted

I Love U **charm**. Platinum and diamonds. Cartier New York, 1945.

Telephone **charm**. Platinum and diamonds. Cartier New York, 1936.

Airplane **charm**. Platinum and diamonds. Cartier New York, 1936.

Book **charm**. Platinum, rubies, and diamonds. Cartier New York, 1939.

Facing page: Detail of the Academician's sword made for Jean Cocteau, based on his own design. Cartier Paris, 1955.

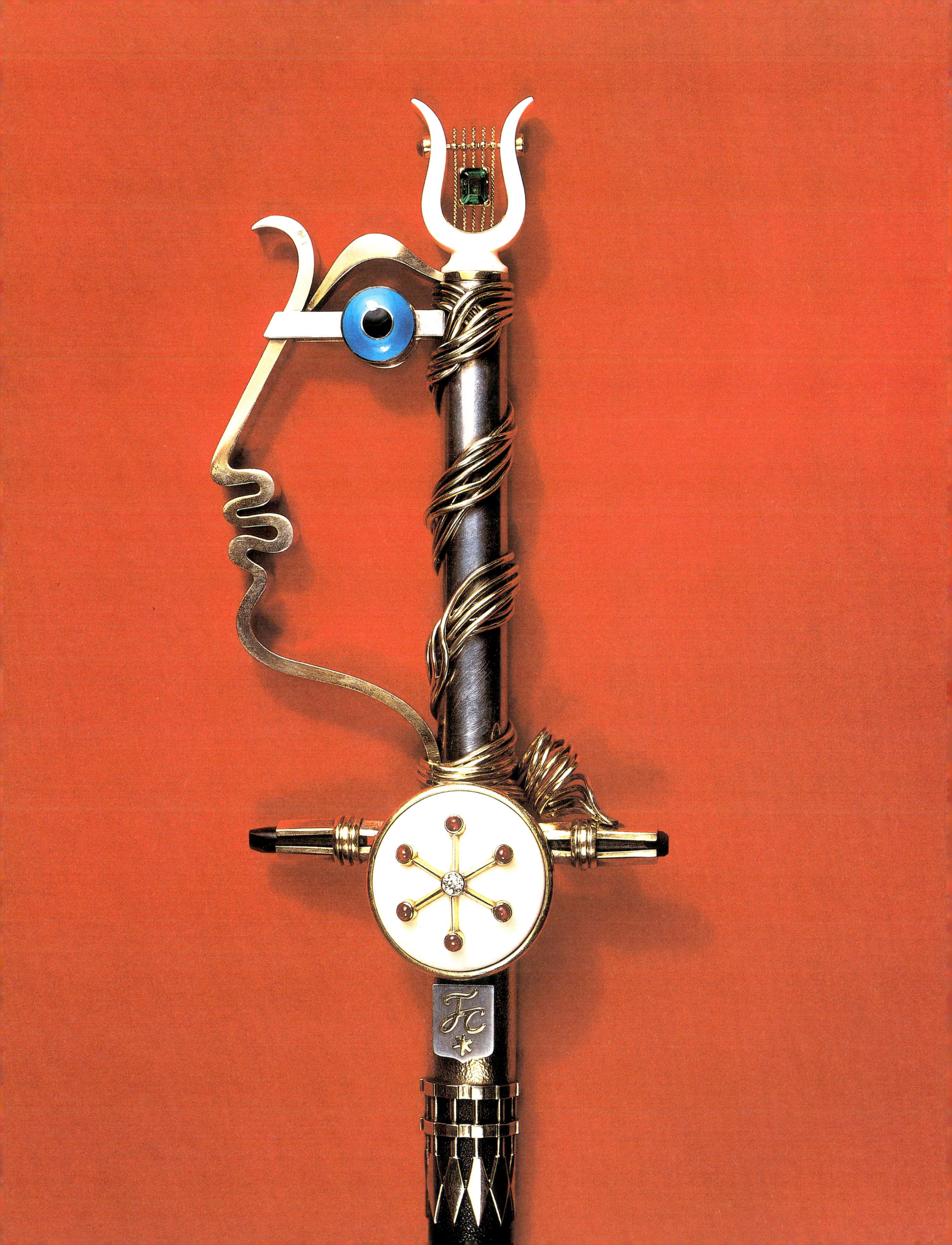

Academician's sword made by Cartier for Maurice Genevoix. Silver, ivory, and steel. Cartier Paris, 1947.

Academician's sword made by Cartier for Jean Hamburger. Silver, bronze, quartz, and steel. Based on a design by Hamburger's architect son, Bernard. Cartier Paris, 1975.

Academician's sword made by Cartier for Louis Pauwels. Burnished silver, gold, silver-gilt, and steel. Based on a design by Pierre-Yves Trémois. Cartier Paris, 1986.

Proposal for an Academician's sword for the duke of Lévis-Mirepoix, 1953.
Jean Cocteau, c. 1950.
Photo: Luc Fournol.

member. Decorative hilt, pommel, and cross guards illustrate a theme, an oeuvre, a discovery, a career. The first of Cartier's swords, executed in 1931, was made for the duke of Gramant, whose scientific research was symbolized by the North Star, constellations, a comet, and microscopes. Then came the swords of François Mauriac in 1934, Jacques de Lacretelle and James Hyde in 1938, André Maurois in 1939, Jules Romains in 1946, Maurice Genevoix and Jacques Rueff in 1947, Joseph Kessel in 1964, and Maurice Druon in 1967. The most naturalistic was certainly the one made for Georges Duhamel (1936), the most sober being the ones for Jean Hamburger (1975, designed by his son Bernard, an architect and avowed enemy of allegory) and Louis Pauwels (1986, the work of Pierre-Yves Trémois, who was elected to the Académie des Beaux-Arts three years later). The most respectful of its owner's genealogy was the one executed for the duke of Lévis-Mirepoix (1954), and the most famous was the one for Jean Cocteau (1955), who designed it himself, his friends supplying, as custom requires, "the wherewithal for jacket and sword."[4] Coco Chanel gave him an emerald, Francine Weisweiller (whose home in Saint-Jean-Cap-Ferrat Cocteau had decorated with frescoes) contributed rubies and the diamond, and his Spanish friends supplied the Toledo blade. As for Picasso, he offered a few penciled and somewhat tardy sketches, just a week before Cocteau's induction into the Académie: an Hors-d'oeuvre Sword (decorated with an open can of sardines), a Breakfast Sword (with cup and croissant), a Nocturnal Sword (with candle), etc. Jean Marais recalled his intense emotion on seeing Cocteau's sword and described it as he saw it just before he left his apartment: "the profile of Orpheus and his lyre, the five-pointed star, the draftsman's charcoal holder, the curtains of the ancient theater, the gates of the Palais-Royal and, at the very tip, the tiny bronze hand on the ivory snowball from Les Enfants terribles."[5]

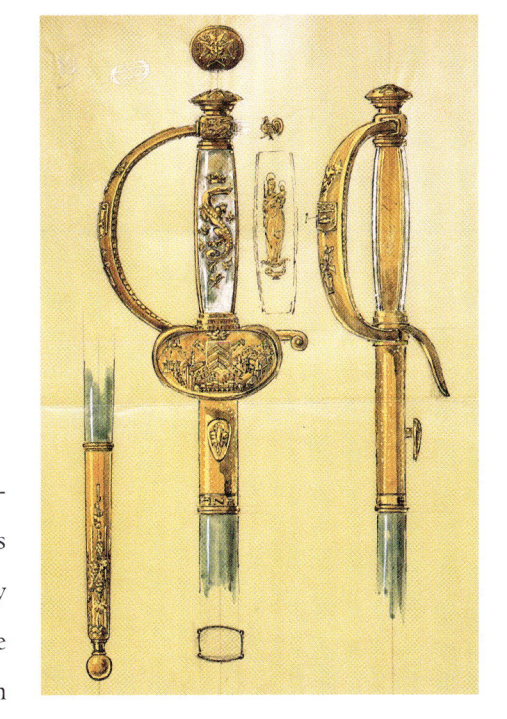

4. Jean Cocteau, quoted in Henry Gidel, Cocteau (Paris: Flammarion, 1998).

5. Jean Marais, quoted in Gilberte Gautier, La Saga des Cartier (Paris: Éditions Michel Lafon, 1988).

57

Lady with White Panther brooch. Gray gold, diamonds, and emeralds. Detachable chain. Cartier Paris, 2003.

French novelist Colette poses on a lion skin, covered with a panther skin, 1909.

Brooch. Gray gold, yellow gold, one briolette-cut diamond, one orange diamond, fancy yellow diamonds, emerald eyes, onyx, and brilliants. *Inde Mystérieuse* collection. Cartier Paris, 2007.

Facing page: *Panther* **brooch**. Platinum, diamonds, emeralds, and onyx. The head pivots, the legs and tail are articulated. 1978.

Rembrandt Bugatti, *Two Panthers*. Bronze with black patina.

Cats

The *enfants terribles* or "dreadful children" in France during World War II were certainly the youngsters known as "Zazous." Their insolent attitude, the irritating onomatopoeic phrases they constantly mumbled, and the yards and yards of scarce cloth they consumed to make their outrageous baggy suits all revealed their contempt for a tragic situation that would eventually catch up with them. Their provocation later became more explicit, and some Zazous went so far as to wear a yellow Star of David on which they stitched not the word "Jew," but "Swing."[6] In their own way, Zazous prefigured the confusion of the postwar years that engendered total despair and a burning desire to party. Two schools faced off against each other, their members often bumping into one another (as had been the case in the cafés on boulevard des Italiens in the late nineteenth century). On the left (bank, that is), there were the existentialists, who danced to be-bop till dawn and read Sartre. A new sexual freedom blossomed, and sleek young women dressed all in black, led by Juliette Gréco and Annabel, henceforth refused to wear makeup.[7] On the right (yet also left, if we're still discussing the banks of the Seine), were the magnificent parties that began in 1947, the year the New Look was launched. Thanks to Dior, women recovered their femininity. Waists were narrow, shoulders rounded, skirts were flowing and longer. Evening dress was ample and sumptuous, while diamonds, as De Beers proclaimed, were "forever."[8] Notorious balls and parties included the Bal du Panache (decorated with a profusion of plants and feathers by Christian Bérard), the Grande Nuit de Paris, the Bal de la Rose, the Bal de la Violette (where Léonor Fini wore a lighted lamp on her head) the Bal du Ruban, the Bal des Oiseaux, the Bal de l'Infante, the Bal des Rois et des Reines (where Christian Dior incarnated the king of beasts).[9] Women, whether devoid of makeup and artifice or super-sophisticated, appeared to be dangerous (the demimonde ladies whose professional occupation involved fleecing their game were dubbed "lionesses"), or at least that's what Jacques Tourneur seemed to suggest in

6. Patrice Bollon, *Précis d'extravagance*, illustrated by Stefano Canulli (Paris: Éditions du Regard, 1995).

7. Bollon, *Précis d'extravagance*.

8. The slogan "A diamond is forever" was launched by De Beers and the Ayer ad agency in 1947.

9. Jean-Claude Daufresne, *Fêtes à Paris au XX siècle: Architectures éphémères de 1919 à 1989* (Paris: Pierre Mardaga Éditions, 2001).

Necklace. Platinum, brilliants, onyx, and emeralds. Cartier Paris, 1986.

Tiger **brooch.** Platinum, single-cut diamonds, onyx. Cartier Paris, 1929.

Facing page: Edith Dussler wearing *Tiger* earrings. Lapis lazuli, fancy yellow diamonds, onyx, and emeralds, 1967.

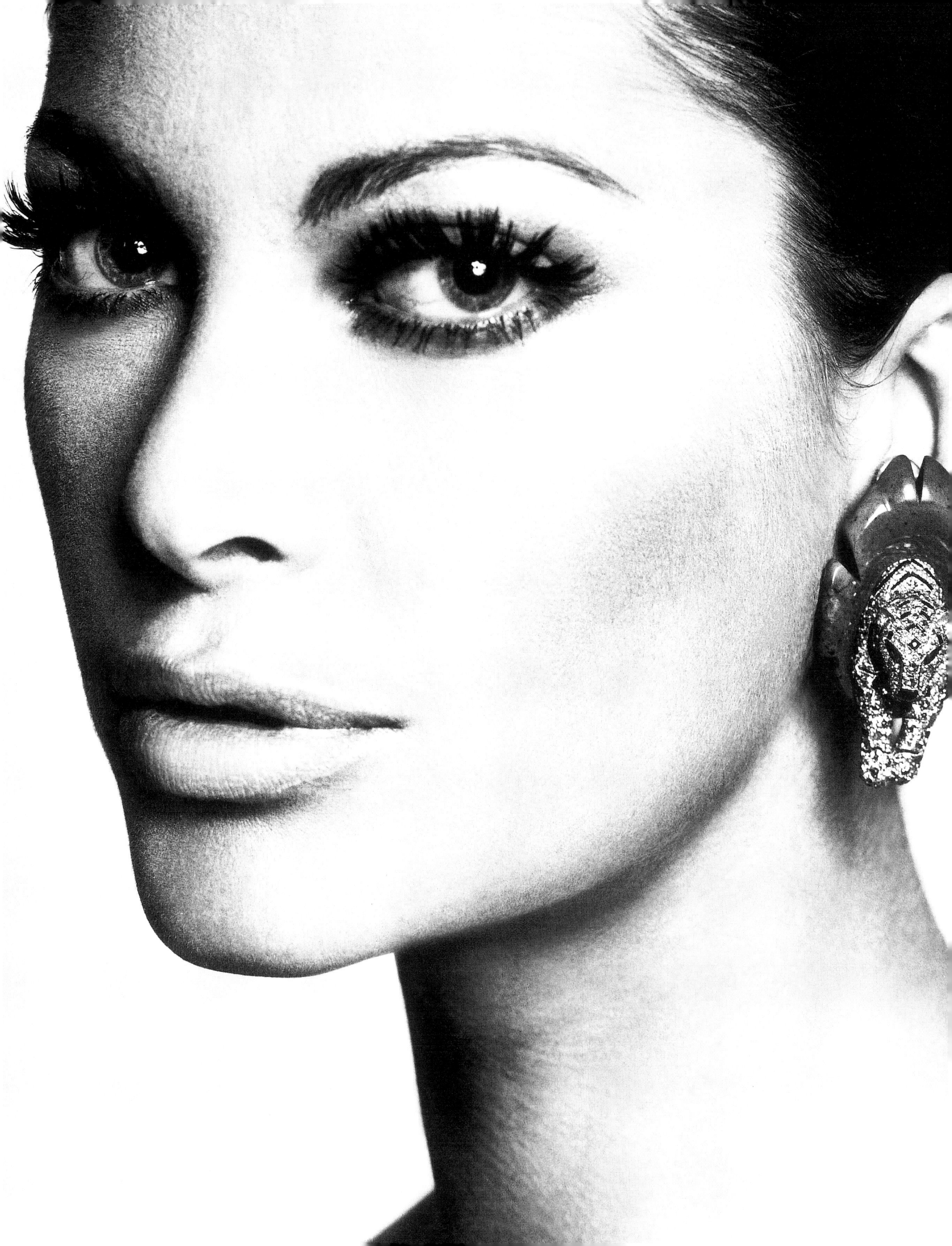

Panther **clip brooch**. Platinum, white gold, single-cut diamonds and pear-shaped fancy yellow diamonds, one 152.35 Kashmir sapphire cabochon, and sapphire cabochons. Formerly the collection of the Duchess of Windsor. Cartier Paris, 1949.

Facing page:
Panther **bangle**. Platinum, white gold, brilliant- and single-cut diamonds, sapphire cabochons, marquise-shaped emeralds, and onyx. This bangle opens with a swivel action. Formerly the collection of Princess Sadruddin Aga Khan. Cartier Paris, 1958.

63

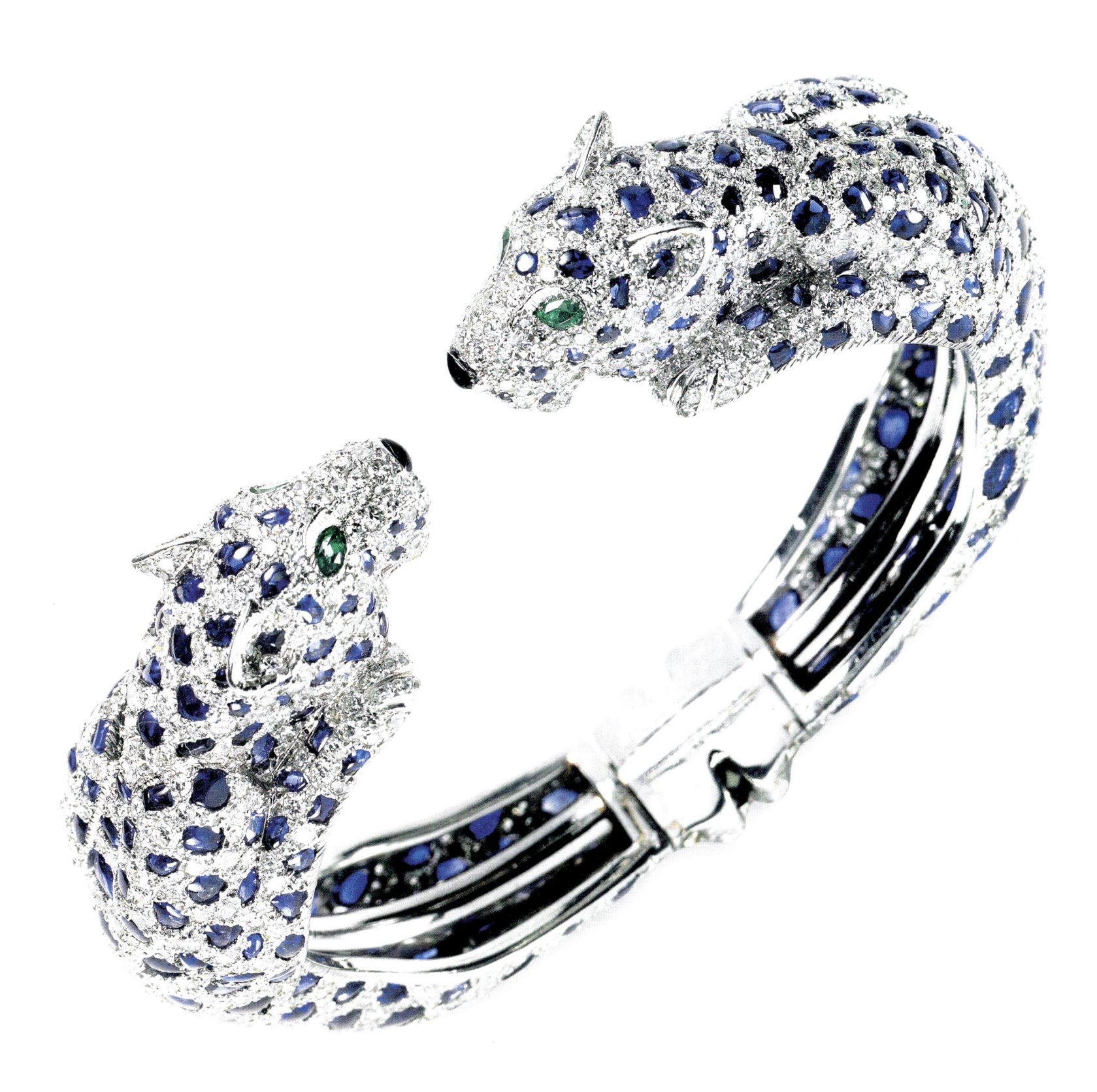

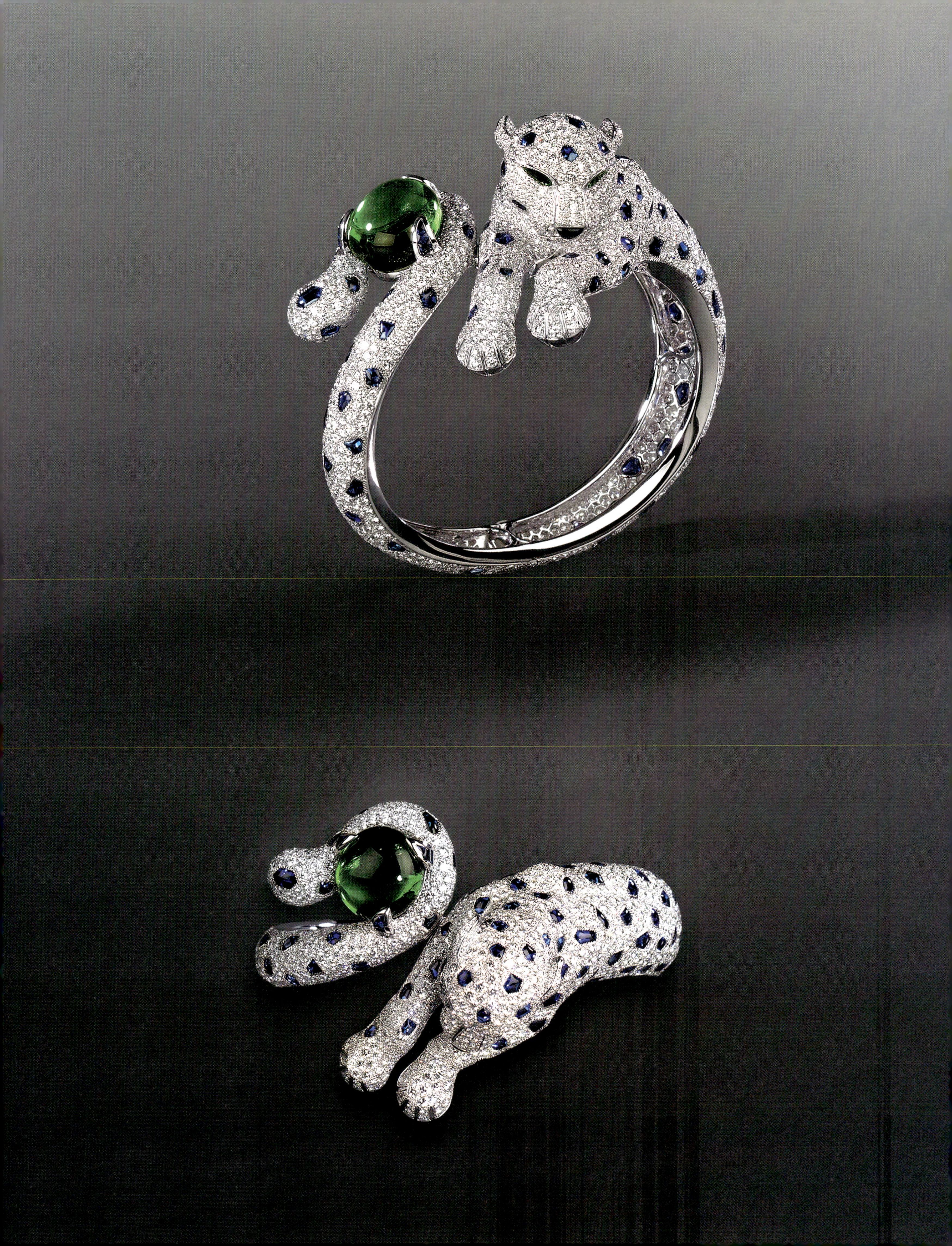

Jooghi **brooch**. 453 brilliants studded with 68 sapphires. Cartier Paris, 1988.

Facing page: *Panther with gem* **bracelet**. Platinum, brilliants, sapphires, one 17.45-carat emerald cabochon, and emeralds. Cartier Paris, 2006.

his 1942 film for RKO, *Cat People*. This new kind of science-fiction film implied more than it showed, an exercise at which femmes fatales excelled—love turned Irena, the protagonist, into a wild, blood-thirsty panther.

After the war, panthers would become one of the most powerful symbols of Cartier creativity, thanks to Toussaint's felicitous collaboration with Peter Lemarchand. Many other jewelers would adopt the panther motif, yet none of them handled it so consistently and so subtly, with so much inspiration and virtuosity. Cats were part of Toussaint's aesthetic universe—she is said to have been the first woman to wear a tiger coat made by Révillon with pelts from Kenya. It is also reported that during a foreign trip with Louis she spotted a wild cat crouching in the shadows and that this vision inspired her. It is furthermore claimed that, while she was paying a visit to Marquise Casati in 1925, a stuffed panther fitted with an automatic mechanism leaped at her face, sparking an emotion that reinforced her desire to transform this beast into a truly exceptional jewel.[10] As the designer, Lemarchand had a thorough mastery of his craft and a love of painting that were complemented by frequent visits to the Vincennes Zoo outside Paris, where he spent countless hours observing these fascinating carnivorous beasts. Toussaint's vision, Lemarchand's draftsmanship, and the remarkable skill of the gem-setters turned this shared vision into reality.

The first three-dimensional panther—almost a piece of animal sculpture—dates from 1948. Made of yellow gold with black enamel spots, it was set on an oblong emerald cabochon weighing over 116 carats and came with a pair of ear clips in which the cats' claws clutch either a round sapphire cabochon or openwork strands of polished gold, so fashionable at the time, depending on the whim of the wearer. The Duke of Windsor bought this set for the duchess who the very next year received a new version of the same species—a true incarnation of perfection. Poised on a 152.35-carat sapphire cabochon, pavé-set with diamonds and spotted with caliber-cut sapphires, it conveys ferocity through its yellow-diamond gaze and half-open jaws. The expressiveness is so accurate and intense that animal sculptors such as Barye and Bugatti come to mind. While the first panther also displayed superb modeling, this one is a sparkling technical feat that positively rivets the eye. The panther motif was certain to enjoy a long life once a few famous women were seduced by it.

10. Gautier, *La Saga des Cartier*.

Panther **cliquet pin.** Platinum, white gold, brilliant- and single-cut diamonds, sapphire cabochons, and green garnets. The cap over the tip could be replaced by a 30.67-carat sapphire surrounded by diamonds, or else the panther could be detached from the pin and set directly on a large coral cabochon. Formerly the collection of Nina Aga Khan. Cartier Paris, 1957.

George Barbier, *Woman with a Black Panther*, watercolor. Invitation for a 1914 exhibition, used as an ad in the 1920s.

They included Mrs. Reginald Fellowes, née Daisy Decazes, whose connections and sure yet bold sense of taste earned her a job as the head of the Paris bureau of *Harper's Bazaar*. A friend and rival of the Duchess of Windsor—both competing for the fashion magazine's title of "the world's most elegant woman"—Daisy Fellowes bought, that same year, a panther of diamonds and sapphires attached to a ring of baguette-cut diamonds, probably inspired by the Golden Fleece that Jason brought back to King Pelias. An ancient vase made in 340–330 BC, now in the Louvre, perfectly illustrates the form of the ram's fleece (which a 1970 pendant would directly evoke by conveying the flexibility of the pelt thanks to the use of gold mesh). A press report in December 1949, titled "Cartier's Panther," recounted the opening of Cartier's exhibition of diamonds; in it, even before listing "Mademoiselle Toussaint's sensational new items," the reporter referred to "an atom bomb in the central display case . . . within two hours, all of Paris had heard about the panther and its owner, Daisy Fellowes."[11] The duchess, however, continued to build her own collection. Three years later, she acquired a panther bracelet whose spots were made of caliber-cut onyx, and whose eyes were marquise-shaped emeralds (as was a matching clip of 1966). The bracelet was fully articulated, as its successors would be, lending it such suppleness that the shape of the wrist seemed to engender feline curves: the body stretches around the arm, one paw slightly pulled back, while the tail is attached to the head by an invisible clasp. The tiger motif, which appeared as early as 1954, was also netted by the insatiable duchess, first in the form of a gold-and-enamel lorgnette: the emerald-eyed animal was portrayed frontally, walking, head held high; the rear limbs served as the handle, while the glasses were hinged to its neck (and could be slipped back into the body after use). René Bouché described the lady and the accessory for American *Vogue*, proclaiming that "lorgnettes are back in fashion." There followed an articulated bracelet in 1956 and a clip brooch in 1959. These two pieces inaugurated the yellow-and-black combination of fancy yellow diamonds and onyx (set in gold), whereas the black-and-white combination of onyx and white diamonds (set in platinum) dated back to a panther wristwatch of 1914.[12] This pattern had been the invention of Charles Jacqueau, and Cartier archives hold a similar design, dated 1913, for a watch that

11. *Paris Presse*, (December 20, 1949).
12. The setting was called a "tiger" pattern at the time.

Panther **clip brooch**. Brilliants, pear-shaped emeralds, and onyx. Formerly the collection of the Duchess of Windsor. Cartier Paris, 1966.

Panther **bracelet**. Brilliants, marquise-shaped emeralds, and onyx. Formerly the collection of the Duchess of Windsor. Cartier Paris, 1952.

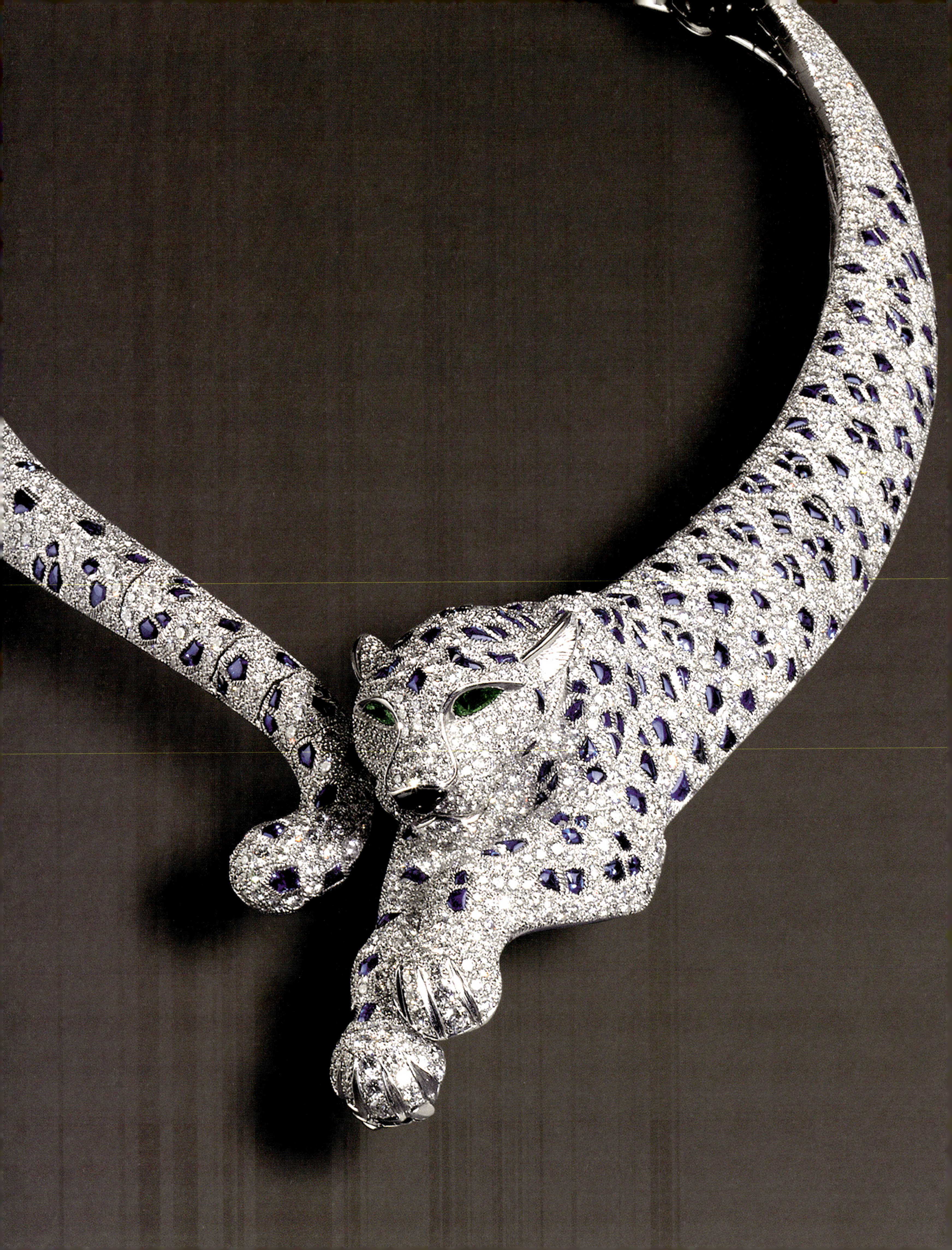

Necklace. Platinum, yellow gold, 435 yellow diamonds weighing 2.9 carats, 443 brilliants weighing 8.38 carats, one briolette-cut yellow diamond weighing 7.89 carats, one yellow sapphire weighing 1.48 carats, emeralds, and onyx. *Inde Mystérieuse* collection. Cartier Paris, 2007.

Facing page:
Necklace. Platinum, pear-shaped emeralds (eyes), sapphires (spots), and brilliants. Cartier Paris, 2006.

was never executed. In 1915, these irregular black spots, whose modern spirit is worth stressing, could be seen on a superb, rectangular panther-pattern watch-brooch attached to a hoop decorated with the same motif (bought by Pierre Cartier). This nature-inspired abstract pattern would grace other watches, as well as clasps (on a handbag of 1925, on a fluted coral-bead bracelet of 1930, etc.). The first figurative depiction of a panther appeared in 1919, in profile, on a vanity case made for Jeanne Toussaint. The same year another panther, also of onyx and brilliants, but this time lying in wait in the landscape, was depicted on a cigarette case made for Louis Cartier. A very fine lacquer vanity case of 1928, with diamond corners, boasts a panther of lacquer and brilliants placed between two emerald cypress trees. Panther handbags then followed, whereas figurative brooches appeared as early as 1927. The first was a reclining panther of onyx and diamonds set in platinum, while a black-and-white tiger was ready to leap by 1929.

Panthers and leopards (African panthers) had appeared in a few sophisticated interiors prior to the First World War. Cecil Beaton, enthusiastically describing celebrity figures in *The Glass of Fashion*, wrote that Cécile Sorel, who was able to benefit from the advice of the socialite Count Boni de Castellane (a friend of Louis Cartier) and the architect Whitney Warren, "turned her nobly proportioned apartment on the quai Voltaire into a thing of extravagant beauty. Everywhere she displayed her penchant for leopard skin … [in a] taste derived from Largillière and Nattier."[13] Beaton illustrated his comments with a drawing of a spotted skin negligently draped over a sofa. Beaton also appreciated the aesthetic taste of the famous American interior decorator Elsie de Wolfe (Lady Mendl), although he suspected her of having pinched the idea of upholstering furniture in leopard skin from Cécile Sorel or Marquise Casati.[14] In Paul Poiret's salon on the Rond-Point des Champs-Élysées, skins covered the floor and adorned armchairs. Later, Mainbocher would cover its showroom in leopard skin. In an entirely different register—less sophisticated if equally novel—Alfred Machin, a forgotten movie pioneer who shot a color film

13. Beaton, *The Glass of Fashion*.
14. Ibid.

Panther **clip brooch**. Gold, black enamel, emeralds, and emerald cabochon. Formerly the collection of the Duchess of Windsor. Cartier Paris, 1948.

Khana two-tiger **necklace**. Yellow gold, 618 brilliants, 619 fancy yellow brilliants, four pear-shaped faceted emeralds, and onyx. Cartier Paris, 1988.

Tiger **brooch**. Gold, diamonds, fancy yellow diamonds, onyx, and marquise-shaped emeralds. Cartier Paris, 1997.

Siddartha **brooch**. Yellow gold pavé-set with 245 brilliants and 268 fancy yellow diamonds, onyx, and one 196.6-carat emerald cabochon. Cartier Paris, 1993.

Tiger **brooch**. Yellow gold, yellow diamonds, onyx, and emeralds.

in 1914, *Maudite soit la Guerre* (*War Be Damned*), had cast his pet panther Mimir as the star of several movies as early as 1912. Many women were fascinated by these powerful cats, such as Sarah Bernhardt and Ida Rubenstein. Colette used to walk a magnificent snow leopard, while Sorel had her photo taken with tigers, as did Josephine Baker. Boldini, who in 1908 painted Marquise Casati surrounded by her greyhounds, could have portrayed her a few years later as an animal tamer at the Bal Longhi, where she appeared in the company of a leopard. In 1914, Louis Cartier asked Georges Barbier to produce a cardboard "Lady with Panther" for an exhibition, which was later used as an advertising image for the firm. The animal in all its forms—from sculpture to painting, from movies to interior decoration, from the furs displayed in Renaissance "cabinets of curiosities" to the print media of the 1950s—has carried such a symbolic charge that everyone still dreams of acquiring its strength, elegance, pride, and prowess.

Once three-dimensional panthers and leopards became the rage at Cartier in the late 1940s, Nina Dyer, the Princess Sadruddin Aga Khan, acquired some magnificent and complete sets of jewelry, pavé-set with brilliants and sapphires (a combination that would not be replaced by onyx until 1973). Dyer, a young and ravishing Englishwoman, moved to France in 1947. She became a model highly appreciated for her beauty, her presence, and her sense of repartee. Her first husband, the extremely rich Baron von Thyssen (nephew of the German steel magnate), presented her with, among other extraordinary gifts, a leopard and a black panther; her second husband, Prince Sadruddin Aga Khan (youngest son of Mohammed Shah

Banghai **bracelet**. Yellow gold, lacquer, and emeralds. *La Route des Indes* collection. Cartier Paris, 1991.

Kublai **bracelet**. Yellow gold, lacquer, and emeralds. *La Route des Indes* collection. Cartier Paris, 1991.

Genghis Khan Tiger **bracelet**. Yellow gold, lacquer, and emeralds. *La Route des Indes* collection. Cartier Paris, 1991.

Evening bag of satin with gold clasp, emeralds, diamonds, and black enamel. Ordered by Barbara Hutton for her sister-in-law, Princess Nina Mdivani. Cartier Paris, 1961.

Necklace with clip brooch. Gold, brilliant-cut fancy yellow diamonds, brilliant-cut diamonds, emeralds, and onyx. Cartier Paris, 1986.

Aga Khan), who over his lifetime assembled one of the largest collections of Islamic art and calligraphy, settled for precious miniatures of these wild beasts. A panther with green garnet eyes on a 1957 clip brooch, although given a pose similar to the brooch owned by the Duchess of Windsor, has nothing cruel about it. It is perched on a cliquet pin whose tip is capped either by diamonds or by a sapphire of over thirty carats surrounded by diamonds; or the pin can be removed and the animal set on a coral cabochon. Its companion, with emerald eyes and onyx nose (1958), is shown from the bust, one hind paw brought forward, as though its designer saw it perched at a certain height. Entirely articulated, it can be used as a clasp on a necklace of several strands of pearls. The princess's set was completed by a ring (1959), a small panther entwined around the finger, and two bangle bracelets (1958; the body of one is pavé-set, the other is gold), both of which terminate in two heads (the heads of the latter bracelet can be transformed into earrings or an evening-bag ornament, the body serving as handle).

In contrast, the poetic artistry of Cartier's languid tigers was favored by Barbara Hutton, somewhat unkindly christened a "poor little rich girl" by the press. Hutton's mother, Edna Woolworth, heir to the retail chain of the same name, died when Barbara was six; ignored by her father, she became one of the richest women in the world on reaching her majority. She then married seven times, never finding happiness, consoling herself with jewelry and magnificent homes. Her first cats—a 1957 clip brooch and 1961 earrings—were bent double like the Golden Fleece, as though suspended from the middle of the body. The articulated head, legs and tail lent remarkable expressiveness to this pose of abandonment. A bracelet made the following year emphasized the strong nose and the light halo of white diamonds that ring the animal's features from maw to ears, making the portrait all the more striking. In 1961, Hutton ordered for her sister-in-law, Nina Mdivani, a black satin handbag adorned with an N topped by a crown of brilliants; the clasp was a striding tiger of yellow gold with black enamel stripes. As to the inimitable actress María Félix, in 1967 she ordered a bangle that ended in the heads and forepaws of two panthers that

Tiger **clip brooch**.
Gold, single-cut diamonds and brilliants ranging from vivid yellow to white, onyx, and marquise-shaped emeralds. The head, legs, and tail are articulated. Formerly the collection of Barbara Hutton. Cartier Paris, 1957.

Barbara Hutton wearing her *Tiger* brooch of fancy yellow diamonds, onyx, and yellow gold, made in 1957. Photo: John Brenneis.

Facing page:
Tiger **ear pendants**. Formerly the collection of Barbara Hutton. Cartier Paris, 1961. Photo: Ettore Sottsass.

overlap, without facing one another. The reign of Jeanne "the Panther" Toussaint lasted long past her death. In Paris, London, and New York, numerous versions of her emblematic beast—full-length models or evocative patterns—graced watches, clocks, lighters, rings, necklaces, and bracelets, continuing to pay tribute to her as existing poses were enriched and reworked in new incarnations. In the early 1930s, the panther-skin pattern had appeared on a few original jewels, a concept reinterpreted in the early 1970s for a bracelet decorated with a gold hoop. Brooches from the mid-1960s, meanwhile, incorporated panthers and tigers depicted frontally, copying the pose of the lorgnette, alone or next to a cub. Sometimes only the heads of mother and cub would appear. Then the cats began to leap, or to lie in wait, crouching on a rock of yellow jasper or a cabochon of lapis lazuli, pouncing from a coral flower. Twisting strands of stone beads might close with a clasp composed of two heads, skull to skull, while another bracelet (three strands of pearls) was graced by a reclining tiger, and still others—totally rigid hoops—were abstract patterns punctuated with black dots, like the spotted, preciously sober, irreproachable Creole pieces made in the late 1960s. Elsewhere, the bust of a panther, paws joined together, hid the dial of a watch. Over the years, the animal came to be presented in a gentler, more friendly light, the fur sometimes being that of a snow leopard, notably for some of the "golden fleece" pieces. In the early 1990s, Mouna Ayoub and Luisa Fanti Melloni opted for cats lying along branches of lapis lazuli, paws dangling like some big domestic cat. The October 1982 issue of *Vogue* reproduced a magnificent panther set of diamonds and onyx, including a bangle with facing heads, Creole earrings, and a two-strand necklace of emerald beads whose ends meet at a panther-head clasp. That same year, Paul Schrader directed a remake of *Cat People,* forty years after Jacques Tourneur's original film. Meanwhile, Micheline Kanoui had taken over Cartier's fine jewelry department, and since she, too, loved gems and animals, it was normal that big cats continued to enjoy their "lion's share." Throughout the 1980s, the press constantly praised Cartier's bestiary, both historic and contemporary, and the workshop continued to turn out many remarkable items, both figurative and abstract—bracelets, earrings, rings,

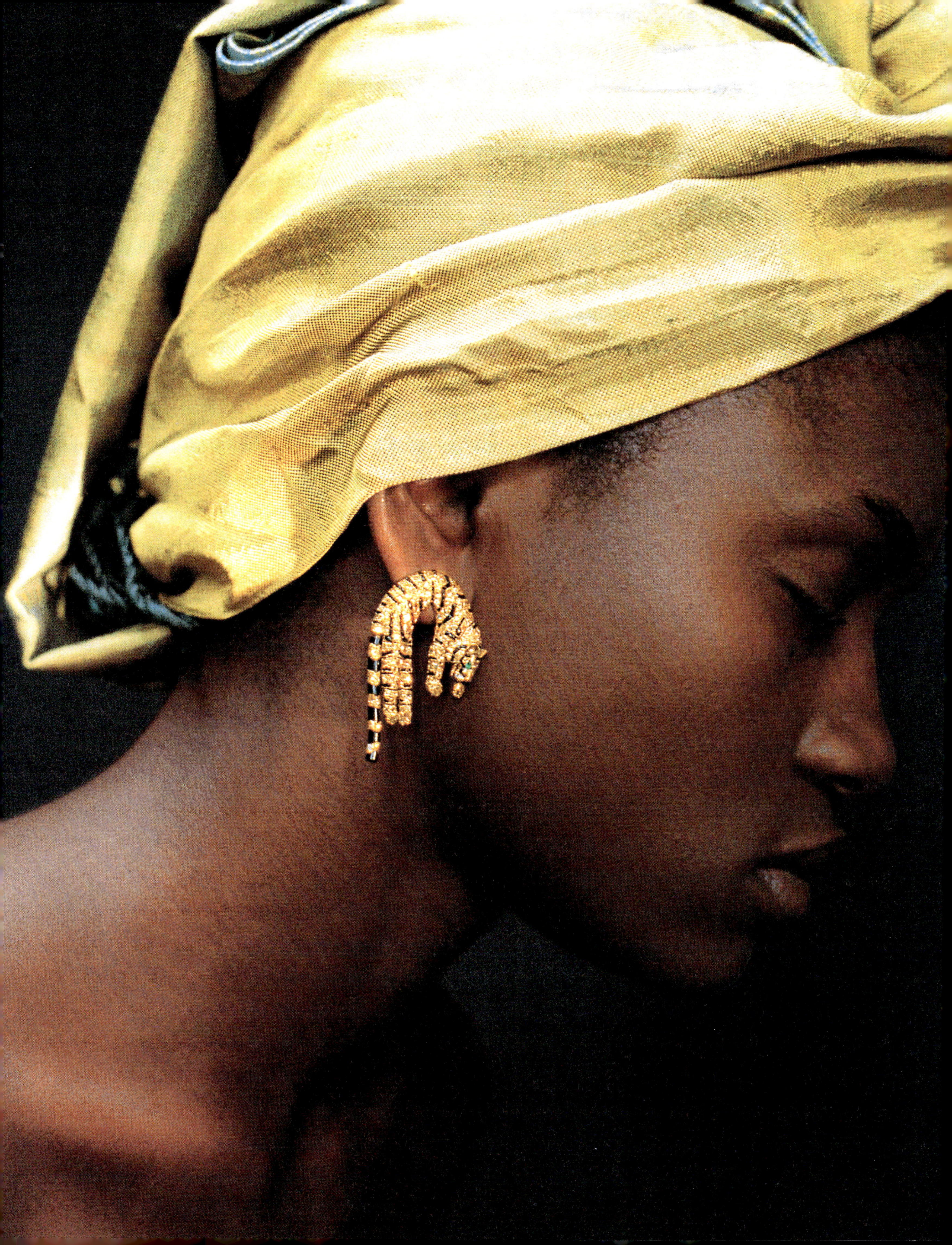

Tiger **brooch.** Brilliants, onyx, and emeralds. Cartier Paris, 1991.

Magadi-Loulou **brooch.** Gold, diamonds, emeralds, and onyx. Cartier Paris, c. 1995.

Lion head **brooch.** Chased yellow gold and rubies, c. 1970.

Creole clips. The Khana necklace of 1987 was particularly magnificent—two tigers, heads almost touching, crouch on a branch of rattan. Career women in those years wore cinch-waisted, wide-shouldered suits that Thierry Mugler revived from the ashes, and such jewelry was wonderfully suited to these "female tigers" who henceforth measured their worldly success in terms of market share.

Cartier also made some spectacularly creative timepieces. In 1986, a mystery clock incorporating 1,500 carats of rock crystal featured two panthers who jointly gaze at a raw black diamond of 97.14 carats. The next year, another mystery clock—this time a Portique (or Shrine Gate) model—placed the two animals back to back. Also in 1987, a big cat stared at an egg sitting on a cushion-shaped aventurine rimmed with diamonds: pressing the forepaw would spring open the dial. One loses count of time spent at work—over three thousand hours were required to make this little marvel.

Four years earlier, journalists were focusing attention on a cigarette lighter. It was the beauty and value of this object that generated all the talk: the oval lighter, topped by the bust of a panther, its head resting on a paw, was set with 1,121 diamonds and 260 sapphires (over 40 carats in total), making it the most expensive lighter in the world. It had been stolen from the Cartier boutique in Cannes by a gentleman thief, Bruno Sulak, whose exploits and tragic death made the headlines. During these same years, new panther incarnations were born, such as a panther watch in 1984 (henceforth a classic Cartier item) and Panthère de Cartier perfume in 1987 (in a diamondlike bottle hugged by two cats). The mid-1980s also saw the launch of the Silverium collection, combining gold with black silver. Reviving a few of the firm's archetypes, although deliberately favoring stronger modeling and flat zones of color, these pieces prefigured more recent ones that have imitated their shape while simultaneously borrowing the materials of the Duchess of Windsor's lorgnette. For example, there is a highly stylized panther-head ring whose spots are geometric and whose jaws are wide open to receive the wearer's finger; on another ring, only the gold and black pattern—harmonizing with a citrine—evoke the panther. Today, the cat theme is so present that there is greater latitude for freedom of expression. Lions have sometimes joined the menagerie: one of them is an amazing cross between a Gorgon and a wild beast, so cruel is its expression, so sharp its teeth, so tangled and wild its mane. Carved in coral, this "lion head" handbag watch belonged to Josette Day, whom Jean Cocteau had cast six years earlier, in 1946, as Beauty alongside Jean Marais's Beast in his movie adaptation of the eighteenth-century fairy tale.[15] At the sight of this object, it is hard not to think of the extraordinary makeup used on Jean Marais to recreate a chimerical character who would recover his true appearance through love. Thus love, which renders women "fatale," apparently makes men authentically handsome.

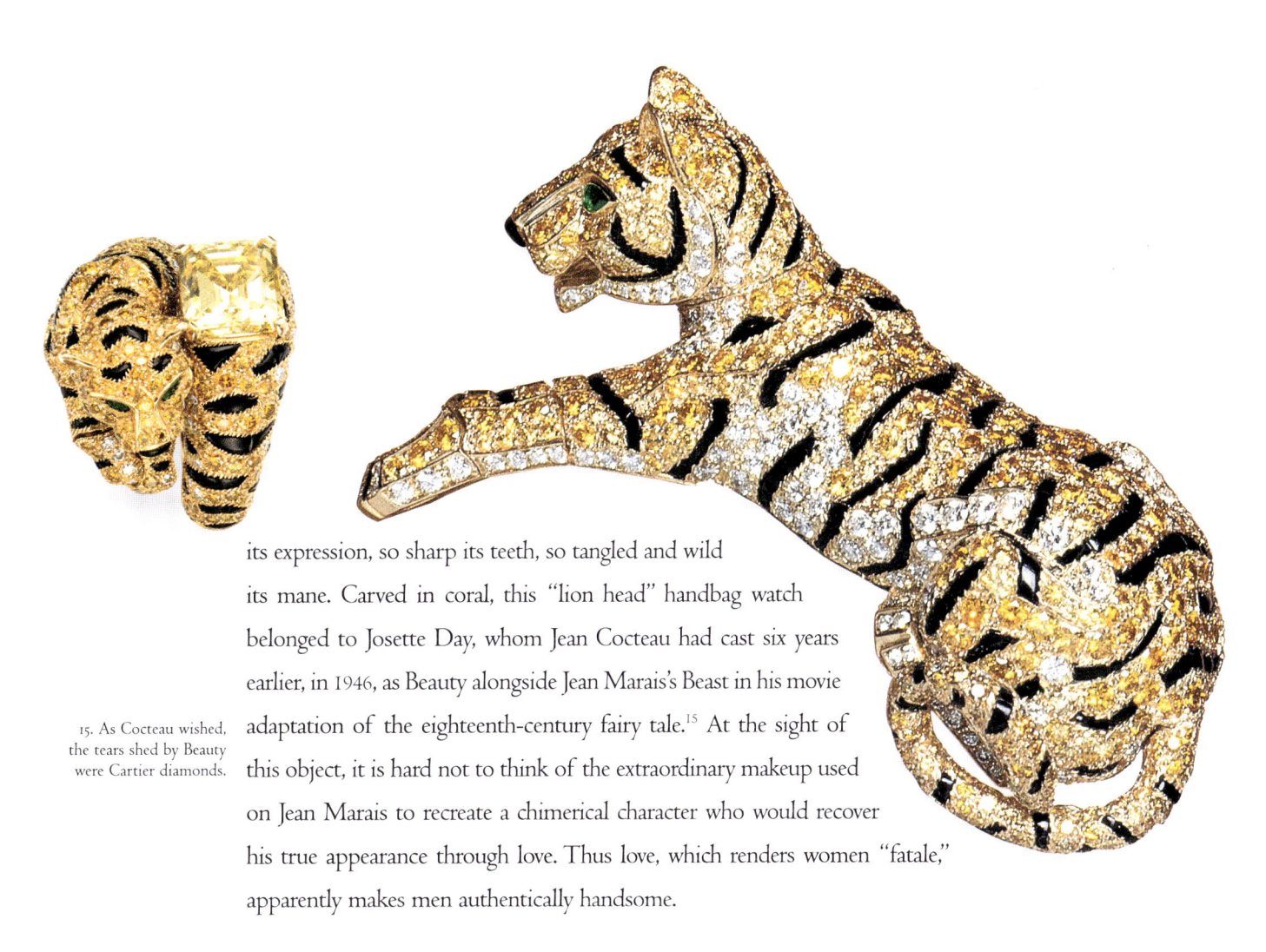

15. As Cocteau wished, the tears shed by Beauty were Cartier diamonds.

Ring. Yellow gold, fancy yellow diamonds, brilliants, emeralds, and onyx. *Inde Mystérieuse* collection. Cartier Paris 2007.

Tiger **bracelet-watch**. Yellow gold, diamonds, fancy yellow diamonds, onyx, and emeralds (eyes). Cartier Paris, 1988.

Tiger **ring**. Yellow gold, fancy yellow diamonds, emeralds, and onyx. Cartier Paris, 1995.

Snake **necklace**. Platinum, white, and yellow gold, 2,473 brilliant- and baguette-cut diamonds weighing 178.21 carats in total, emeralds, and green, red, and black enamel. Articulated around a complex armature of platinum and gold. Formerly the collection of María Félix. Cartier Paris, special order, 1968.

Facing page:
Chimera **cliquet pin**. Platinum, gold, round old- and single-cut diamonds, one fluted emerald bead, emerald cabochons and buff-top emeralds, carved and fluted coral, onyx cabochons, black enamel, and natural pearl. Cartier Paris, 1923.

Chimeras, Crocodiles, and other Reptiles

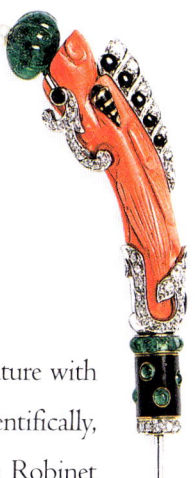

The chimera is a strange animal. The daughter of one of the Gorgon sisters, it is a mythological creature with the head of a lion, the body of a goat, and the tail of a dragon. Every now and then it would spit fire. Scientifically, its genetic blend is highly improbable; symbolically, it expresses an exalted state of imagination. When Robinet Testard was commissioned in 1480 by Charles of Angoulême to produce a book on the world's "marvels" that included the "secrets of natural history," he blithely included unicorns, dragons, and human-headed snakes alongside crocodiles and elephants. Cartier's chimeras, however, whose formal foundations were laid in the early 1920s, have little in common with this image, apart from the indispensable ingredients of creative imagination and evocative name. As Hans Nadelhoffer explained, the idea derives from the Indian *makara*, a hybrid aquatic creature associated with fertility, as well as from the Chinese dragon, a mythological, protective animal; the *makara* can be seen on certain bracelets dating from the sixteenth to nineteenth centuries, while the dragon has figured on bracelets from the seventeenth century onward.[16] The structure of Cartier's bangles, meanwhile, evolved from ancient armbands with animal heads.[17]

Dragons and chimeras appeared on Cartier vanity cases and compacts in the 1920s. A superb mystery clock made by Cartier New York in 1926 also featured a Chinese agate chimera dating from the nineteenth century. But the first depiction of the creature that interests us here—and which would become fashionable again the 1940s, presenting a powerful image of the firm—dates from 1923. It was a cliquet pin bought by Louis Cartier himself. Only the chimera's slightly tilted head and very long neck are represented, carved from coral; a crest of diamonds is dotted with onyx cabochons, while the black, almond-shaped eye, has a slit of gold, and the mouth holds a fluted emerald bead set with a natural pearl; the nose is flat and strong, while the grooves engraved along the neck might evoke folded wings. The following year, a fairly similar beast appeared as a fully articulated spiral of coral ringed with black enamel and studded with diamonds. Chimera bracelets would then follow from 1927 to 1929, including

16. Hans Nadelhoffer, *Cartier* (London: Thames & Hudson, 1984), 225–26.

17. Cartier bangles that ended in similar motifs, whether figurative or not, were variously described by the firm as Egyptian, Sudanese, or Indian.

Dragon **bracelet.**
Platinum, gray gold, brilliants, round faceted emeralds, and baguette-cut rubies. Cartier Paris, 1998.

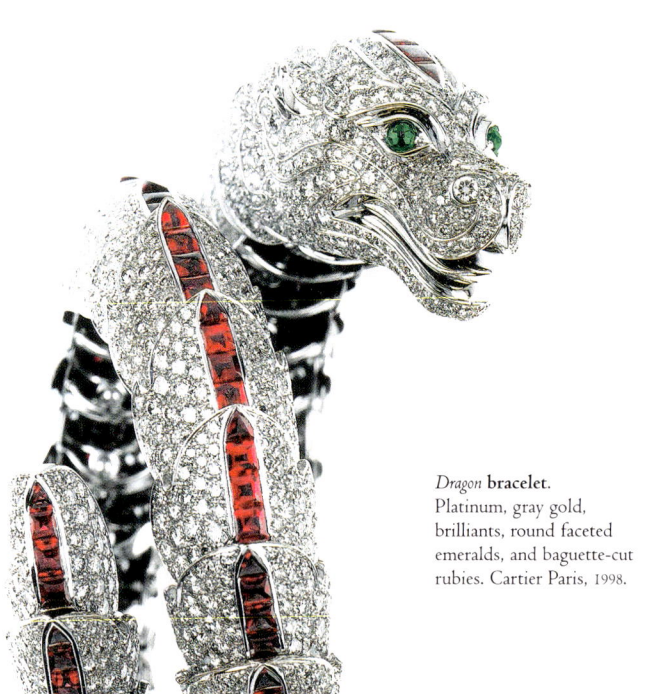

one worn by Ganna Walska, an opera singer of Polish origin whose social talents were more appreciated than her vocal ones. (Orson Welles was apparently thinking of Walska, then married to Harold Fowler McCormick, when he created the character of his hapless opera singer for *Citizen Kane*). She nevertheless showed a sure sense of taste when it came to jewelry, as demonstrated by a superb bracelet she bought in 1928 (and sold again in 1971, along with other Cartier items from her collection, in order to finance her botanical garden in California): two coral heads terminating in fluted emerald beads (like the cliquet pin) stare at one another; their black enamel eyes, set with inverted cushion-shaped diamonds, create a disturbingly high relief that adds a touch of savagery, while the body of the bangle is decorated with ornamental patterns in blue and green enamel. Another chimera bangle, made in 1929, was entirely made of platinum set with precious gems; this pair of chimeras has turned-up noses (as would many later models), although they are not necessarily friendlier than their predecessors, for their bulging eyes are set with bullet-shaped sapphires. A softer, friendlier expression appeared in 1930 on a "sea monster" necklace.

Toussaint later put new life into this motif, to which Cartier gave powerful expression by stressing a formal ambiguity related to the very essence of the mythical creature. Halfway between abstraction and representation, it retained its spirit and structure even as its appearance changed. Coral often dominated, lending an impression of warmth and a feeling of authenticity—the Greeks thought coral was the petrified blood of the Gorgon Medusa—but some jewels were entirely covered with precious stones or with yellow gold flecked with spots of color. In 1945 a striking Indian model of yellow gold set with diamonds, sapphires, and emeralds twisting along the back of the bracelet, terminated in two heads that share a carved ruby. It was the Duchess of Windsor, once again, who in 1947 chose a remarkably orchestrated piece—coral heads encrusted with diamonds and emeralds, the body of gold being worked in various ways—whose balanced, clear-cut forms subtly combine representation with geometry. In 1954

Snake **bracelet**. Platinum, gold, rose-cut diamonds, pear-shaped emerald cabochons, coral, and black enamel. Cartier Paris, 1924.

Chimera **bracelet**. Platinum, white gold, brilliant- and marquise-cut diamonds, fluted coral beads and buff-top coral cabochons. Cartier Paris, special order, 1954.

81

Twin Chimera-Head **bangle.** Platinum, white gold, yellow gold, pear-shaped and brilliant-cut diamonds, emerald cabochons and faceted emeralds, and carved and engraved coral. Formerly the collection of Daisy Fellowes. Cartier Paris, 1961.

Twin Chimera-Head **bangle.** Platinum, yellow gold, white gold, marquise-, baguette- and brilliant-cut diamonds, round faceted rubies, and round and oval faceted emeralds. The heads swivel to allow the bracelet to open. Cartier Paris, 1960.

Chimera **bangle.** Platinum, gold, cushion-shaped, single-, pear-, and baguette-cut diamonds, fluted emeralds beads, one carved emerald, buff-top emeralds and emerald cabochons, leaf-shaped carved sapphires, sapphire cabochons and buff-top sapphires, carved coral, and green, blue, and black enamel. Formerly the collection of Ganna Walska. Cartier Paris, 1928.

Chimera **bangle.** Yellow gold, rubies, and diamonds. Cartier Paris, 1976.

Twin Chimera-Head **bangle**. Yellow gold, white gold, brilliant-, baguette-, and single-cut diamonds, and ten oval faceted rubies. Cartier Paris, 1957.

Dragon **bracelet** with swivel hinge. Gold, coral, single-cut diamonds, emeralds, and rubies. Formerly the collection of the Duchess of Windsor. Cartier Paris, 1947.

Chimera bangle. Platinum, sapphires, and yellow and white diamonds. Cartier Paris, c. 1960.

Chimera bracelet. Pear-shaped, round old-, single-, and French-cut diamonds, sapphire cabochons, buff-top emeralds and sapphires, and gadrooned rock crystal. Cartier Paris, 1929.

Facing page:
Chimera bracelet. Platinum, brilliant-cut diamonds, emeralds, and sapphires, including a 20.76-carat oval sapphire cabochon from Ceylon. Cartier Paris, 2005.

three rows of fluted coral beads were given a clasp of a superb head pavé-set with diamonds. In New York in 1957, the countess of Boisrouvray bought a black velvet handbag topped by two chimera heads of coral, diamonds, and emeralds; one head looked right, the other left. In 1961, a twist of black pearls was fastened by a head of coral, similar to a piece that Barbara Hutton would buy the following year, but with a clasp of yellow brilliants and white diamonds. A bangle made by the Paris workshops in 1973 featured two heads very similar to an Indian *makara*. In the early 1980s there appeared torsade necklaces decorated with facing heads—or a single head—holding a carved stone. Henceforth the chimera was often more appealing, and might be mistaken for a fish—which it isn't—such as a ravishing dolphin in yellow gold outlined by countless brilliants—which can't really be a dolphin, for that matter, since its body is finely carved with scales. But then, perhaps the dolphin is really another mythical animal.

In 1972, María Félix ordered a chimera of coral, diamonds, and emeralds—a classic Cartier combination. The head is appealing: up-turned nose, friendly eye, well-defined mouth. Seen in profile, this depiction is

84

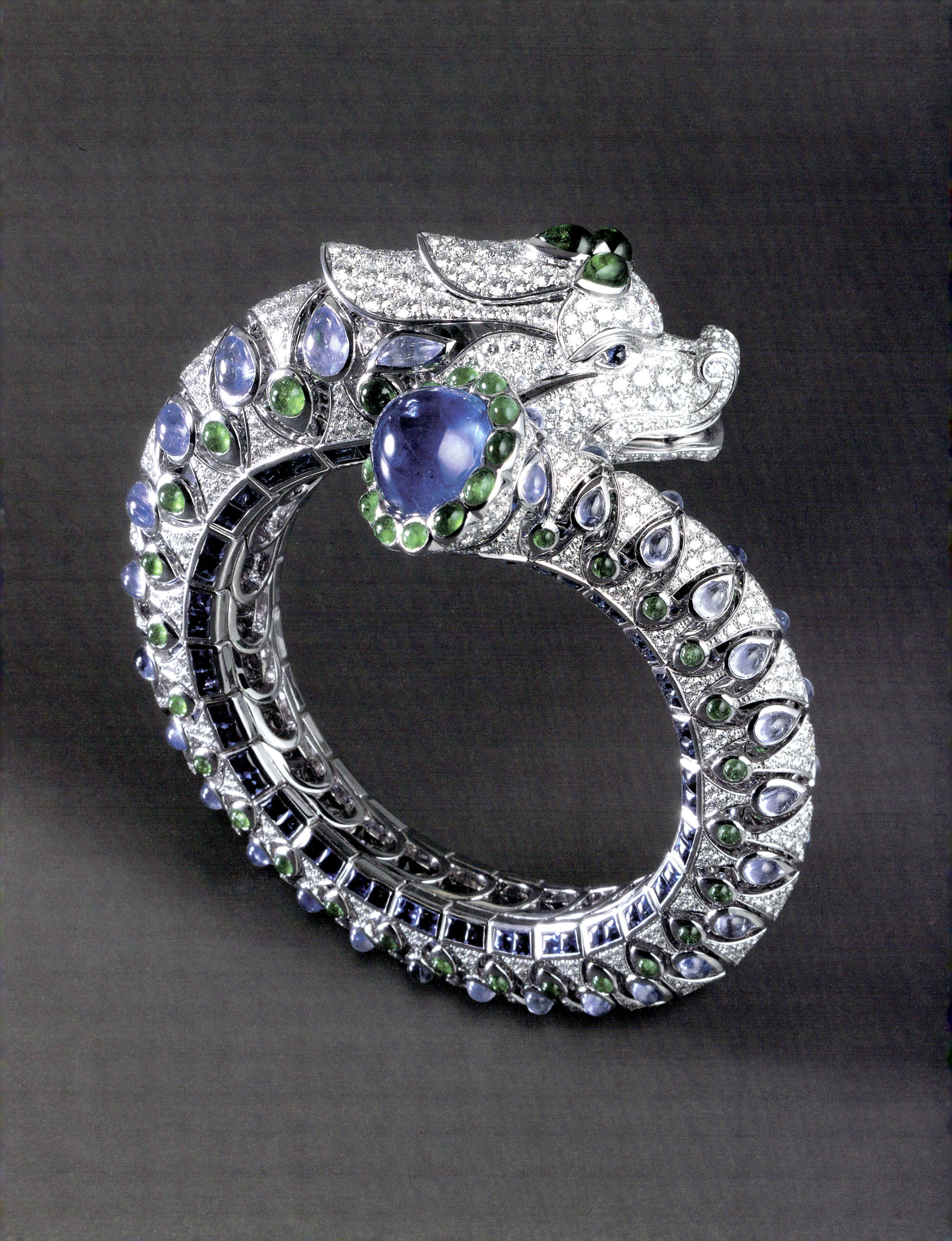

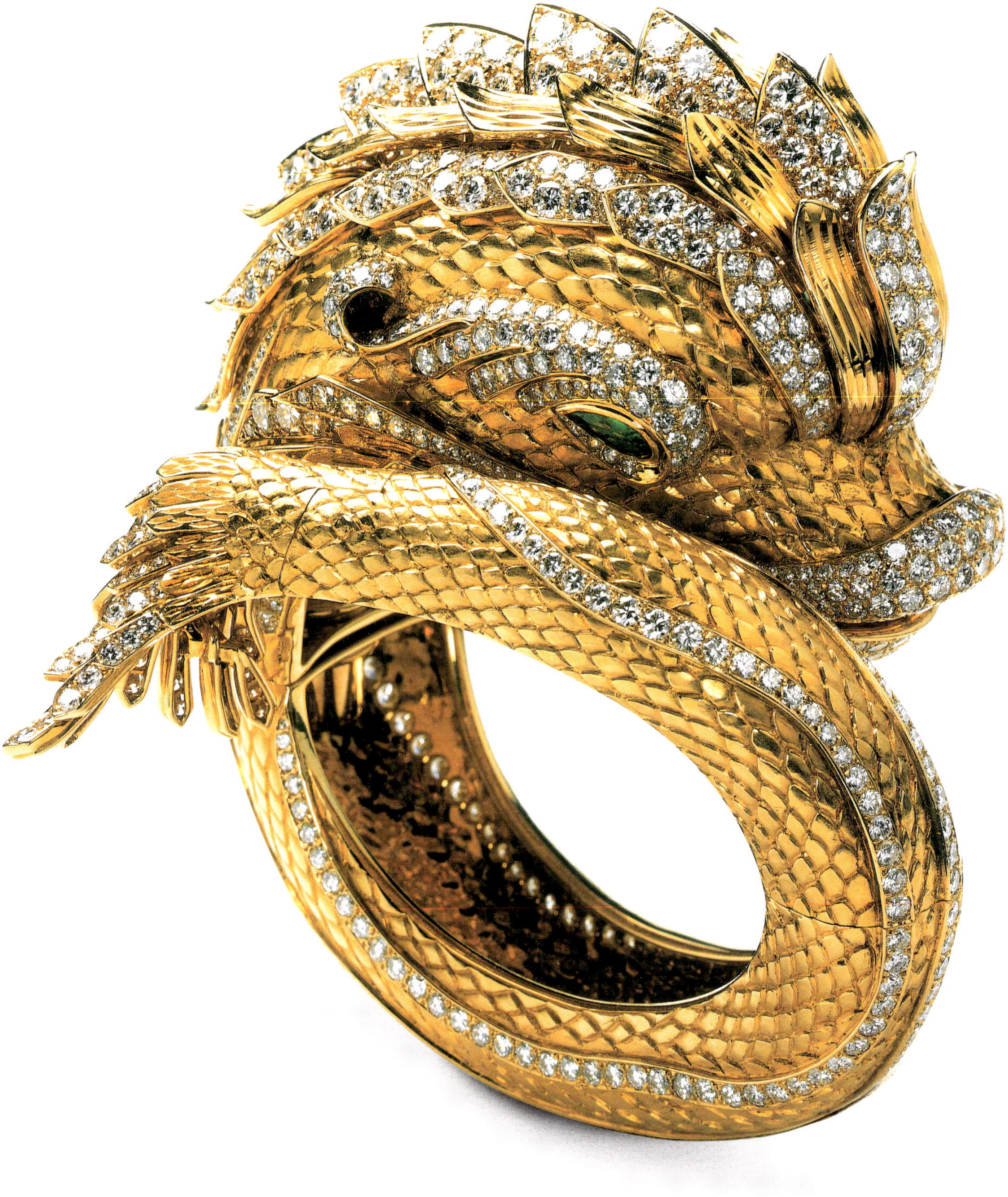

Original design for a *Lizard* **brooch** of yellow gold and diamonds, 1960. The brooch belonged to actress Jacqueline Delubac.

Facing page: *Dolphin* **bracelet**. Engraved gold, 1,028 brilliant-cut diamonds weighing a total of 33.73 carats, and two pear-shaped emeralds. Cartier Paris, special order, 1969.

charming; seen from above, the remarkable construction looks abstract. Snakes can also be abstract. A snake is a line that suddenly comes to life; it represents mankind's origins and contradictions—positive and negative, phallic and feminine. Félix, the most famous of Mexican actresses, described herself as a "woman with a man's heart." Even more than beauty she projected unsettling strength, haughty comportment, and a dark, imperturbable gaze. Her movie career lasted some two decades, during which she performed in a few films shot in Europe (*La Belle Otéro, French Cancan, Les Héros sont Fatigués, La Fièvre Monte à El Pao*). Félix was always faithful to the role her public expected her to play, namely a Hispanic Doña. Her love of serpents spurred her to order snakes and crocodiles from Cartier. The snake is amazing: measuring over 20 inches (50 cm) long, and 2 inches (5 cm) in diameter, it is set with 2,475 diamonds (brilliant-cut and baguette-cut, totaling 178.21 carats) and required two years of work by the Paris workshop. Each ring is independent, and the structure that connects them all is extremely complex, endowing the jewel with the suppleness of a living animal. To make the underside of this necklace smoother, it was paved with tiny plaques of green, red, and black enamel. Félix hired an airplane to have the necklace specially delivered to her estate in Mexico. Earrings followed three years later, and then in 1975 she ordered an absolute marvel, a necklace made of two entirely articulated crocodiles—incomparable replicas whose every movement is frightening and whose lifelike gaze is alarming to anyone who fears these uncompromising predators. Only the magnificence of their cloaks distinguishes them from their live models: one is made of fancy yellow diamonds (60.02 carats), the other of emeralds (66.86 carats). The eyes of the former are emeralds, of the latter, rubies. The inner feet are removed when this piece is worn as a necklace, to avoid scratches from the claws; if the feet are retained and the two crocodiles separated, they can be worn as brooches.

Cartier's terrarium includes lizards in the form of brooches and bracelets whose naturalistic impression is contradicted by the color and arrangement of gems. On a brooch made in 1945, a series of small round stones

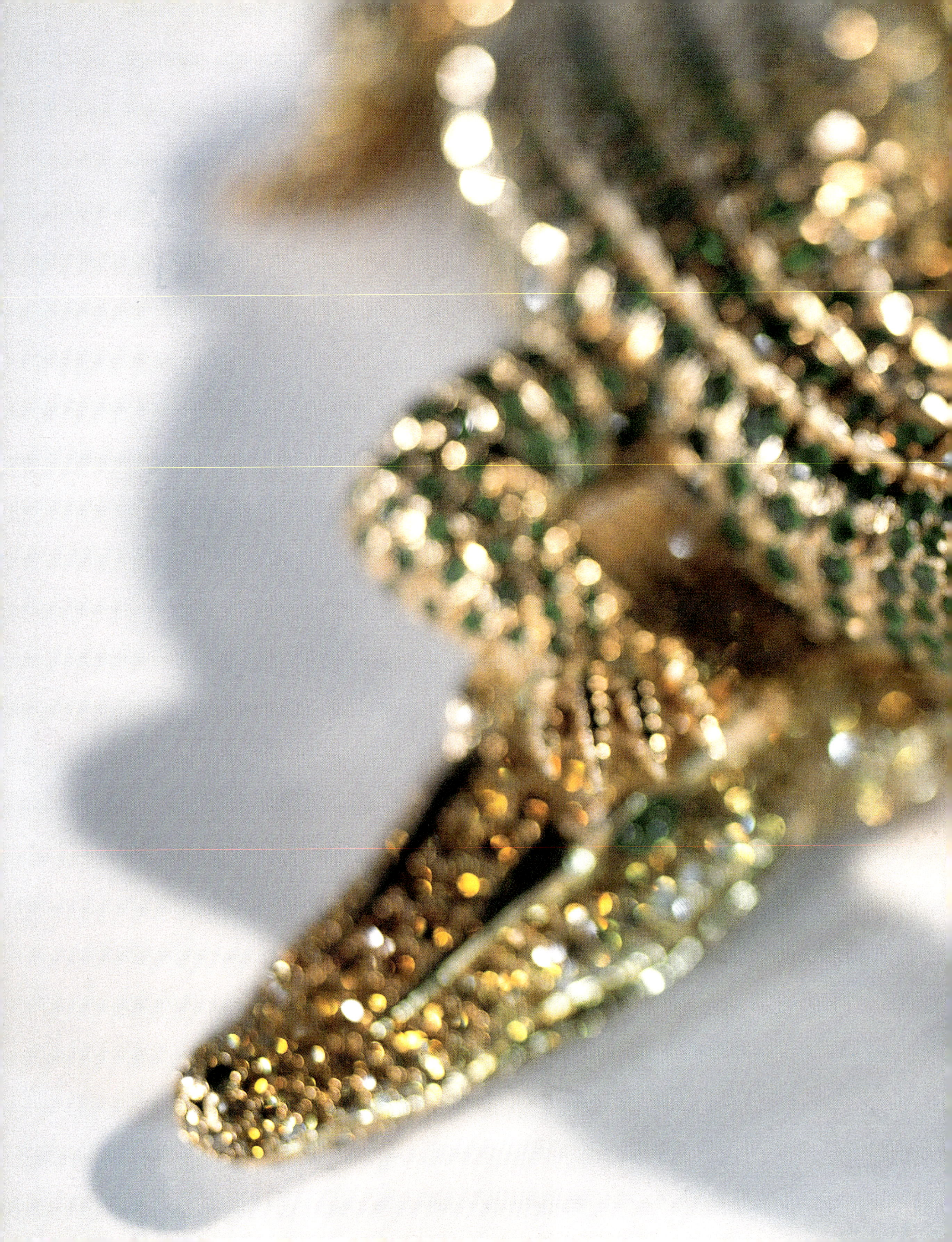

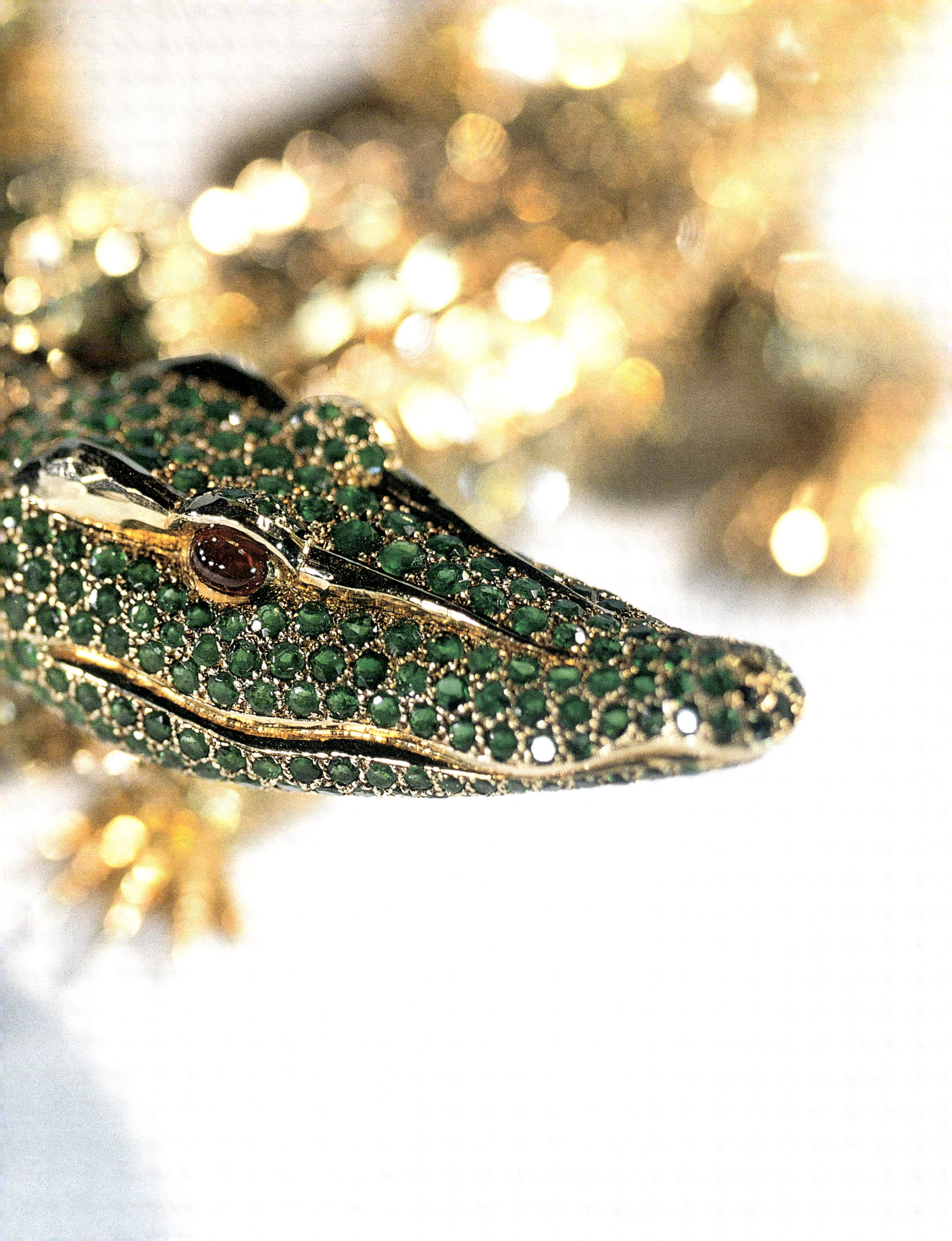

set in squares yields a geometricized portrait of a lizard. Josette Day later chose a bangle whose stones were set in gold circles (1972), while Jacqueline Delubac owned an articulated brooch of chased gold studded with intense yellow brilliants (1958). Reptiles (and their scaly motif) have been a recurring source of inspiration to the house of Cartier since the nineteenth century. Recent pieces illustrate two complementary trends. In an Eternity necklace of 1997, the snake's scaly motif of diamonds and overall design—in which the head joins the tail, symbolizing an eternal recommencement—is similar to a model of 1919, but whereas the latter hides its clasp at the exact point of juncture, the recent version flaunts two emeralds of over two hundred carats each, from the same rough stone. As to the Cobra from Cartier's Inde Mystérieuse line (2007), it wraps its slinky body around the wearer's arm, protected by 2,400 scales of white and brown diamonds. A crocodile bracelet in diamonds (2006) whose tail encircles the wrist looks just like the real thing, except for its cheerful, almost smiling expression. Finally, the links of the bracelet on the Doña watch (2006) are an extremely stylized version of scales and reptilian silhouettes.

Snake **necklace**. Platinum, diamonds, and emeralds of which two weigh over two hundred carats each. *Les 150 Ans* collection. Cartier Paris, 1997.

Facing page: *Lizard* **bangle**. Gold, brilliant-cut fancy yellow diamonds, brilliant-cut and pear-shaped diamonds, round faceted emeralds, round faceted sapphires, and ruby cabochons. Formerly the collection of Josette Day. Cartier Paris, 1972.

Pages 88–89: *Crocodile* **necklace**. Gold. One crocodile: 1,023 brilliant-cut fancy yellow diamonds weighing 60.02 carats in total and two emerald cabochons; the other crocodile: 1,060 emeralds weighing 66.86 carats in total and two ruby cabochons. Each crocodile is completely articulated. Can be worn as brooches or joined to form a necklace, in which case the feet are replaced by clawless paws. Formerly the collection of María Félix. Cartier Paris, special order, 1975.

Snake **necklace**. Platinum, round old-cut diamonds, millegrain setting. Cartier Paris, 1919.

Facing page:
Bracelet. Platinum, 68 fancy yellow and bronze-colored diamonds weighing 3.67 carats, and 2,347 brilliants weighing 68.66 carats. Cartier Paris, 2007.

Bracelet. Platinum, two table-cut diamonds of 6.38 and 6.68 carats; 2,900 diamonds weighing 71 carats. Cartier Paris, 2000.

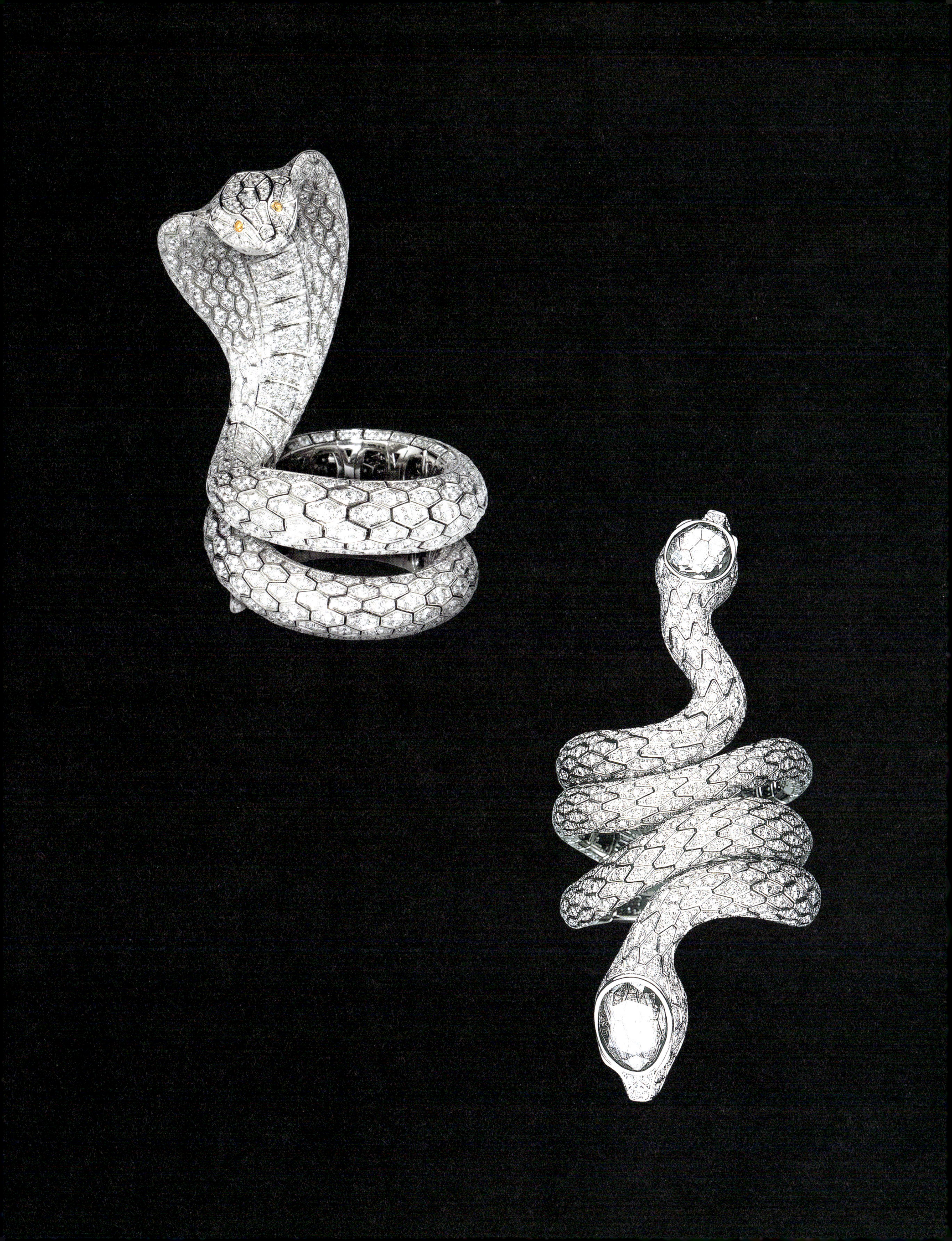

LARGE AND SMALL

Dachshund **brooch**.
Gold, rubies, and enamel.
Articulated legs.
Cartier Paris, c. 1960.

Pug **clip brooch**. Gold,
citrines, enamel, and
collet-set topazes on gold.
Formerly the collection
of the Duchess of Windsor.
Cartier Paris, 1955.

Poodle **brooch**. Gold,
pearls, rubies, and sapphires.
c. 1960.

Terrier **brooch**. Gold,
diamond, rubies, and black
enamel. Cartier Paris, 1964.

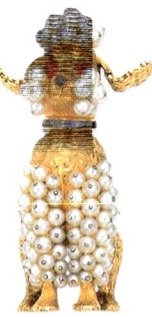

The animal kingdom is infinite, and many of its terrestrial, aerial, and aquatic members, large and small, simple or decorative, have inspired Cartier at one time or another. Dogs for example, have had a good show, from London's 1940s dachshunds (geometricized by caliber-cut citrines) to the Duke of Windsor's pug (a three-dimensional, very nineteenth-century portrait whose enameling accurately renders a pug's always moist eye), to poodles set with pearls or diamonds (1950s), via the strange little terriers of the 1950s (heads topped by tufts of golden twine that almost look like today's dreadlocks), the bichons frises (made of gold wire as though it were ordinary wire), and the basset hounds (with pointy noses and enamel-speckled fur). Nor should we forget the rabbits, squirrels, or highly realistic and charming donkey of carved gold, whose baskets contain bouquets of precious flowers (London, 1960), nor all the fawnlike "Bambis" and the contented cats of mabe pearls. Luisa Fanti Melloni, mentioned above as the owner of a Cartier cat, notably liked elephants of plain gold or set with diamonds. She also owned a giraffe with gracefully angled head, one foot raised, whose hide of diamonds and onyx recalled panther fur. Zebras, meanwhile, nuzzle up to one another on a double-headed bracelet set with diamonds and onyx (1992).

Tropical fish, flying fish, fish draped in aquamarine bubbles, starfish, and conch shells—they bring to mind the blond, fragile Marilyn Monroe (the perfect antithesis of María Félix) wearing a gold off-the-shoulder dress striped like a seashell; or else Brigitte Bardot singing "*Sur la plage abandonnée*" ("On a deserted beach of shells and shellfish."). One necklace now in the Cartier Collection evokes both the hullabaloo of hunters and finery of a Papua medicine man. From three strands of polished gold beads there dangles, like a fetish or trophy, a perfectly orchestrated jumble of gold shells, baroque pearls, sapphires, and emerald beads. This necklace dates from 1972, when Flower Power encouraged people to pick up guitars and bedeck themselves in flowers, those symbols of "peace, love, and innocence."

Bantu **bracelet**. Gold, emeralds, and black lacquer. Cartier Paris, 1991.

Nagar **bracelet**. Yellow gold and rubies. Cartier Paris, 1991.

Zebra **bracelet**. Platinum, diamonds, and onyx. Cartier Paris, 1992.

Giraffe **brooch**. Platinum, brilliants, emeralds, and onyx. Cartier Paris, 1999.

Fish **brooch**. Platinum, yellow gold, opal, rubies, and diamonds. Cartier London, 1962.

Fish **brooch**. Yellow gold, onyx, emeralds, and diamonds. Cartier Paris, 1992.

Fish **brooch**. Gold, tourmaline, and aquamarine cabochons. Cartier Paris, c. 1960.

Starfish **brooch**. Gold and brilliant-cut diamonds, c. 1958.

Chinese Fish **clip brooch**. Gold, diamonds, white agate, and coral. Cartier Paris, 1950.

Shell **necklace**. Chased and polished gold, natural and baroque pearls, carved emeralds, and emerald and sapphire beads. Cartier Paris, 1972.

Flowers, Foliage, Bouquets, and Palm Trees

Orchid **brooch**.
Platinum, gold,
amethyst, and diamonds.
Cartier New York, 1969.

aFacing page:
Open-and-shut flower **clip brooch**. Gold wire, platinum, brilliant-cut diamonds, round faceted emeralds, sapphires, and rubies. Designed in 1962, the petals of the rose can be opened by pressing and then sliding the emerald between the leaves. The gems are set on "tremored" stems. Cartier Paris, 1969.

Flower **clip brooch**. Yellow gold, platinum, amethysts, turquoises, and diamond. Cartier London, 1948.

Reversible petal flower **clip brooch** (one side gold, one side diamonds). Gold wire and twisted gold, platinum, and baguette-, round old-, and single-cut diamonds. Cartier Paris, special order, 1946.

Flower **brooch**. Rubies and baguette-cut and marquise-shaped diamonds. The 12.84-carat diamond in the center was originally a pearl. Cartier New York, 1940.

W hen World War II was declared, Henri Matisse moved south to Nice, then to Vence, all the while continuing to draw flowers and foliage until his hand instinctively knew their shapes. In 1943 his famous paper cutouts finally enabled him to "cut directly into color," an experience that gem cutters also share. Matisse's *Reader against a Black Background* (*The Pink Table*), whose center is occupied by a large, luminous bouquet of daisies and scabious in all their expressive simplicity assumes today the value of a parable: the year was 1939, the world was growing dark—could nature lead mankind back to the light? The plant kingdom has always fueled inventiveness in the decorative arts by generating motifs that stick more or less close to reality. Cartier's approach to flowers, meanwhile, had already undergone many metamorphoses by the time the war loomed. The garland style had taken the form of perfectly balanced compositions of foliage, sprays, palmettes, petals, and blossoms, based on symmetry and repetition to create a perfect balance; in contrast, decorative objects—pots of lily of the valley or other small flowers, or hydrangea—imitated the colors and textures of nature through use of enamel, opaline, jade, agate, and moonstone; exotic influences, meanwhile, had inspired original settings, shapes, and colors, such as the famous Tutti Frutti style with its carved leaves and fruit; and art deco, finally, flaunted its bold geometry.

During the 1930s, curves came back into play. Early in the decade flower motifs appeared, often set with diamonds enhanced by a colored gem in the center, on clip brooches whose lines and volumes showed more affinity with nature; similar designs could be combined in twos and threes on wide bracelets. The Cartier workshops thus began producing a profusion of flowers, playing with great freedom on different cuts of stone, various techniques of articulation, and subtle mechanisms.

Soberly drawn flowers of gold or gems, removed from their stems, were perfect for clip brooches, such as anemones made of a few petals whose tips were slightly turned up. And they could be adapted to bracelets and necklaces, leading

99

Thistle **brooch**. Platinum and brilliant- and baguette-cut diamonds The stem is articulated, c. 1940.

to novel variants; in 1942 a flower ring had diamond petals with, at their center, a sapphire from Kashmir weighing over forty-three carats. When set lightly atop their stem, Cartier's flowers displayed incomparable grace, combining the fragility of a simple row of square- or baguette-cut stones with the magnificence of a fully open blossom. Their simplicity conveys a universal quality, like the tiny flowers held between two fingers by the lady (or courtesan) in Bartolomeo Veneto's *Ideal Portrait of a Woman* (c. 1550). Cartier New York produced very fine examples of such flowers. On a diamond brooch ordered by Lady Mendl in 1940, the stem was dotted by four baguette-cut diamonds arranged on both sides, the flower being composed of narrow, tight petals that opened around a center of marquise-shaped diamonds. That same year, another flower was simply sketched in a childlike design of a round pearl surrounded by eight rubies cut in different shapes. The following year, a more complex model of emeralds and sapphires underscored its asymmetry with diamond curls. In the same spirit, during these years, Paris composed a fully open flower around a core of diamonds—tear-shaped gaps between the petals suggested that they were about to fall. Similar structures of a segmented, articulated stem topped by a gem ringed with openwork petals might be executed in yellow gold, popular throughout this period.

Roundness sometimes gave way to an elongated shape, as seen in a 1944 piece now in the Cartier Collection, an open thistle with its bulb crowned by baguette-cut diamonds supporting a large diamond; on the stem, a line of baguettes forms an artful contrast with the skillful disorder of the round diamonds composing a curved leaf. Sometimes roundness was combined with rigidity: in the 1930s, baguette-cut stones could be used for the center of a curving blossom or the petals of stylized leaves, while square or rectangular stones yielded geometric flowers. In 1949 the Duchess of Windsor bought a brooch of such flowers, knotted with a simple but no less imposing ribbon, all made of sapphires dotted with little round diamonds.

Cartier London displayed virtuoso skill in combining gems with semiprecious stones, notably rectangular citrines set in yellow gold. Many of its compositions were complex, such as a pair of brooches specially

Pair of *Floral Bouquet* **brooches**. Platinum, emeralds, sapphires, and diamonds. Cartier London, 1964.

Leaf and Flower **clip brooch**. Platinum, white gold, and baguette-, round old-, and single-cut diamonds. Cartier Paris, special order, 1944.

Flower **clip brooch**. Platinum, white gold, and round old- and single-cut diamonds. Cartier Paris, special order, 1941.

Flower **clip brooch**. Platinum, white gold, and round old- and single-cut diamonds. The stem is articulated. Cartier Paris, special order, 1941.

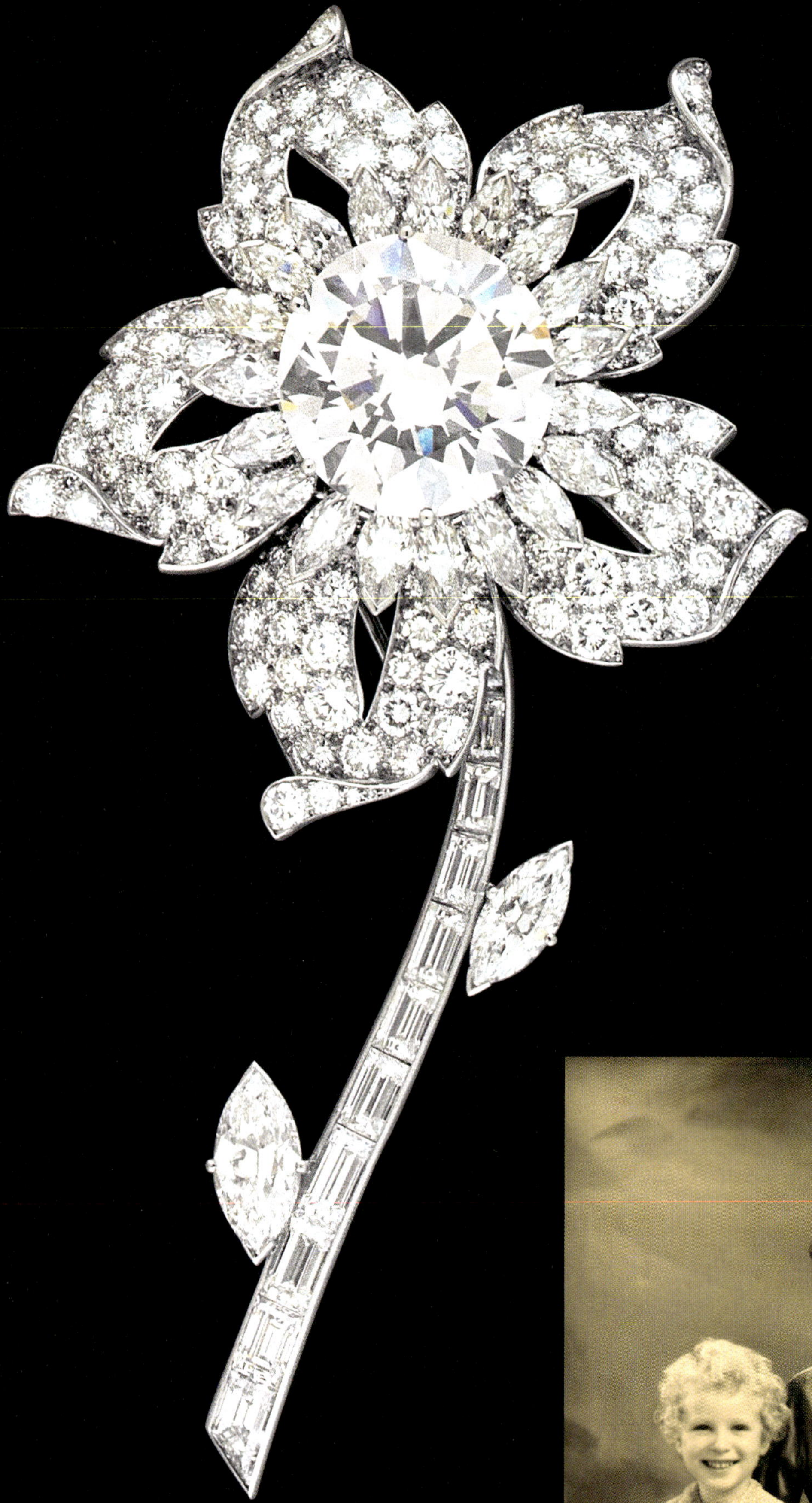

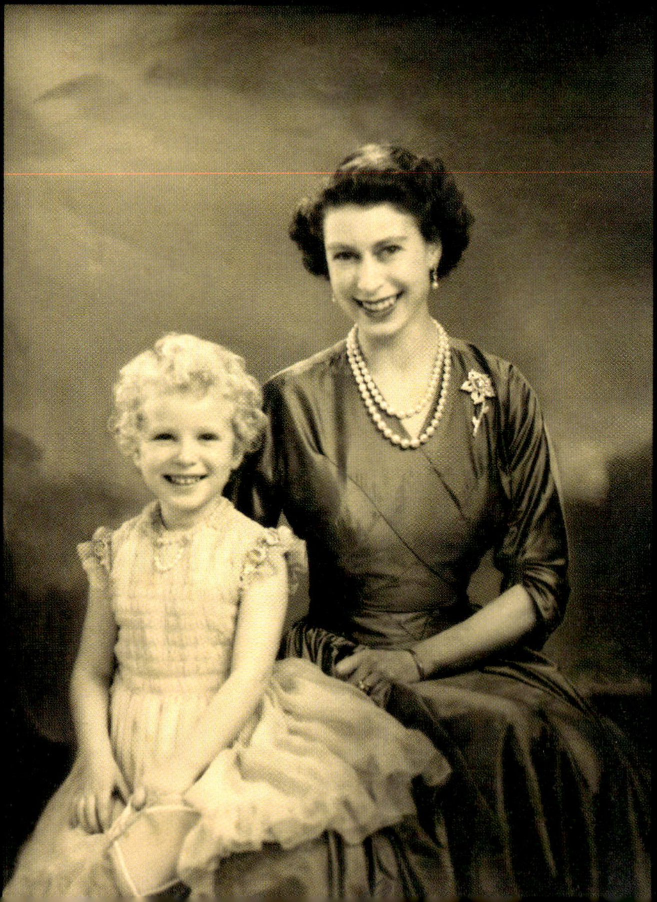

Flower **brooch**. Gold, 96.9-carat citrine, diamonds, and quartz. Cartier London, c. 1950.

Flower **brooch**. Platinum and diamonds. The 102.07-carat "Allnatt" diamond in the center was found in 1881 and set by Cartier in 1952.

Flower **brooch**. Gold, diamonds and yellow and blue sapphires. Cartier London, c. 1945.

Facing page:
Portrait of Queen Elizabeth II of Great Britain and her daughter, Princess Anne. The queen is wearing her **Edelweiss brooch** of marquise-shaped, brilliant-, and baguette-cut diamonds. The 23.6-carat pink Williamson diamond is set in the center. Cartier London, 1953.

ordered in 1946: two flowers—one of square sapphires ringing an emerald, the other of emeralds ringing a sapphire, one curved left, the other right—were topped by briolette-cut emeralds, all surrounded by a charming jumble of variously cut stones.

For her wedding in 1947, the future Queen Elizabeth received a remarkable brooch—among other Cartier foliate clip brooches—featuring a remarkable pink diamond of 23.6 carats (from a raw diamond of 54.5 carats). The giver was John T. Williamson, a Canadian geologist who, at age thirty-three, discovered a deposit of diamonds at Mwadui, Tanganikya (now Tanzania), which became the largest mine in the world. In 1947 a child brought Williamson this fabulous stone, which would be cut by Briefel and Lemer in London. Williamson included a few small white diamonds in the gift, but also wished to add other pink diamonds, which obliged the princess to wait until 1952, the year she became queen, before Frederick A. Mew of Cartier London could compose a superb, edelweiss-style flower around the Williamson diamond.

Another outstanding flower was fashioned that year. It, too, was formed of five openwork petals that lent light and majesty to a stone that was none other than the Allnatt, a cushion-cut, intense yellow diamond of 102.07 carats that Porter Rhodes presented to Queen Victoria and Empress Eugénie in 1881. The diamond was

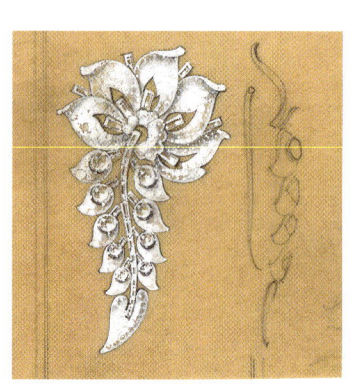

Flower **brooch**. Platinum, gray gold, rose of coral, drop diamonds, and round- and baguette-cut diamonds. c. 1940.

Design for a *Flower* **brooch** of gold, platinum, diamonds, and sapphires. Cartier Paris, 1943.

Design for a *Flower* **brooch** of platinum, gold, diamonds, coral, pearl, and jade. Cartier New York, 1956.

Design for a *Flower* **brooch** of platinum and diamonds. Cartier Paris, 1940.

Design for a *Flower* **brooch** of platinum and diamonds. Cartier Paris, 1942.

Design for a *Flower* **brooch** of platinum, gold, diamonds, coral, and jade. Cartier New York, 1956.

Design for a *Flower* **brooch** of gold, diamonds, and coral. Cartier New York, 1958.

Design for a *Reversible Petal Flower* **brooch** of gold, platinum, rubies, and diamonds. Cartier Paris, 1946.

Design for a *Flower* **brooch** of platinum, diamonds, and sapphires. Flexible stem. Cartier New York, 1960.

Design for a *Bouquet* **brooch** of platinum and diamonds. Cartier Paris, 1939.

Flower **brooch**. Platinum, white gold, coral, and diamonds. The diamond leaf is articulated. Cartier Paris, 1964.

Merle Oberon,
New York, 1942.
Photo: Horst P. Horst.

Flower **clip brooch**. Platinum, diamonds, coral, and emerald. Cartier Paris, 1953.

Flower **brooch**. Platinum, coral, and diamonds. Cartier Paris, 1955.

Flower **brooch**. Platinum, white gold, coral; diamonds underscore the quivering petals. Cartier Paris, c. 1940.

105

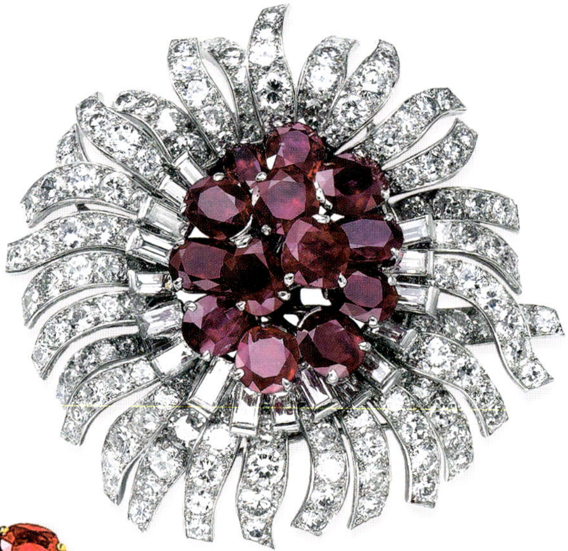

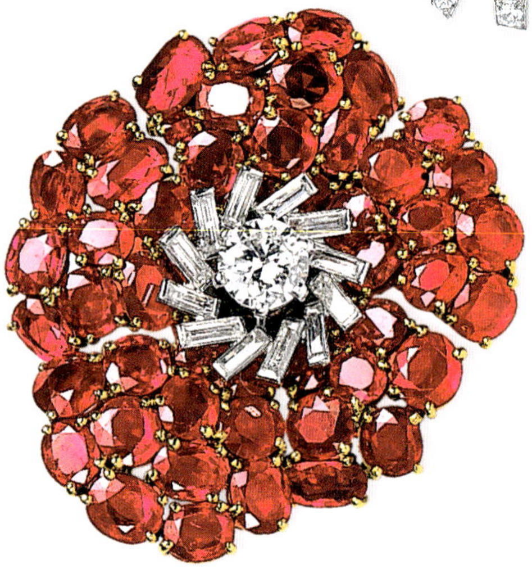

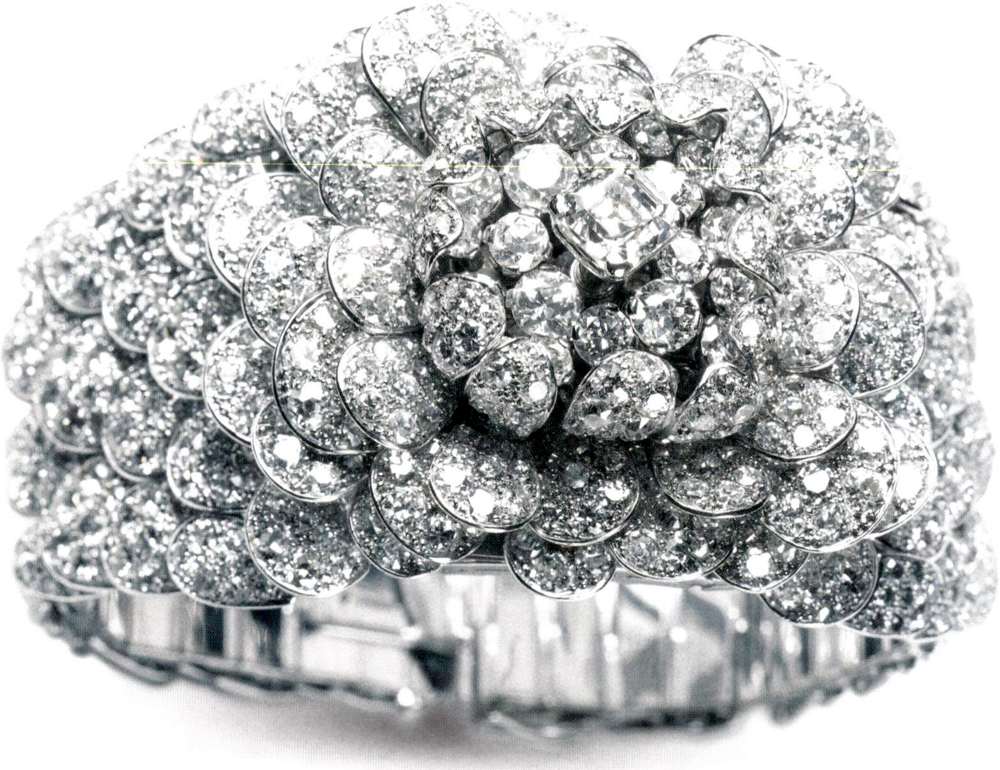

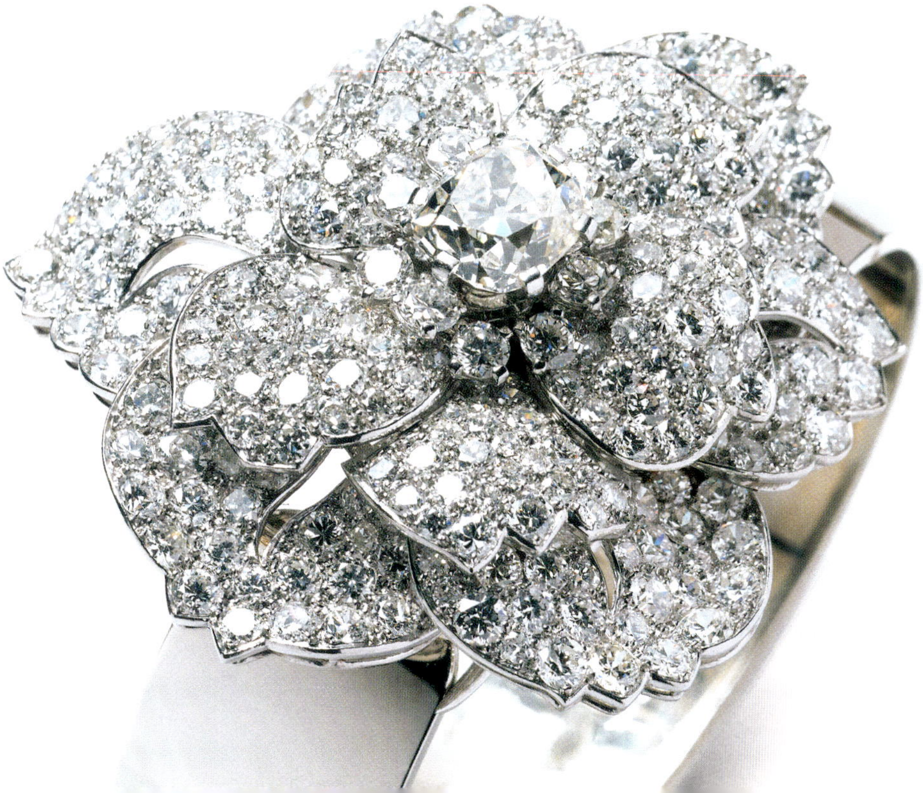

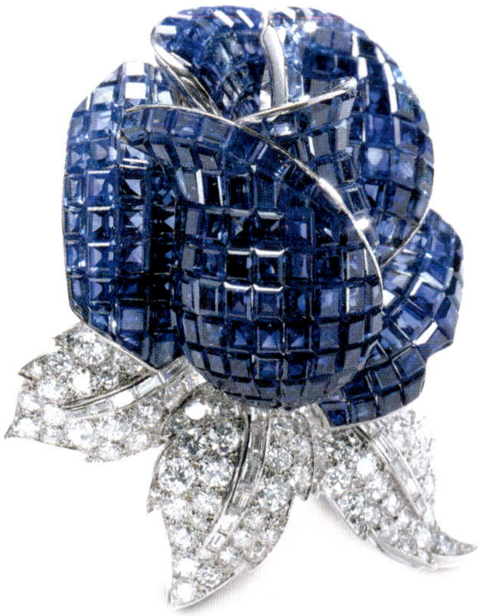

Flower **brooch**.
Gold and diamonds.
Cartier London, c. 1940.

Facing page:
Flower **brooch**.
Platinum, gray gold, rubies, and diamonds. Cartier London, 1939.

Flower **clip brooch**.
Platinum, gold, brilliant- and baguette-cut diamonds, and fifty-three oval and round faceted rubies weighing 39.31 carats in total. Cartier Paris, 1938.

Bracelet with *Flower* **clip brooch**. Platinum, white gold, one cut-cornered square-shaped 2.34 carat diamond, and round old-, single-, and rose-cut diamonds. The central motif can be detached from the bracelet and worn as a brooch. Cartier Paris, 1931.

Bangle with *Flower* **clip brooch**. Platinum, white gold, one cushion-shaped diamond weighing approximately 4.5 carats, and brilliant- and round old-cut diamonds. Cartier Paris, special order, 1939.

Blue Rose **clip brooch**.
Platinum, white gold, brilliant- and baguette-cut diamonds, faceted and caliber-cut sapphires. This stylized, three-dimensional rose is one of the few pieces ever made with an "invisible setting." Cartier Paris for New York, 1959.

named after Alfred Ernest Allnatt, one of its owners, who entrusted it to Cartier. Auctioned at Christie's Geneva in 1996, the stone sold for 3,043,496 dollars.

The delicate feel and harmonious color that gold can bring to fine jewelry were marvelously evident in a laurel-leaf clip brooch made by Cartier Paris in 1943. Along a lightly curved stem, highly realistic leaves were set opposite four oblong cabochon sapphires of dark and pale blue. The stones were set on platinum, obviously, but the gold leaves contribute crucial warmth and glow (as proven simply by imagining the entire composition in white and blue). This precious flora also yielded splendid, cascading arrangements of whites, including a dense, teeming spray called a "bunch of leaves" (1948), which magisterially combined the natural curve of the branches with the stylization of the flowers; a series of leafy lines are tipped in diamonds, a light and scintillating motif that would recur on other compositions.

The use of gold in the 1950s, notably in assemblages where voids played a role as important as solids, had already been heralded in the second half of the 1940s, as mentioned above. Worth citing are clip brooches with reversible petals, one face being of engraved gold while the other is set with diamonds. In 1962 gold with finely chased, juxtaposing lines lent an almost shredded look to a blossom whose gem-crowned stamens were given a "tremored" setting; between the two leaves on the stem was an emerald that served as a slider to open, and then to close, the petals.

There were finely lined roses of coral and ivory, decorated with diamonds or a "dewdrop" pearl (one of which belonged to Daisy Fellowes); there were buds of precious white or fancy yellow diamonds, and flowers that masked the dial of a watch on a ring; vibrant flowers that sprang to life with the least movement of the body; other flowers decorated clocks, and still others had petals of exotic woods (1970s); there were bouquets (one of which—yellow and blue sapphires dotted with brilliants—belonged to Andy Warhol) and leaves made of emeralds (for American heiress Doris Duke) or simply of gold wire. And there were also palm trees.

107

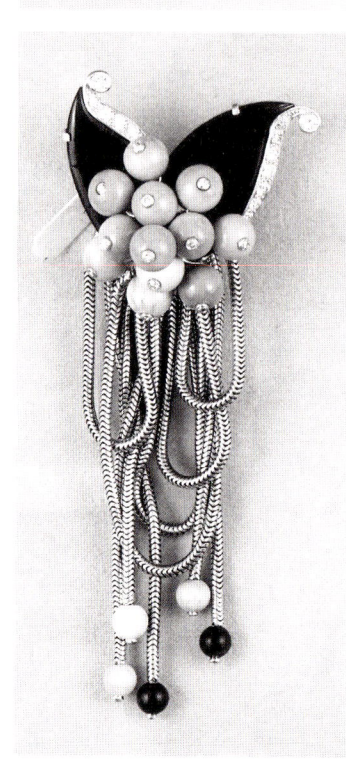

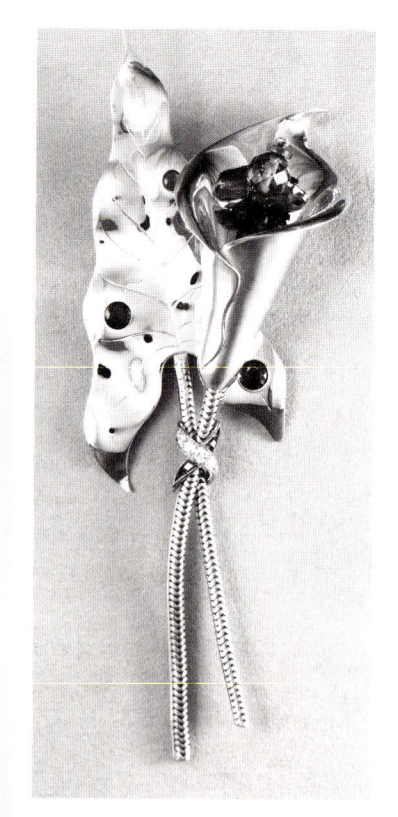

Flower brooch. Platinum, gold, diamonds, sapphires, and emeralds. Cartier New York, 1941.

Brooch. Yellow gold, diamonds, and coral. Cartier New York, 1940.

Lily of the valley **clip brooch**. Yellow gold, sapphires, topaz, and lapis lazuli. Cartier New York, 1941.

Flower **clip brooch**. Platinum, pink and yellow gold, pearls, and diamonds. Cartier New York, 1940.

Clip brooch. Gold, onyx, diamonds, and turquoise. Cartier New York, 1941.

Floral Bouquet **brooch**. Platinum, gold wire and twisted gold, brilliant-cut diamonds, sapphires, round faceted rubies, and emerald cabochons. Cartier London, 1959.

Facing page:
A diamond **brooch** on a dress by Elsa Schiaparelli, with a diamond bracelet on the wrist. 1937. Photo: A. Durst.

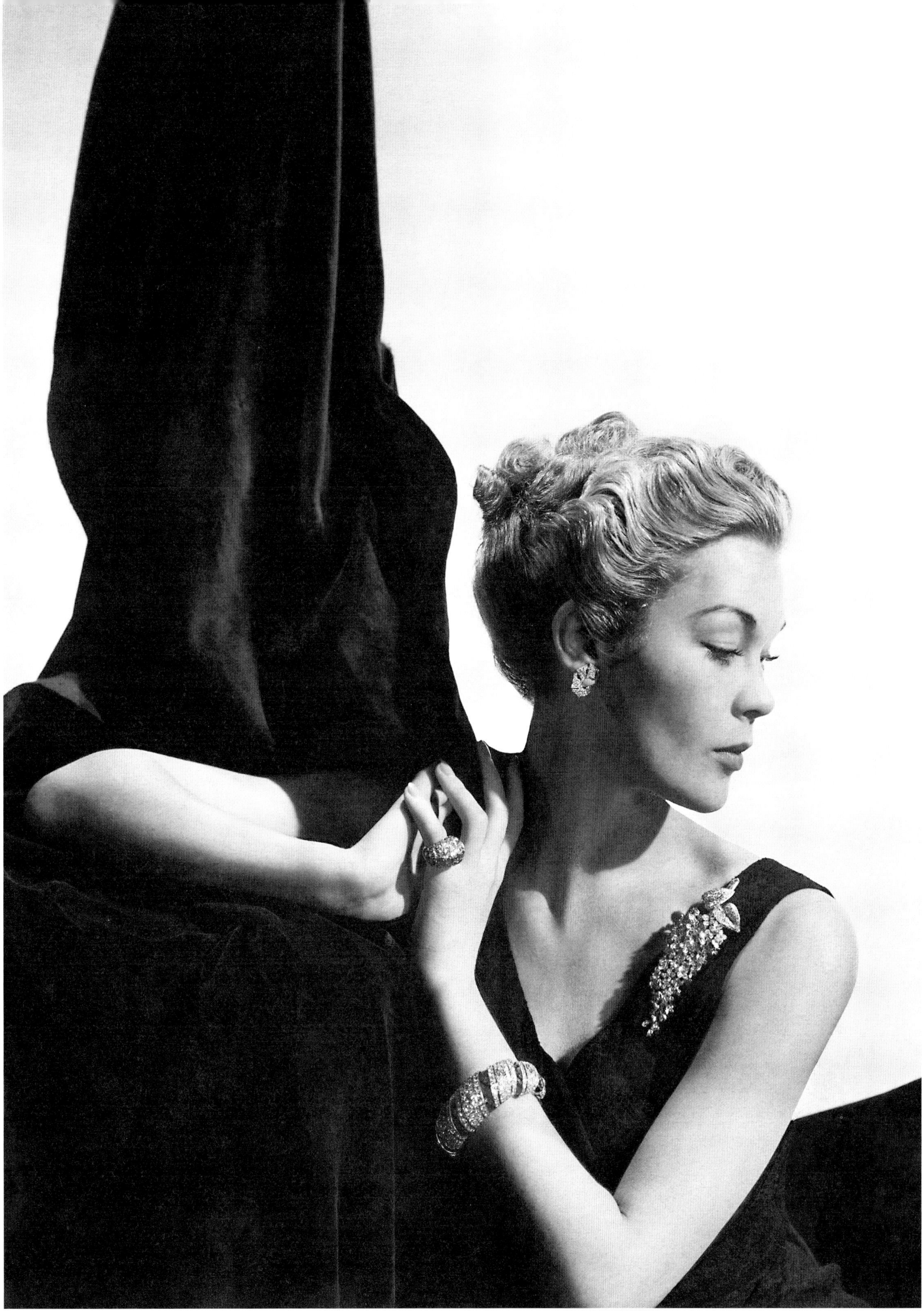

Necklace. Gold, emeralds, and diamonds. The three emerald bouquets can be detached and worn as brooches, c. 1940.

Bracelet. Gold, diamonds, and rubies. Cartier Paris, 1938.

Clip brooch. Sapphires and diamonds. Formerly the collection of the Duchess of Windsor. Cartier Paris, 1949.

Laurel **clip brooch**. Platinum, gold, brilliant-cut diamonds, and four sapphire cabochons. Cartier Paris, 1943.

Flower **clip brooch**. Platinum, gold, sapphires, and diamonds. Cartier Paris, 1943.

Gas-pipe **necklace**. Gold, rubies, and sapphires. Cartier London, 1945.

Bracelet. Platinum, diamonds, and rubies. Cartier New York, 1943.

Bracelet. White gold, diamonds, and pearls. The three floral motifs can be detached and worn as brooches. Cartier New York, 1947.

Facing page: Model flaunting earrings with two unique natural pearls, together weighing 430 grains; a necklace whose central pearl weighs 92 grains; and a diamond rivière with three flower-clips of round baguette- and marquise-cut brilliants with a Ceylon sapphire in the middle. *L'Officiel de la couture et de la mode* (December 1960).

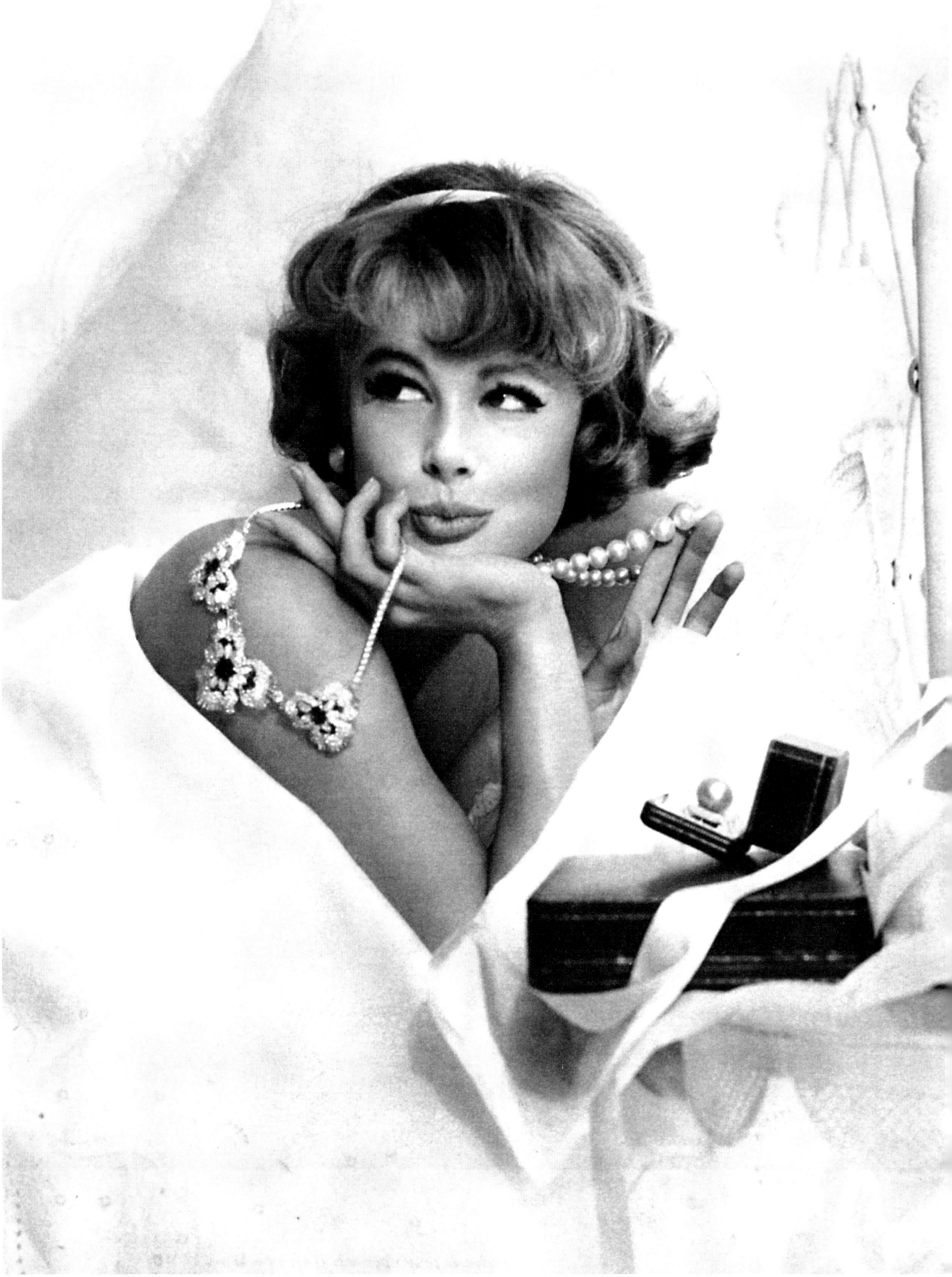

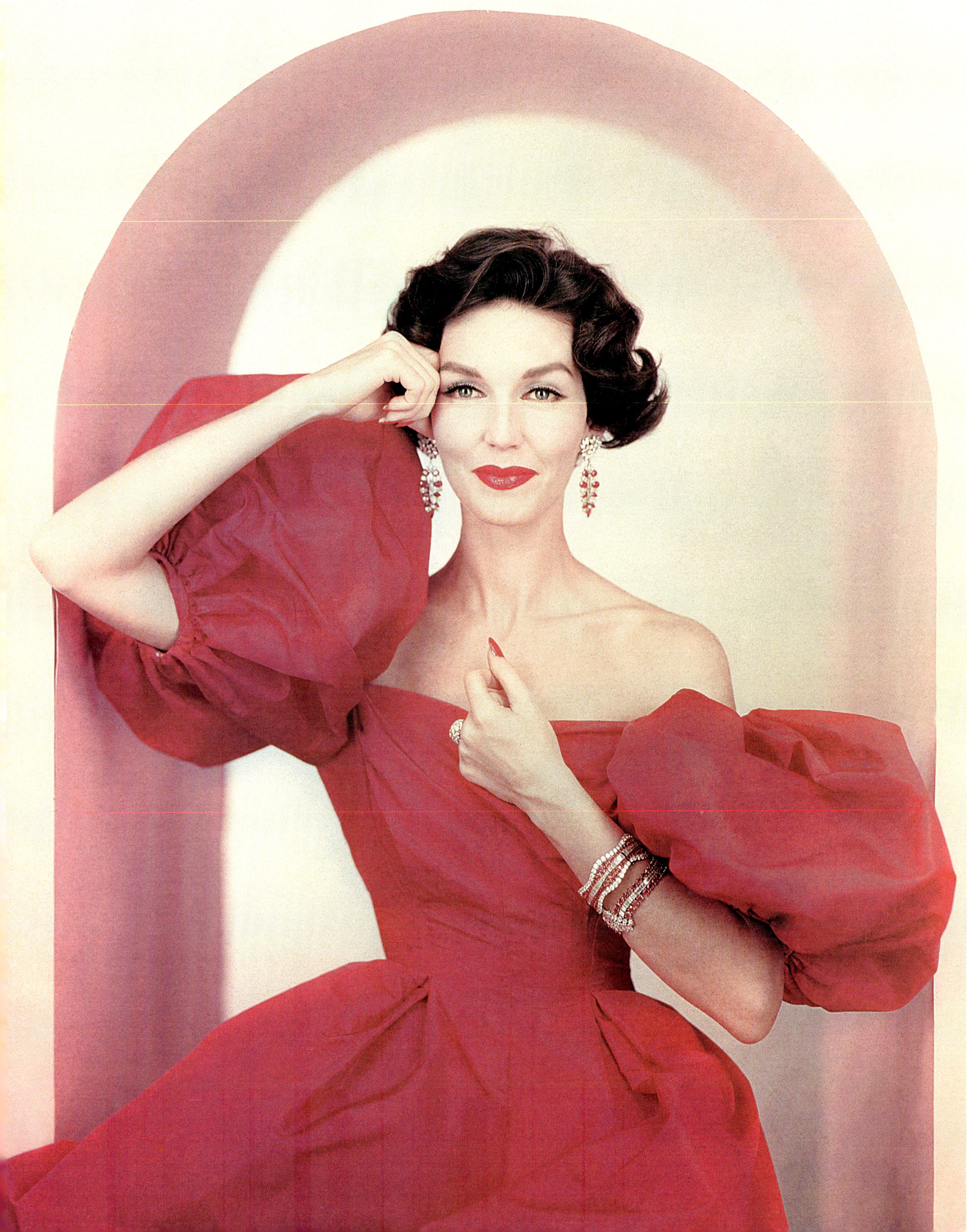

Palm trees—set with diamonds, stylized, with articulated trunks—first appeared in the late 1930s, perhaps inspired by the opening of Cartier boutiques in Monte Carlo and Cannes. The fronds might drip with diamonds or turquoises (for Simone del Duca). One of them is a now a key part of the Cartier Collection: particularly imposing in size, interesting for its use of baguette-cut diamonds that structure each frond depending on its position on the trunk, endowed with movement, it features seven magnificent cushion-shaped Burmese rubies of rare quality (totaling 23.1 carats). It was the work of Georges Rémy, one of the firm's great jewelry designers. Orchids, too, can be complex and fascinating: the 2005 Caresse d'Orchidée collection presented orchids that are startling in their exceptionally natural modeling and their free handling of color. When worn, they display a sensuality surprising for such large pieces, because each curve, each stone is conceived as a function of the overall flower and its movement. Current techniques of design and manufacture, which allow designers to express a sculptural vision, plus the use of both precious and semiprecious stones with infinite hues, impart greater life to these hybrid jewels that borrow the best from both reverie and reality.

Open-and-Shut Flower **earrings**. Platinum, gold wire, brilliant-cut diamonds, sapphires, emeralds, and round faceted rubies. The flowers bloom when the petals are opened. Cartier Paris, 1967.

Palm **earrings**. Yellow gold, emeralds, and diamonds. Cartier Paris, 1957.

Six-Petal Flower **ear clips**. Platinum, yellow gold, and white and fancy yellow diamonds. Cartier Paris, 1965.

Earrings. Platinum, gold, emeralds, and diamonds. c. 1940.

Ear clips. Platinum, yellow gold, citrines, and diamonds. Cartier London, 1944.

Facing page:
Diamond and ruby **parure** composed of earrings, bracelet, and ring. 1956. Photo: R. Rutledge for *Vogue* magazine.

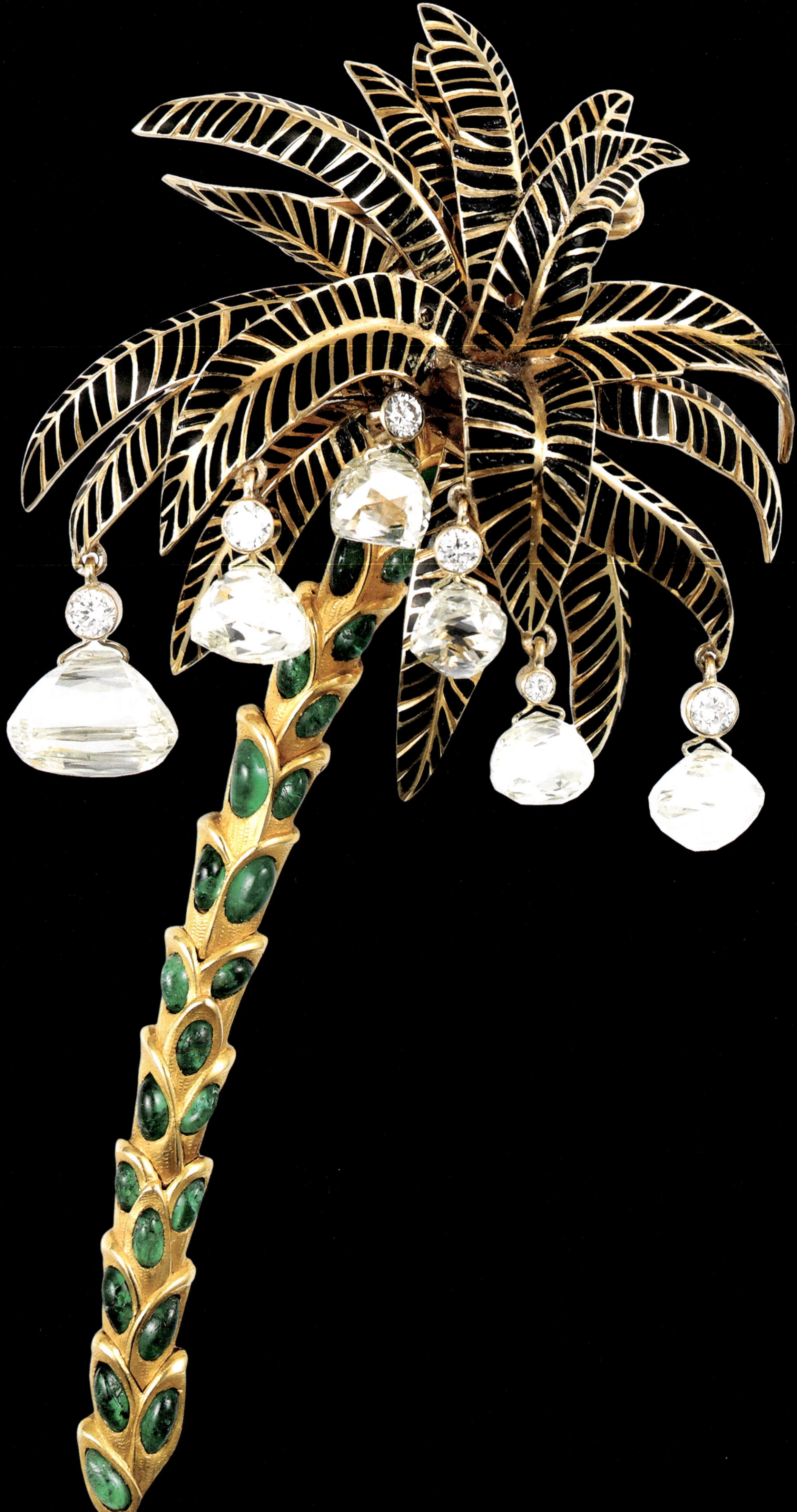

Palm-Tree **clip brooch**.
Platinum, white gold,
brilliant- and baguette-cut
diamonds, and seven
cushion-shaped Burmese
rubies weighing 23.1 carats
in total. Cartier Paris,
special order, 1957.

Palm-Tree **brooch**.
Platinum and diamonds.
Cartier Paris, 1948.

Palm-Tree **brooch**.
Platinum and diamonds.
Cartier Paris, 1950.

Palm-Tree **brooch**. Platinum,
gray gold, round diamonds,
turquoise cabochons, and
seven dangling pear-shaped
turquoises. Formerly the
collection of Simone del
Duca. Cartier Paris, 1965.

Palm-Tree **brooch**.
Platinum and diamonds.
Cartier Paris, 1939.

Facing page:
Palm-Tree **clip brooch**.
Yellow gold, enamel,
emeralds, and diamonds.
Cartier Paris, 1939.

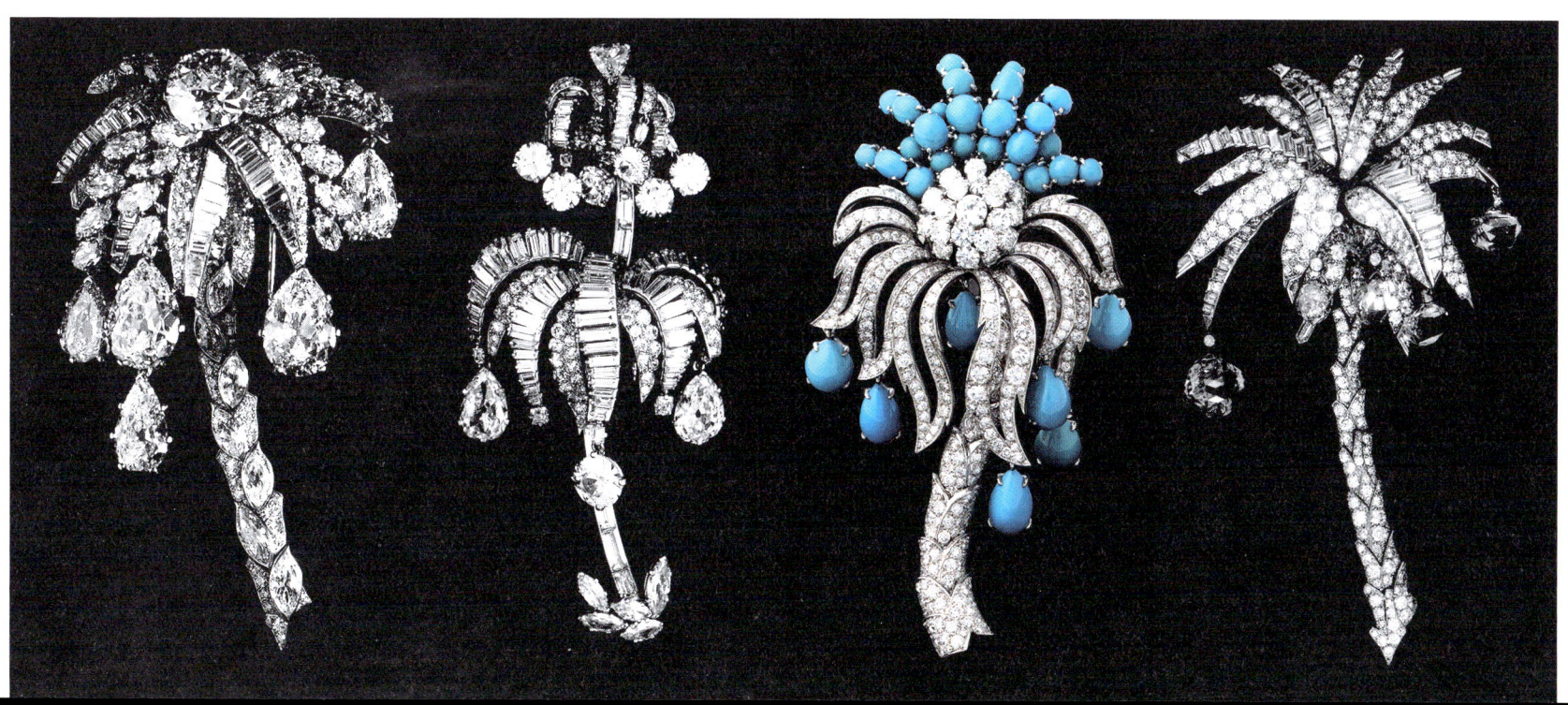

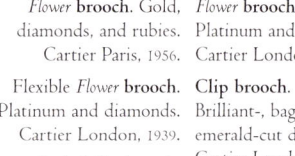

Flower **brooch**. Gold, diamonds, and rubies. Cartier Paris, 1956.

Flexible *Flower* **brooch**. Platinum and diamonds. Cartier London, 1939.

Rosebud **clip brooch**. Yellow and pink gold, brilliant-cut fancy yellow diamonds, brilliant- and single-cut diamonds, emeralds, and green enamel. Cartier Paris, 1965.

Flower **brooch**. Platinum, gold, diamonds, and coral beads. Cartier London, 1955.

Flower **brooch**. Platinum and diamonds. Cartier London, 1938.

Clip brooch. Brilliant-, baguette-, and emerald-cut diamonds. Cartier London, 1939.

Flower **brooch**. Platinum and diamonds. Cartier Paris, 1961.

Brooch. Platinum and diamonds. Cartier Paris, 1960.

Necklace that can be transformed into a head ornament. Platinum, pearls, and diamonds. Cartier London, 1972.

Page 120:
Cartier advertisement. *L'Officiel de la couture et de la mode* (December 1969).

Page 121:
Floral Bouquet **clip brooch**. Yellow gold, palladium, tourmalines, rubies, and diamonds. Cartier London, 1945.

Brooch. Platinum, pink gold, round faceted rubies, and single-cut diamonds. Cartier New York, c. 1948.

Anemone **clip brooch**. Platinum, yellow gold, rubies, emerald, and diamonds. Cartier Paris, 1941.

Flower **clip brooch**. Platinum, yellow gold, citrine, and diamond. Cartier London, 1942.

Flower **clip brooch**. Platinum, gold, round old-, brilliant- and single-cut diamonds, pale marquise- and pear-shaped faceted topazes, and intense round and pear-shaped faceted citrines. Cartier London, 1943.

Cartier

JOAILLIERS

13, RUE DE LA PAIX

PARIS

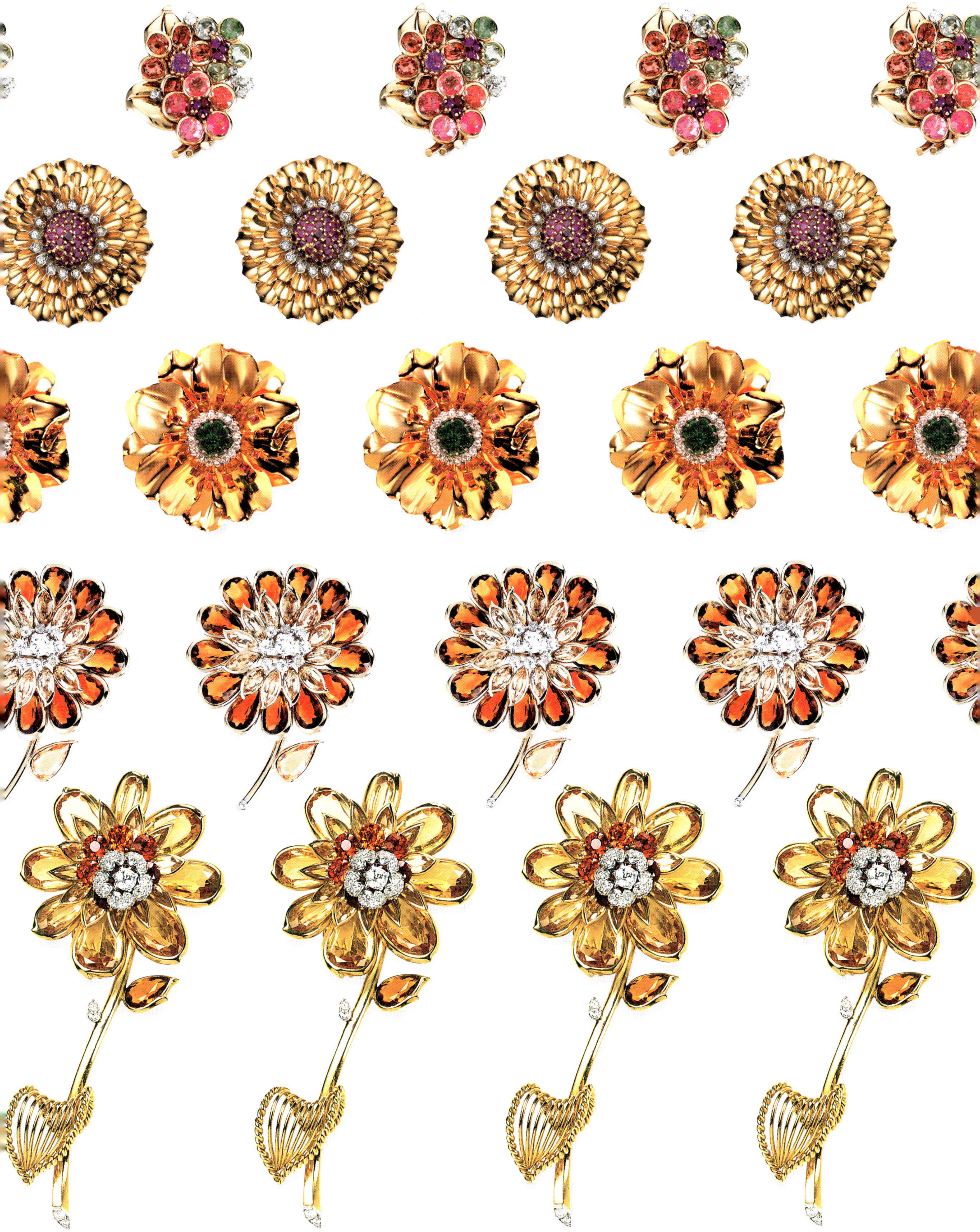

Flower **clip brooch.** Platinum, white gold, brilliant- and baguette-cut diamonds, and one octagonal step-cut yellow sapphire weighing 12.49 carats. Cartier Paris, special order, 1962.

Ring. Platinum, diamonds, and one 43.8-carat sapphire cabochon. Cartier Paris, 1942.

Flower **brooch.** Platinum, gold, octagonal faceted emerald, and square-shaped, baguette-, and brilliant-cut diamonds. Cartier Paris, 1959.

Facing page:
Necklace and detachable brooch. Platinum, 952 diamonds weighing 15.11 carats, two rubellite drops weighing 28.11 carats, and one cushion-shaped faceted rubellite weighing 12.51 carats. *Caresse d'Orchidées par Cartier* collection. Cartier Paris, 2005.

Flower **brooch.** Platinum and pear-shaped and baguette-cut diamonds. Cartier London, 1953.

Rose **clip brooch.** Platinum and round old-, baguette-, and single-cut diamonds. Formerly the collection of HRH The Princess Margaret, Countess Snowdon. Cartier London, 1938.

Flower **brooch.** Platinum, sapphires, and brilliant-cut diamonds. Cartier Paris, 1991.

123

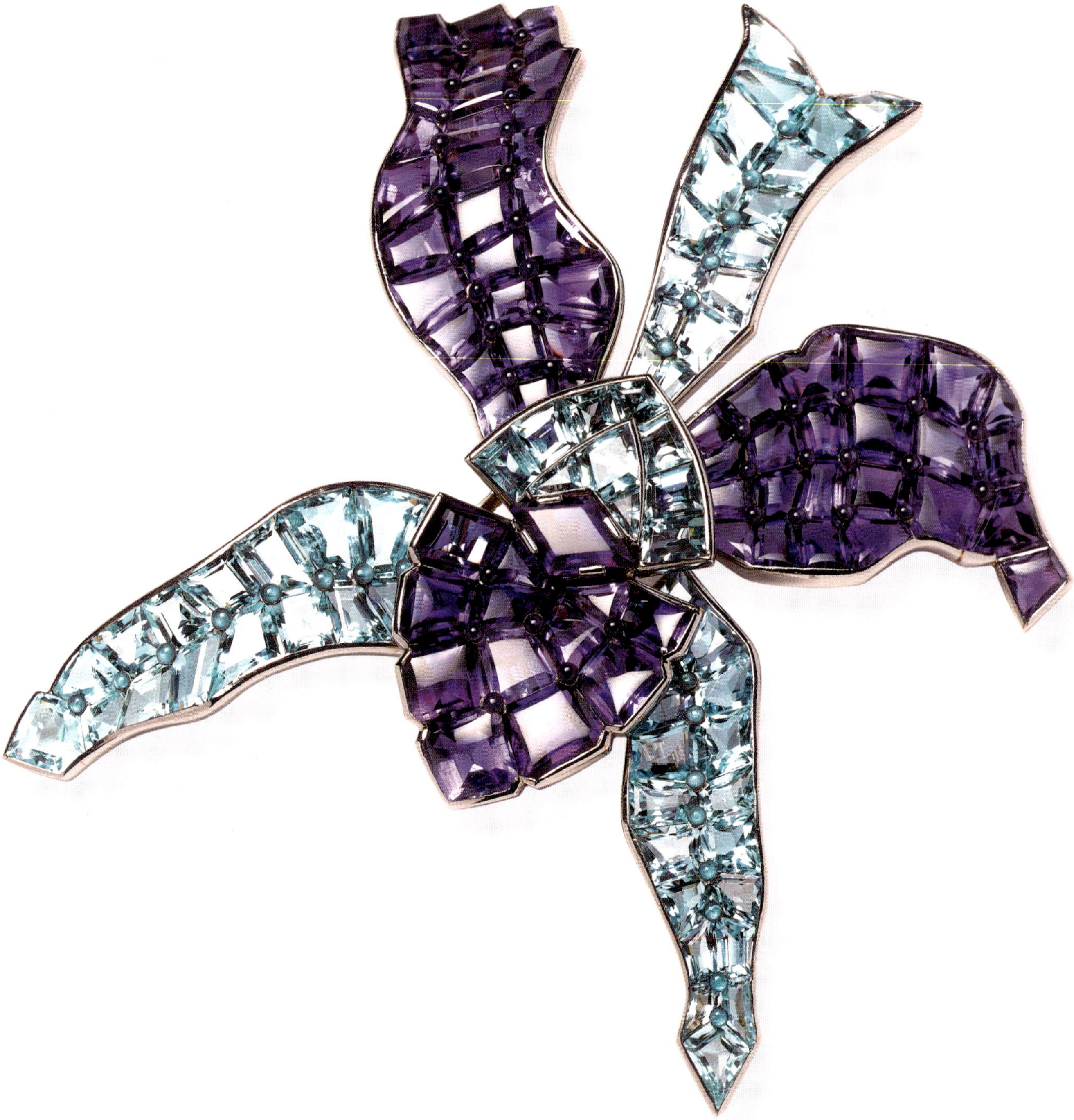

Necklace and **clip brooch**. Gray gold, diamonds, rubellites, and pink faceted sapphires. *Caresse d'Orchidées par Cartier* collection. Cartier Paris, 2005.

Brooch. Gray gold, diamonds, spinels, demantoid garnets, mandarin garnets, and one 30.38-carat faceted spinel. *Caresse d'Orchidées par Cartier* collection. Cartier Paris, 2005.

Facing page: *Orchid* **brooch**. White gold, faceted amethysts and aquamarines, and pale blue and mauve enamel studs between the stones. Cartier Paris, special order, 1937.

Necklace. Gray gold, diamonds, rubies, one faceted 18.4-carat rubellite, fifteen rubellite drops weighing 74.04 carats, and 189 emerald beads weighing 656.58 carats. *Caresse d'Orchidées par Cartier* collection. Cartier Paris, 2005.

Facing page:
Earrings. Platinum, white and fancy yellow diamonds, and ruby drops. *Caresse d'Orchidées par Cartier* collection. Cartier Paris, 2005.

Ring. Platinum and white, pink, and fancy yellow diamonds. *Caresse d'Orchidées par Cartier* collection. Cartier Paris, 2005. Detail.

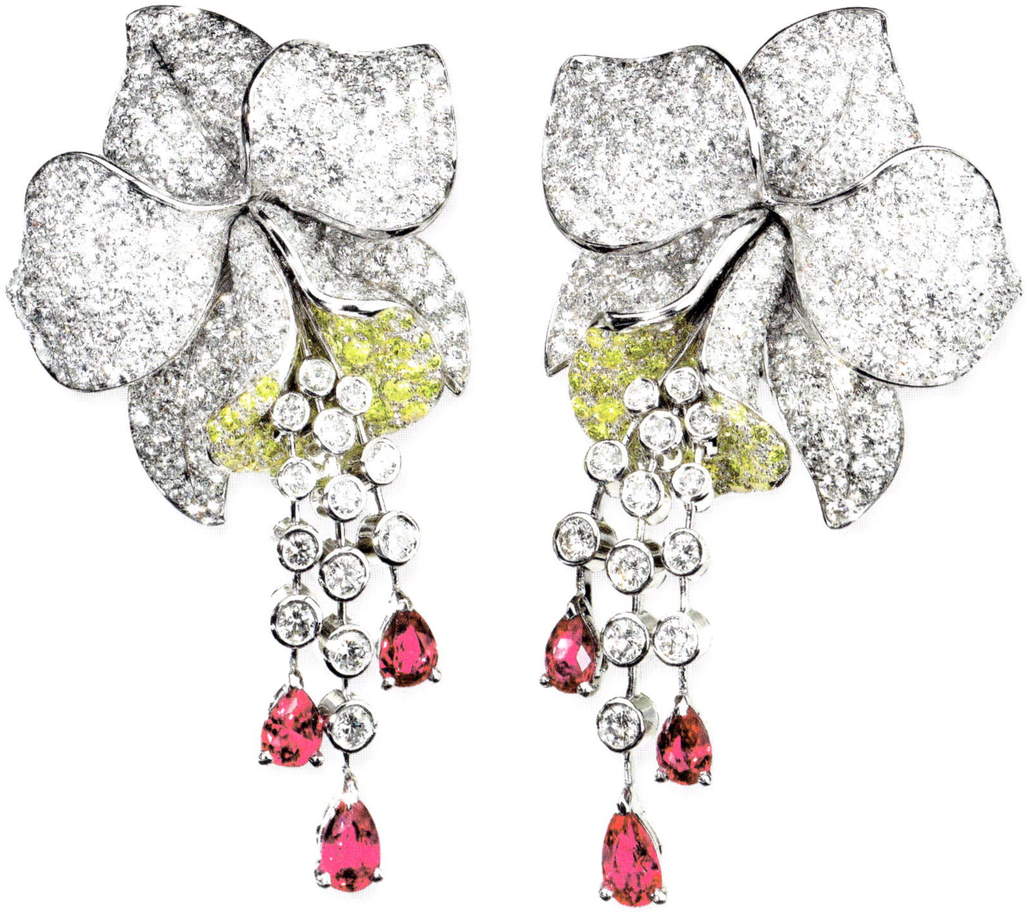

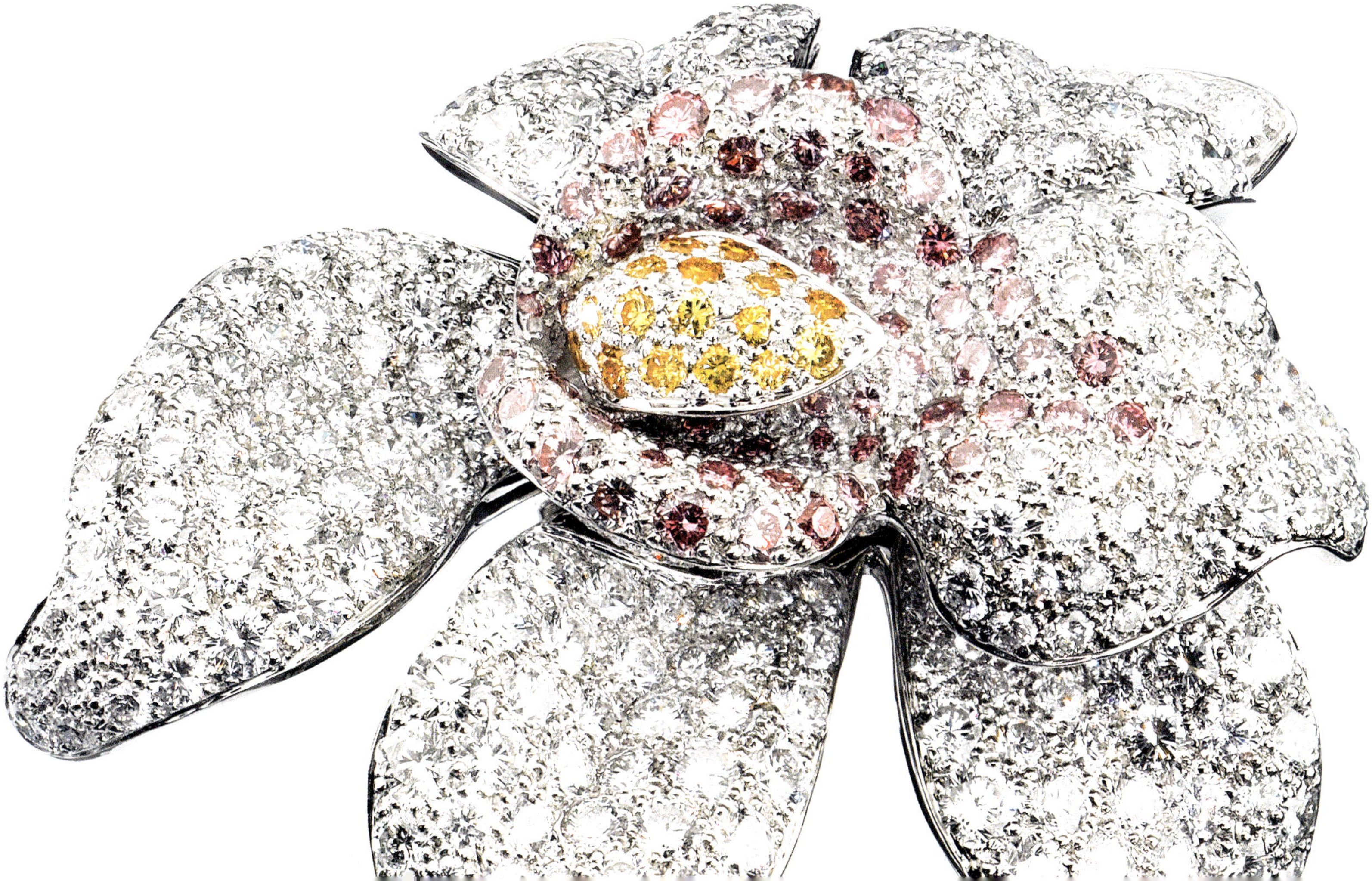

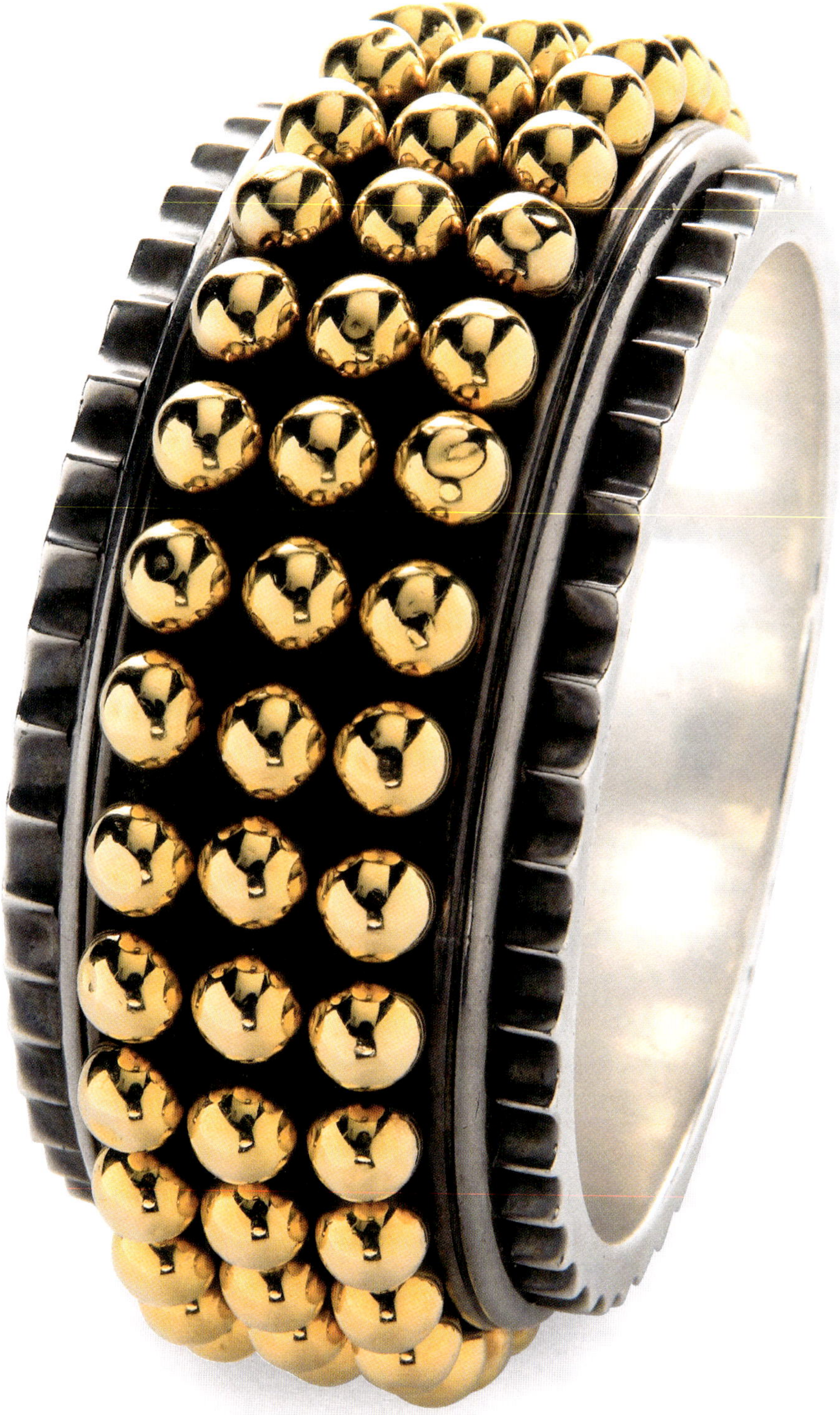

ABSTRACT
JEWELRY

Bracelet. Gold and brilliant-cut diamonds. Cartier Paris, 1951.

Facing page:
Bracelet. Yellow and red gold. Cartier Paris, 1945.

Bracelet. Gold and faceted and caliber-cut sapphires. Cartier Paris, 1938.

Page 128:
Bangle. Silver with three rows of gold beads. Cartier Paris, 1930.

Gold

Of abstraction, artist Michel Seuphor used to the say that it should "contain no reminder of reality, whether or not reality served as the artist's point of departure." Yet the line between abstraction and representation can often be fine, and the decorative arts have always exploited, with great freedom, ambiguities generated by the play of volumes, stylization, and repetition. Furthermore, abstraction is often a question of focus: regardless of the subject, a view of one isolated part of it becomes abstract. Finally, abstraction is an idea that is not rooted in everyday reality—in its own way, it is a kind of chimera.

The uniquely delicate look of Cartier's abstract jewelry during the art deco period was due to the talent of designer Charles Jacqueau. A circle would tame a straight line; a curve would soften the harshness of a square. The abstraction of the 1940s, meanwhile, was more sculptural and encouraged gold to shine. The privileged role of gold can of course be explained by wartime shortages—platinum's many qualities made it essential to strategic industries, while the importation of precious gems into Europe became a thing of a past—but a pronounced taste for yellow gold had emerged several years earlier, probably due to the appeal of Indian jewelry and perhaps to a need for a warmer glow after the wintry splendor of white diamonds. At any rate, even prior to the abysmal rigors of war, in 1937 *Femina* magazine published an article on Cartier titled "Gold Jewelry Has Arrived." Certain bracelets with clean, massive shapes played on a repetitive decorative theme often underscored by caliber-cut stones or cabochons whose outlines accentuated the overall sobriety. Made of thick sheets of polished gold in a rolling pattern, or a succession of yellow-gold "rooftops" linked by red-gold "half-tubes"

Bracelet-watch. Gold, and square and rectangular citrines. Cartier Paris, 1938.

Buckle **bangle.** Platinum, white gold, and brilliant-, baguette-, and single-cut diamonds. Originally, the buckle-shaped clasp could be detached and worn as a brooch. Cartier London, 1937.

Facing page:
Bracelet. Pink gold, platinum, round faceted sapphires, and round old-cut diamonds. Cartier New York, c. 1945.

133

(Cartier Paris, 1945), they sometimes evoked certain buildings of the late 1930s seen from afar, such as the colonnaded wing of the Palais de Chaillot. Others, lighter in appearance, played on the alternation of round links and oblong ones, or disks and rings, or scrolls and semicircles. Still others were made of flat bands of overlapping patterns of flat disks (Cartier Paris, 1945), or rows of little domes adorned with brilliants (London, c. 1940), or Chinese hats, often with engine-turned decoration. Necklaces were draped with motifs of stripy little leaves that retained only the sharp outlines and central vein of their original models. One bracelet suggested rows of eyes with blue, green, and red irises (sapphires, emeralds, and rubies) that look around in every direction—"Big Brother is watching you!" warned George Orwell in 1948 in his novel *1984*. Yet Cartier always avoided the pitfall of heavy-handedness thanks to numerous imperceptible details such as the subtle rounding of sharp angles, the tiny spaces left between two motifs, or differences in color and polishing techniques. Examples of rigid bracelets and bangles, decorated with costly gems in geometric designs, include a wide strap whose end loops through a ring of circular diamonds (Cartier London), and a series of thick, curved plaques adorned with bulging rows of caliber-cut sapphires that seem to protrude from diamond-studded rectangles. This later model, made by Cartier New York in 1939, belonged to Doris Duke, sole heir to a tobacco and electricity tycoon, whose mother who already owned some very fine Cartier jewelry. When Duke's wardrobe was exhibited in Newport in 2007, Diors, Chanels, and Saint Laurents could be seen alongside Halstons from the best years; a photo from the late 1970s that also made the press showed her at Studio 54, the fashionable New York nightclub, in the company of Andy Warhol, another great fan of Cartier jewelry and watches. Warhol's collection included a beautiful bracelet from that same period, featuring a step-cut aquamarine of nearly thirty-five carats set on a "gas-pipe" bracelet, evoking an aesthetic idiom familiar to Warhol—soup cans, Brillo boxes, gaspipe jewelry. The prosaic term "gas pipe" referred to flexible, reeded gold that created the effect of a tube. Devised during the first half of the 1930s in various, often flattened diameters, it became a highly fashionable motif in the 1940s and was

Necklace. Yellow gold, citrines, sapphire cabochons, and brilliants. c. 1938.

Facing page:
Bracelet. Platinum, yellow and pink gold, old European-cut diamonds, and caliber-cut sapphires. Formerly the collection of Doris Duke. Cartier New York, c. 1939.

135

Gas Pipe **bracelet**. Platinum, gold, round old-cut diamonds, leaf-shaped carved rubies, and one 23.37-carat sapphire cabochon. Cartier Paris, 1945.

Bracelet-watch. Gold, sapphires, and diamonds. Cartier New York, 1945.

Bracelet. Gold, round diamonds, and yellow and blue sapphires, c. 1940.

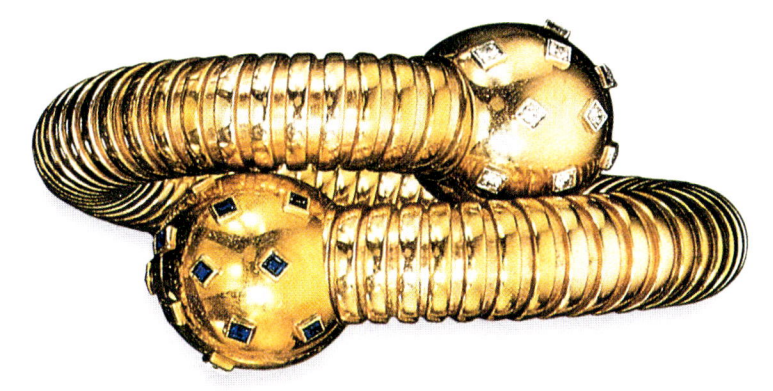

Bracelet. One ball is yellow gold studded with sapphires, the other is pink gold studded with diamonds. Cartier New York, c. 1944.

Ring. Gold and diamonds. Cartier Paris, 1942.

therefore adopted by numerous jewelers. Cartier produced some fine examples that underscored its sobriety and suppleness, notably in bracelets with a clasp in the form of two large loops that extended from each end of a slightly larger "pipe" and then closed around an abstract or figurative motif, such as a flower with ruby petals surrounding a sapphire cabochon weighing 23.37 carats, or an asymmetrical motif of emeralds and diamonds set in the "Hindu" style (Cartier Paris, 1945, 1946). The gas pipe, or *tuyau à gaz*, model, whether single or double, thick or thin, provided an inspiring platform for a series of wrist and neck ornaments that might flaunt overlapping golden spheres studded with diamonds and sapphires, or oblong clusters of ribbed coral beads, or emerald cabochons set in black lacquer claws. Two very sober, very different necklaces—one representational, the other abstract—can serve as examples. The former, held by two rings of polished gold, ends in two floral clips composed of rubies, diamonds, and sapphires (Cartier London, 1945), while the latter merely alternates two gaspipes of different diameters in a play of two polished gold loops whose line suggests a Möbius strip (Cartier Paris, 1947). Nothing could be simpler—or more decorative.

During this same period, a lady's watch was above all an item of jewelry. The dial was often hidden and often very small, a challenge successfully met by Cartier at an early day since, in 1932, the narrow Baguette model, bought by Prince Tikkar of Kapurthala, was fitted with the tiniest existing movement, weighing less than a gram (a record unsurpassed to this day); while in 1938, the smallest watch in the world, created by Cartier, was presented by French President Albert Lebrun to the young Princess Elizabeth during a visit to France by the British king and queen.[18] There are many examples of bracelets designed to hold watches, such as a triple snake chain holding a small Tonneau (Cartier Paris, 1946) or an imposing motif edged in pleated gold and decorated with sapphires and diamonds (Cartier New York, 1945), or scrolled links of pink gold set with rows of brilliants holding a sliding watchcase of green gold (Cartier New York, 1940), not forgetting gas-pipe bracelets (in gold or even platinum) that served the same purpose, notably in the Pineapple watch, whose dial was masked by a curved cover of gold disks dotted with precious gems.

18. Elizabeth lost the watch during a stroll with her dogs at Sandringham. Extensive searches proved vain; in 1957, after she had become queen, the French government presented her with another, equally tiny watch, but this time of platinum and diamonds.

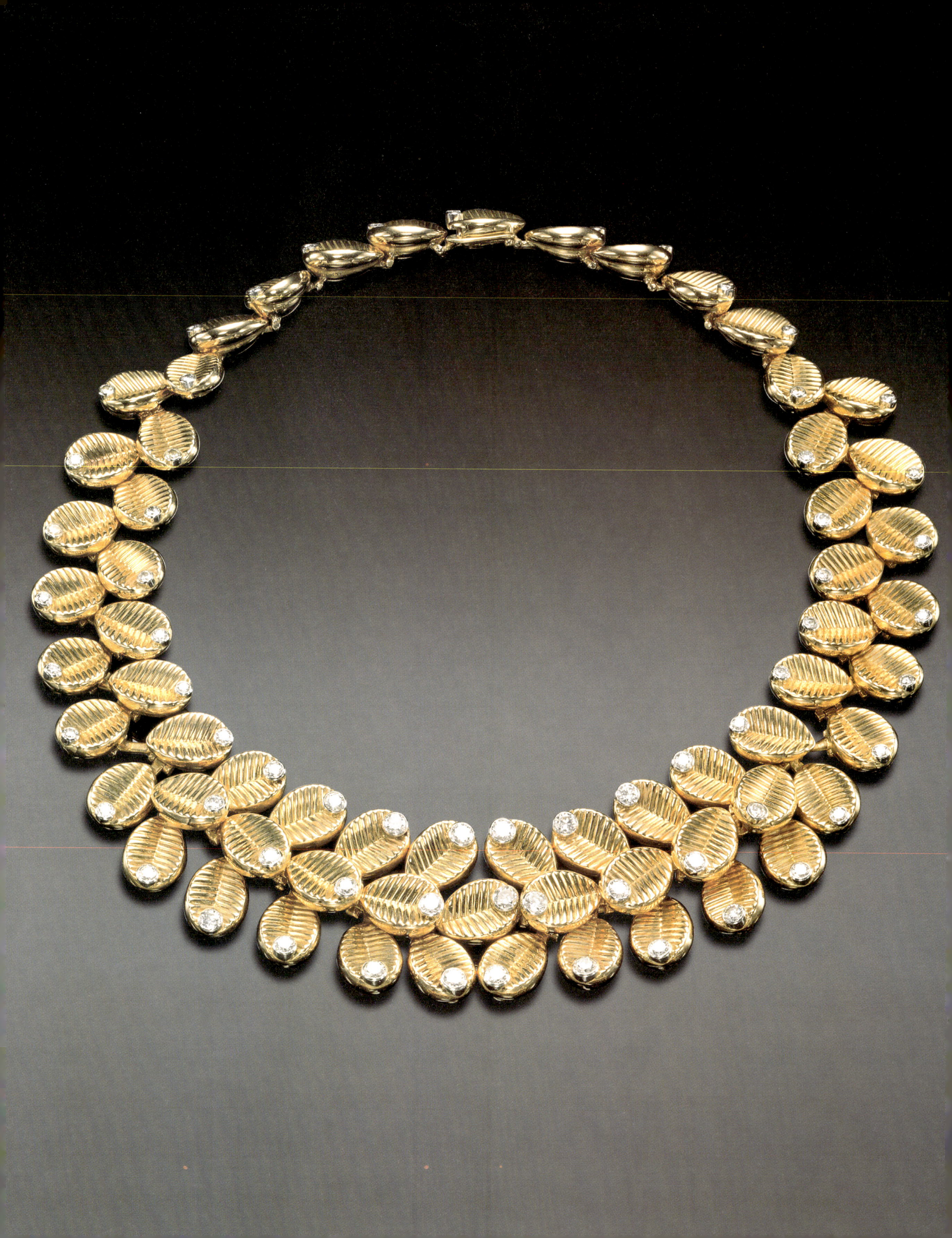

COFFEE BEANS

It is not only the wrist that tells time, as demonstrated by a 1947 watch-brooch in the Cartier Collection. A small dial, worn as a brooch, is ringed by three rows of "coffee beans" dotted with round diamonds. Coffee, it was alleged in the seventeenth century, was discovered by a goatherd whose goats, after having nibbled the leaves and berries of the bush, showed all the symptoms of euphoria. Less convincing, if highly appealing, is the tale that the archangel Gabriel offered coffee to a weakened Muhammad who, after drinking the beverage, fought off forty warriors and then satisfied the desires of forty women.[19] The new drink soon lent its name to new establishments—coffee houses or cafés—where artists, writers, philosophers, and ordinary fellows could meet and chat. By the time Cartier paid tribute to the famous coffee bean in the mid-1930s, the likes of Pablo Picasso and Dora Maar were

19. Lemaire, *Les Cafés littéraires*.

Coffee-Bean **bracelet**.
Yellow gold and diamonds.
Cartier Paris, 1953.

Coffee-Bean **earrings**.
Yellow gold and diamonds.
Cartier London, 1955.

Facing page:
Coffee-Bean **necklace**.
Yellow gold and diamonds.
Cartier Paris, 1953.

meeting in the Café des Deux Magots in Paris. These were also the days of New York's "Café Society" with its notorious hostess Elsa Maxwell, known for memorable parties where she invited people who were "full of beans." In his book *Les Styles,* Philippe Jullian identified Maxwell as "a friend of the Duchess of Windsor" and then set the stage: "Everything could be found on Fifth Avenue—the knickknacks came from Cartier's or Tiffany's—but the chintz with big roses, chosen by Cecil Beaton, came from London, while the chairs came from Paris in honor of Lady Mendl, and the mirror from Venice, a present from Lily Volpi."

Cartier's little coffee beans have the particularity of being ribbed along their central vein, and sometimes dotted with a stone on the tip or one edge. Brooches, necklaces, bracelets, ear clips, and pendant earrings were decorated with this motif: a double row was linked to a simple chain to make a bracelet in 1953; set with rubies and diamonds combined with gold beads, they spiraled around the wrist in a 1938 bracelet; arranged in a sunburst, they became a brooch; arrayed as a flower, ear clips; in rows, pendant earrings. In 1954 a young woman with her hair in a bun wore a tight choker made of three strands of coffee beans and three strands of gold beads; on her ears, petals of coffee beans formed a flower with a diamond at the middle. In 1955 a twist of gray pearls featured a coffee-bean clasp, this time made of coral studded with brilliants.

Coffee-Bean **clip brooch**.
Platinum, gold, brilliant-cut diamond, emeralds, rubies, and sapphires.
Cartier London, 1955.

Coffee-Bean **brooch**.
Platinum, gold, and brilliant-cut diamonds.
Cartier London, 1955.

Coffee-Bean **brooch**.
Yellow gold and diamonds.
Cartier London, 1953.

Coffee-Bean **brooch**.
Gold, diamonds, natural pearl, and carved coral.
Cartier New York, c. 1962.

Coffee-Bean **brooch**.
Platinum, gold, and brilliant-cut diamonds.
Cartier London, 1955.

Coffee-Bean **earrings**.
Yellow gold and diamonds.
c. 1953.

Facing page:
A diamond-studded *Coffee-Bean* **necklace** sits atop three strands of gold beads. *Coffee-Bean* **earrings**. Cartier, 1953. *L'Officiel de la couture et de la mode* 381–82 (1953).

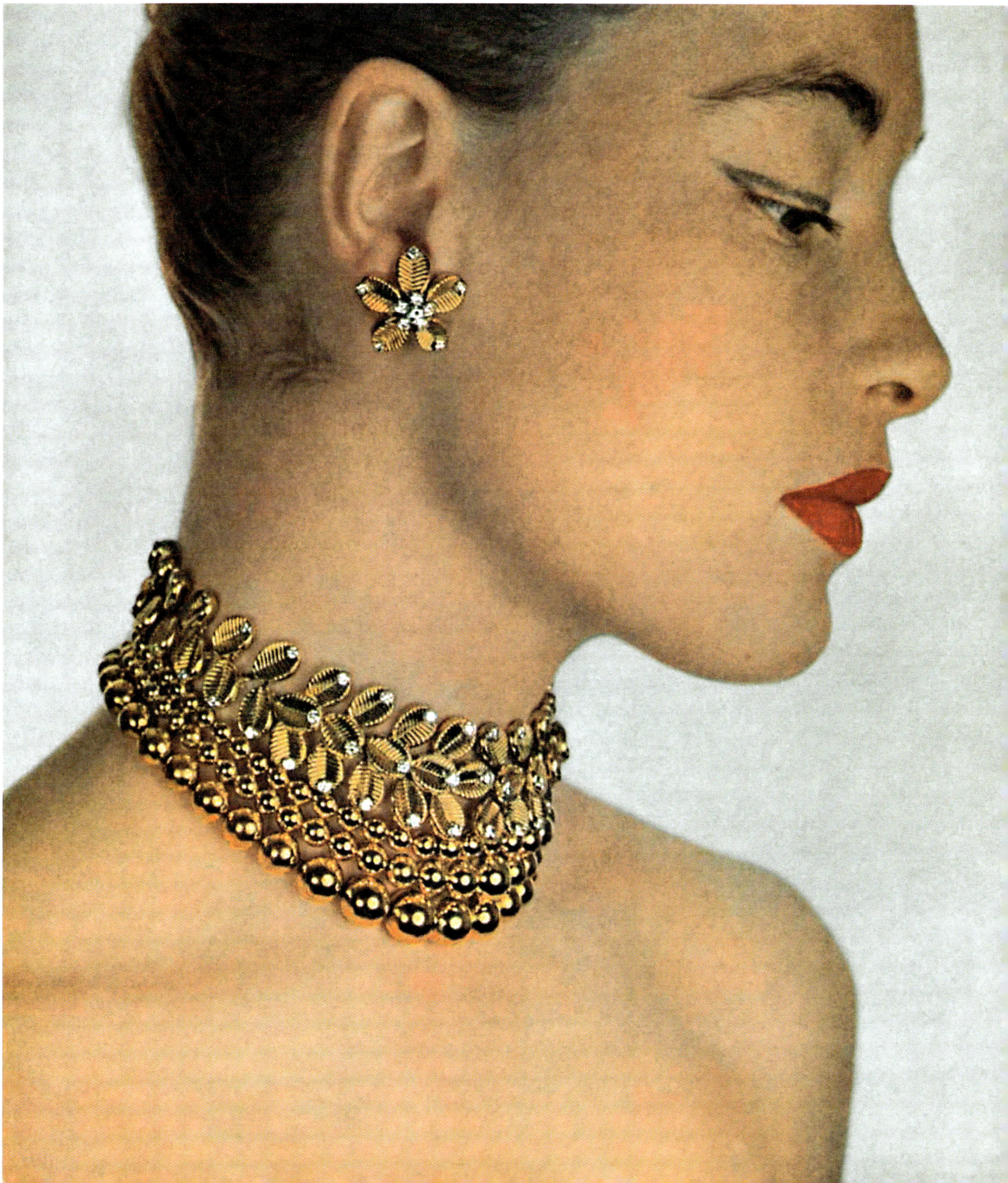

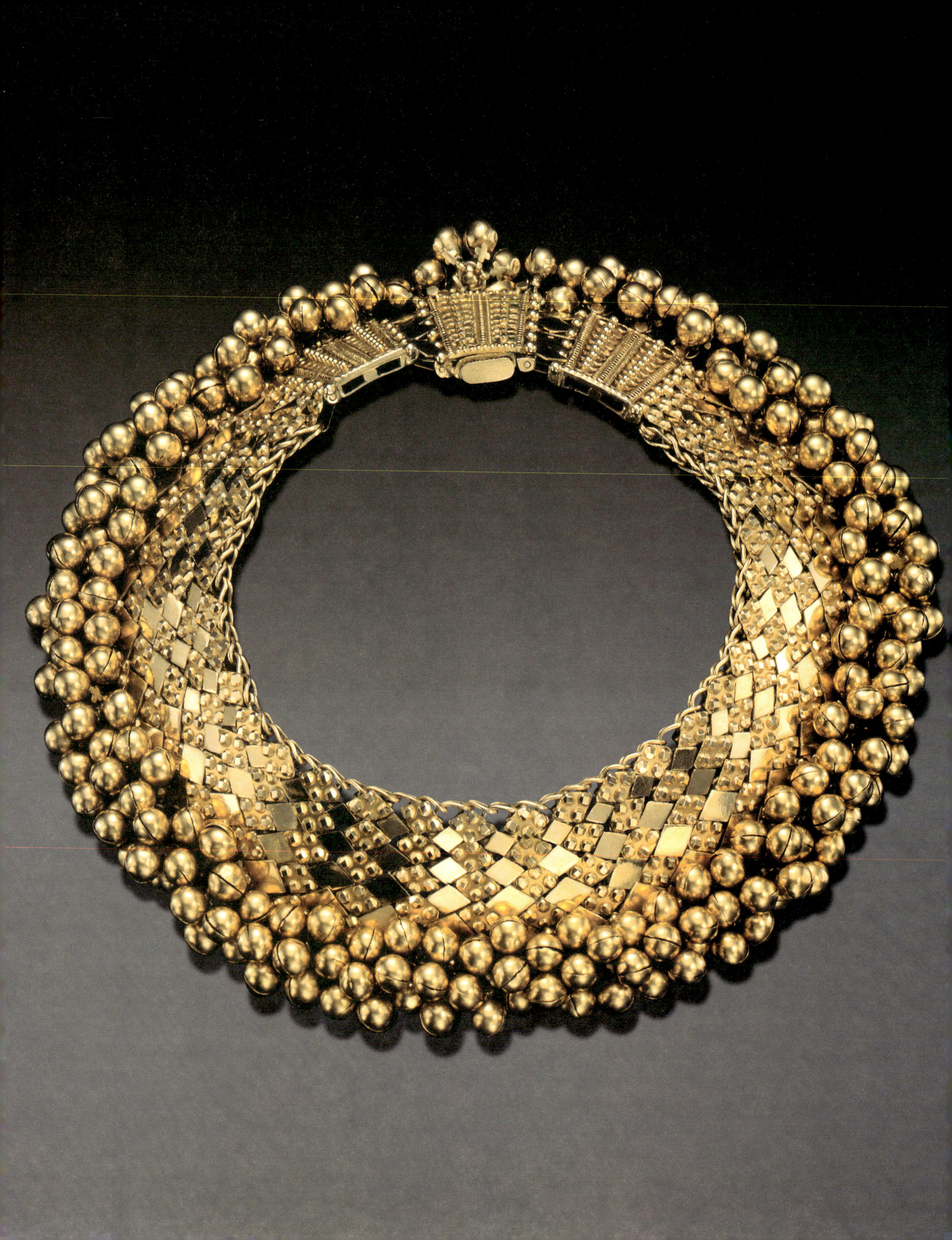

Bracelet. Five strands of reversible disks, gray gold and yellow gold. *La Création* collection. Cartier Paris, 1996.

Facing page: *Indian* **necklace**. Yellow gold. Cartier London, 1939, modified in 1941.

Necklace. Gold
and diamonds.
Cartier New York, c. 1953.

Facing page:
Necklace. Gold
and diamonds.
Cartier Paris, c. 1945.

145

Alchemy

Brooch. Gold, rubies, and brilliant-cut diamonds. Cartier, c. 1950.
Brooch. Gold and diamonds. Cartier Paris, 1956.
Facing page: **Bracelet**. Gold and emerald cabochons—three strips of gold mesh with two tassels. Cartier, c. 1950.

The postwar period was a time of interrogations, of challenges to artistic and narrative codes. Ten years after "degenerate art" shows organized by the Nazis violently rejected any art outside "the norm," the movement that Jean Dubuffet dubbed art brut in 1947 would promote the work of people completely "outside" the cultural scene—as typified by the first exhibition of psychopathological art at the psychiatric hospital of Sainte-Anne in Paris the previous year. Meanwhile, the Cobra group of artists advocated an aesthetic idiom free of any intellectualism; Samuel Beckett was questioning human existence; the "Nouveau Roman" novelists were questioning literature; John Cage was exploring all kinds of sounds while Pierre Schaefer made music "concrete"; the Beat Generation decided to hit the road. In France, artists of the "lyrical abstraction" movement favored the immediacy of the physical gesture, filling the space of a painting with the marks of their unconscious, even as, in the United States, confronted with the blankness of a canvas, Jackson Pollock covered it with an inextricable network of lines. More lines, feverish ones, typified Alberto Giacometti's sculptures of bodies. And lines featured in furniture design, from the intricate trimmings of Gilbert Poillerat to the exuberant reveries of Emilio Terry (who had a major show at the Musée d'Art Moderne de Paris in 1948), via the fine, black tubing that supported Arne Jacobsen's Ant chair (1952) and Serge Mouille's shell-like light fixtures, not forgetting the single, white, blossoming tube of Eero Saarinen's Tulip chair (1955–57). Lines were everywhere, from tailored women's garments (set above thin, high heels) to indoor plants where the stalky shape of philodendrons reigned.

Given this thread, certain ideas suddenly become clear: in jewelry, objects were henceforth being designed in gold wire. Thin and sleek, gold wire created new spaces and gave birth to jewelry of great lightness, based on networks of parallel lines; twisted, it could surround or underscore; plaited, it created links, cords, or even precious meshes.

Many delicate, airy leaves were thus produced, handled in a manner more abstract than representational, as though sketched in a single gesture then hatched to suggest volume.

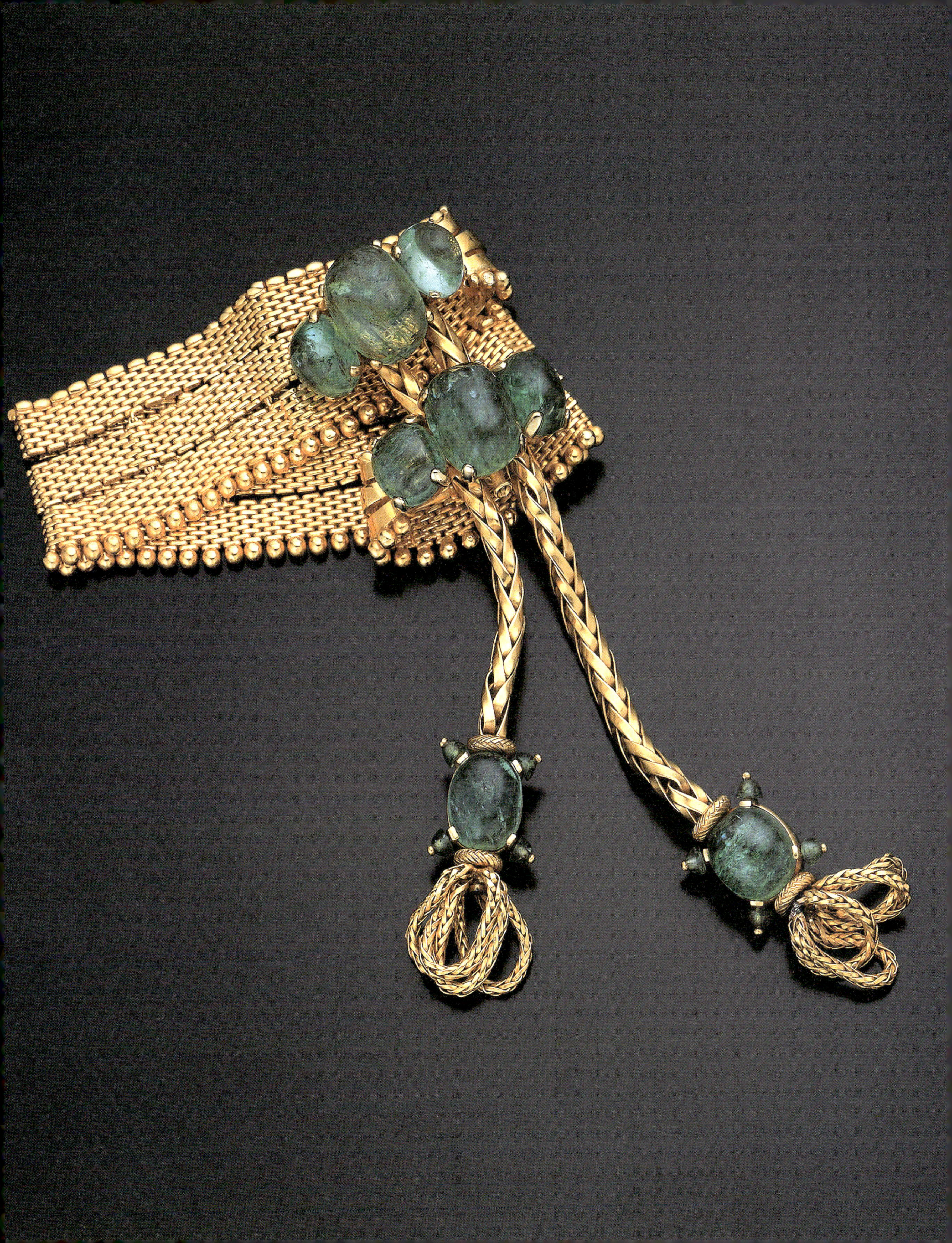

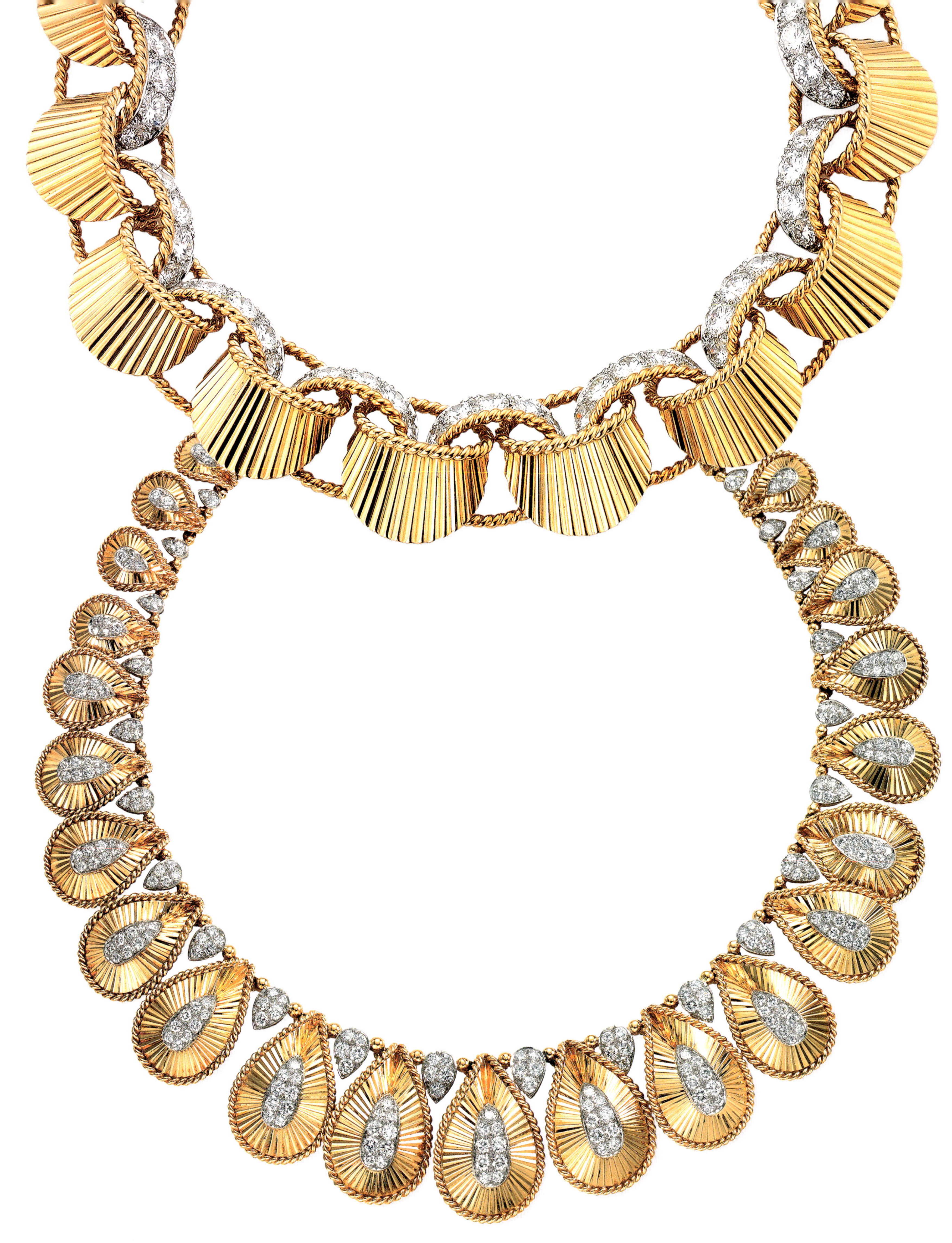

Bow-Knot **brooch**. Platinum,
yellow gold, and diamonds.
Cartier London, 1960.

Flower **clip brooch**.
Yellow gold and diamonds.
Cartier Paris, 1958.

Bracelet. Gold
and diamonds.
Cartier Paris, 1949.

Facing page:
Shell **bracelet**. Platinum,
yellow gold, and diamonds.
Cartier London, 1960.

Sunray **necklace**. Platinum,
yellow gold, and diamonds.
Cartier New York, 1955.

This aesthetic idiom was also reflected in certain armchairs of woven rattan core, whose structure is totally visible, and in an iron chair by Charles Eames (1951). All kinds of forms emerged from the juxtaposition of threads and wires, including necklaces and bracelets made in an endless, springlike spiral (from the mid-1930s), or a rolled, polished braid that thickened toward the middle to hold small, star-set gems, or cone-shaped motifs that held cabochon-cut stones. These threads, when woven in openwork mesh, could adorn neck or wrist in large, flexible ribbons, often studded with diamonds or else holding a large turquoise cabochon, as seen in a ring of 1948. Escaping abstraction, plaited gold might represent the feathers of certain birds or the tufted heads of certain dogs (as discussed above). Or it might be organized in rows of rings set with diamonds and edged with little gold beads, as in a bracelet made in New York in 1955. Two years earlier, also in New York, a supple bracelet was made of five strands of gold braid of decreasing length, ending in openwork cones. In fact, from the latter half of the 1940s gold was woven into fine, fabriclike meshes, yielding wide ribbons in the middle of which could be placed the small round dial of a watch (sometimes hidden beneath a cover). Sometimes the mesh might be rolled into a long cylinder sprinkled with gems. A very beautiful bracelet made in New York in 1948, with matching earrings, is now in the Cartier Collection, as is an extremely flexible belt bracelet of fine, rectangular mesh and a buckle set with brilliants and round faceted sapphires.

Engine-turned decoration was also used on many items, of course, such as two mystery clocks in the Cartier Collection. One, made of reeded gold and rock crystal in 1953, is called the Plate Mystery clock, because it appeared to be a translucent dinner plate ringed in gold; the other, from 1956, had a stepped base of gold supporting a sheaf of grain set with brilliants, above which two diamond-set hands floated

Palm-Tree **necklace.** Platinum, plaited and polished gold, single-cut diamonds, and emerald beads studded with collet-set single-cut diamonds. This necklace was made from stones and two old Hindu motifs (on the sides) supplied by the client. Cartier Paris, special order, 1949.

Fishnet **necklace.** Gold studded with precious stones. Cartier, c. 1940. *L'Officiel de la couture et de la mode* 321–22 (1948).

Ring. Platinum, gold, round old- and single-cut diamonds, one 2.34-carat emerald cabochon, oval-shaped faceted emeralds, sapphires, and rubies. Cartier Paris, 1945.

Three clip brooches on a chain necklace that can be turned into a bracelet. The three floral motifs can be detached and worn as brooches. Platinum, yellow gold, and diamonds. Cartier Paris, 1950.

151

152

Heart **bracelet**.
Yellow gold.
Cartier Paris, 1946.

Facing page:
Necklace that can
be turned into two
bracelets. Platinum,
gold, and diamonds.
Cartier Paris, 1970.
Bracelet. Gold
and diamonds.
Cartier Paris, c. 1950.

mysteriously in a faceted piece of smoky transparent quartz, pointing to a gold chapter ring. Desk clocks, vanity cases, cigarette cases, pens, and evening bags were all woven like precious wickerwork, similar to then-fashionable Sognot chairs and low, anatomical Dumont chairs. Cartier excelled in the creation of useful, harmonious objects that sometimes had several uses—pen-watch or paperknife-watch, etc.—as did their ornamentation—interchangeable floral or abstract clips on vanity cases, and so on. Vivien Leigh, between the release of *Caesar and Cleopatra* and the shooting of *Anna Karenina*, bought a marvelous powder compact at Cartier New York; on his first visit to designer and illustrator Raymond Loewy, cigarette tycoon George Washington Hill (Lucky Strike) commented on taking out his gold cigarette case that only Cartier knew how to make such things; later, in the 1960s, Cary Grant would buy Cartier cufflinks in one of which was set a minuscule watch. A pretty gold handbag decorated with a flower composed of emerald-cabochon petals and diamond leaves came up at auction a few years ago, identified as the property of David Niven—or, more likely, his wife, since even though Niven personified British humor, elegance, and phlegmaticness, it is hard to envision such an item in the hands of the man who played the seducer in Otto Preminger's *Bonjour Tristesse* (alongside the still-young Jean Seberg, who would soon become an icon of the French New Wave cinema).

Some items in the Cartier Collection carry the flag for the jeweler's boldly diverse use of gold. A necklace bearing a long, stylized palm tree, whose figs are none other than diamond-studded ruby beads, combines a loose mesh of plaited gold with old Indian leaf motifs of polished gold plus festoons of fluted gold. A bracelet and ring of 1945, set with emeralds, rubies, and sapphires, are composed of a skillful weave of polished and twisted gold that conveys a teeming impression, as though the inert metal were springing to life in curls, teardrops, and semicircles.

In the 1960s there was a natural shift in taste, from profusion to tautness, from meshes to radiating lines. Gold often became more relaxed, just as hairstyles, attitudes, and morals were more relaxed. The woman of the postwar era had conformed to an ideal promoted by the movies and advertising: dressed up, hair permed, always perfectly feminine. The "American way of life" swept across a world undergoing reconstruction, notably thanks to the Marshall Plan, as the consumer society triumphed with renewed energy due to past frustrations. Political and social upheavals nevertheless followed one another: decolonization, the war in Vietnam, student uprisings. A new balance of social classes was already developing, and changes in attitudes accelerated. The kitchen-appliance manufacturer Moulinex may have claimed in its advertising that it was "freeing women," but such freedom no longer sufficed. Fashion reflected a pressing desire for liberation; it became more democratic and looked to the streets. Swinging London set the tone. Miniskirts, natural hairdos, jeans, pop music, and "teen culture"—Twiggy and the Shrimp (Jean Shrimpton) literally served as models, and mothers began dressing like their daughters. Extreme wealth was no longer flaunted with the same conviction; Jacques Tati made films that ridiculed the increasing uniformity of a car-owning, television-watching society; and Georges Perec composed a literary portrait of a life subject to the laws of consumption. In those years, gold usually appeared cleaner and more sober, although still allowing for handsome models such as a series of finely worked, interlacing gold braids set with diamonds at their intersections. An aesthetic melting pot would soon emerge in all realms of design, responding to society's increasing pluralism. Grand classics were revived, new ones were forged. Highly emblematic in this respect is the Trinity ring, as it was dubbed by Cartier New York. Originally designed by Louis Cartier in 1924 at the request of Jean Cocteau who, as its first owner, perhaps partly inspired the design, this "three-gold rolling ring"—hoops of white, yellow, and pink gold—was a symbol of friendship, faithfulness, and love; it has subsequently offered dazzling proof of the timeless power of these simple ideas. Trinity rings and bracelets have met with unparalleled success through the world, remaining one of the most universal emblems of the house of Cartier. The Tank watch displayed similar qualities. Devised in 1916–17 and presented to General Pershing in 1918, no other watch has been so extensively copied—which, as they say, is the price of fame. Its pure lines, its refined Roman numerals in radial display around a "railroad" minute track, its Breguet hands and its beaded winding crown all made it an archetype that appeals to both men and women (just like the Trinity rings), ranging from Clark Gable to Jackie Kennedy via the prince of Nepal, Catherine Deneuve, Truman Capote (who owned seven), and Marc Bohan. Warhol, who didn't bother to wind his Tank, used to say that "the

Bead necklace/bracelet.
Yellow gold.
Cartier Paris, 1949.

important thing is that it's a Cartier." Made in the Jaegar workshops, by 1921 the watch was being produced in variants such as the Curved Tank, the Tank Chinoise, the small, rectangular Tank Allongée, and so on.

A very fine oval watch with a curved bezel was first designed in 1966, and, like the Tank and Santos, soon became a Cartier classic that enjoyed countless variations. A bracelet of polished gold links lent it a solid 1960s look while a leather strap gave it a timeless feel. During that same decade London produced an unusual watch called the Crash (1967), the idea being that its deformed shape was the result of a car accident. The watch predated by just a few years the famous novel of the same name by J. G. Ballard, a particularly troubling psychoanalytic study of the fascination generated by car crashes. Cartier's Crash watch, however, also evokes the somewhat double-jointed antics of rockers who give free rein to bodily expression, such as Mick Jagger, who also continues to give free rein to his taste for jewelry whenever he passes the Cartier boutique on rue de la Paix in Paris.

In New York, two independent designers were commissioned to produce items for Cartier, namely the Frenchman Jean Dinh Van (in 1967) and the Italian-American Aldo Cipullo. Dinh had already earned his stripes with Cartier before setting up his own company in 1963. His designs favor pure, universal forms, plus a Bauhaus attitude toward the function of art. The Dinh-Cartier duo would collaborate for ten years. As to Cipullo, his most famous creations were joint productions with Cartier. The Love bracelet (1969) was fastened with screws—harking back to the Santos watch—and was sold with a precious screwdriver intended for the lover, since the wearer could not fasten or unfasten it alone: "Make love, not war." The following year, the Nail bangle wrapped a nail around the wearer's wrist. By underscoring the beauty of the useful, these efforts at subversion were followed by square earrings with a screw in the middle (Cartier New York, 1972) and by a jabot pin representing a straight nail (1972). Such inspired humor can be traced back to 1939,

Nail **bracelet**. Gold. Cartier New York, 1971. Designed by Aldo Cipullo for Cartier in 1970.

Handcuff **bangle**. Gold, conical amethyst cabochons, and rectangular caliber-cut citrines. Cartier Paris, 1939.

Love **bracelet**. Gold and brilliant-cut diamonds. Designed by Aldo Cipullo for Cartier in 1970. Cartier London, special order, 1981.

Trinity **ring**. White, pink, and yellow gold. Designed in 1924.

namely to the Handcuff bangle of gold, citrines, and amethysts, whose form justifies the name and whose beauty might be an incitement to lawbreaking. The Love bracelet was inevitably linked to famous love stories: Serge Gainsbourg gave one to Jane Birkin, while Robert Evans (who produced Arthur Hiller's film, *Love Story*) gave one to the leading lady, his wife Ali McGraw, to whom he then offered the role of Carol opposite Steve McQueen in Sam Peckinpah's 1972 *Getaway*. McGraw was soon having an affair as torrid in real life as it was on the screen, where she was obliged to wear the famous bracelet, which wouldn't come off.[20] Dropping one lover for another henceforth came at a cost. Those years also saw the emergence of various geometric ear clips that combined gold, onyx, and semiprecious stones; bracelets of polished gold like a hefty chain bracelet combining oval links with small staggered bricks; and a less heavy "slave bracelet" with articulated tear motifs. They were accompanied by an ad campaign that reflected an era more concerned with symbols than with material possessions: "All you need is a little something from Cartier." Although their designs derived from the 1940s (gold, pure lines, strong outline) and 1920s, the comparison stops there because, as André Arbus, who would later design a chest for Queen Elizabeth's jewelry, pointed out, "unless I'm mistaken, [architects] Gabriel and Mansart exploited old models yet managed to produce new effects. It's the feeling, the idea, and the spirit that have to be new." Necklaces juxtaposed round links with oblong ones and light ones with solid ones, to create long chains (and even a few chokers, although once women opted for liberation these "dog collars" went into retreat). One model of long necklace, first made in 1947, survived into the 1970s; initially called an "Arab sautoir," it was later dubbed a "Muslim prayer-bead necklace" (the name of Allah is engraved on the gold drop of the pendant). It is a series of gadrooned gold beads that end in a long lacy pendant (a kind of upside-down minaret); three motifs of interlacing loops are set on three of the ribbed beads. This interlaced loop motif (which becomes earrings when pearls are added), evoke the bows of diamonds on certain early twentieth-century items, such as a superb necklace dating from 1910, which features two tassels of natural pearls dangling from sapphire disks. It belonged to Mrs. Richard

20. Penny Proddow, Debra Healy, and Marion Fasel, *Hollywood Jewels* (New York: Abrams, 1996).

Muslim prayer-bead **necklace**.
Twisted, polished, and
gadrooned gold. The name
of Allah is engraved on the
gold drop of the pendant.
Designed in 1947, this model
was called an "Arab sautoir."
Cartier Paris, 1970.

Facing page:
Necklace composed
of thirty-four strands
of yellow gold beads for
the *Paris Nouvelle Vague
Cartier* collection.
Cartier Paris, 1999.

Scott Townsend and her great-niece, Mrs. Donald McElroy, heir to the Scott-Strong coal and railroad fortune, a family that perhaps inspired western sagas about the battles between homesteaders and railroad builders, as immortalized in King Vidor's *Duel in the Sun* (1946) and Sam Peckinpah's *The Wild Bunch* (1969)—after all, America still tends to recount its own history via the movies. In 1973, a sautoir made of gold, coral, cultured pearls, and onyx seemed to be a modern adaptation of this model, a less costly but more fashionable, casual, and fun variant—in short, a "youthful" version, as the times demanded. Gold tirelessly pursued its brilliant career with the Paris Nouvelle Vague Cartier collection, the work of Radi Designers in 1999, which exalted simple gold beads by multiplying them to infinity, then endowing these bracelets and necklaces with subtle details betraying Cartier's continued commitment to the world of haute couture, such as precious clasps. One such necklace was a magnificent replica of an early twentieth-century *draperie de décolleté*, that is to say strands of natural pearls that rise high on the neck and sweep down to the shoulders and bust; the lower strands of a similarly draping bracelet lay lightly on the hand.

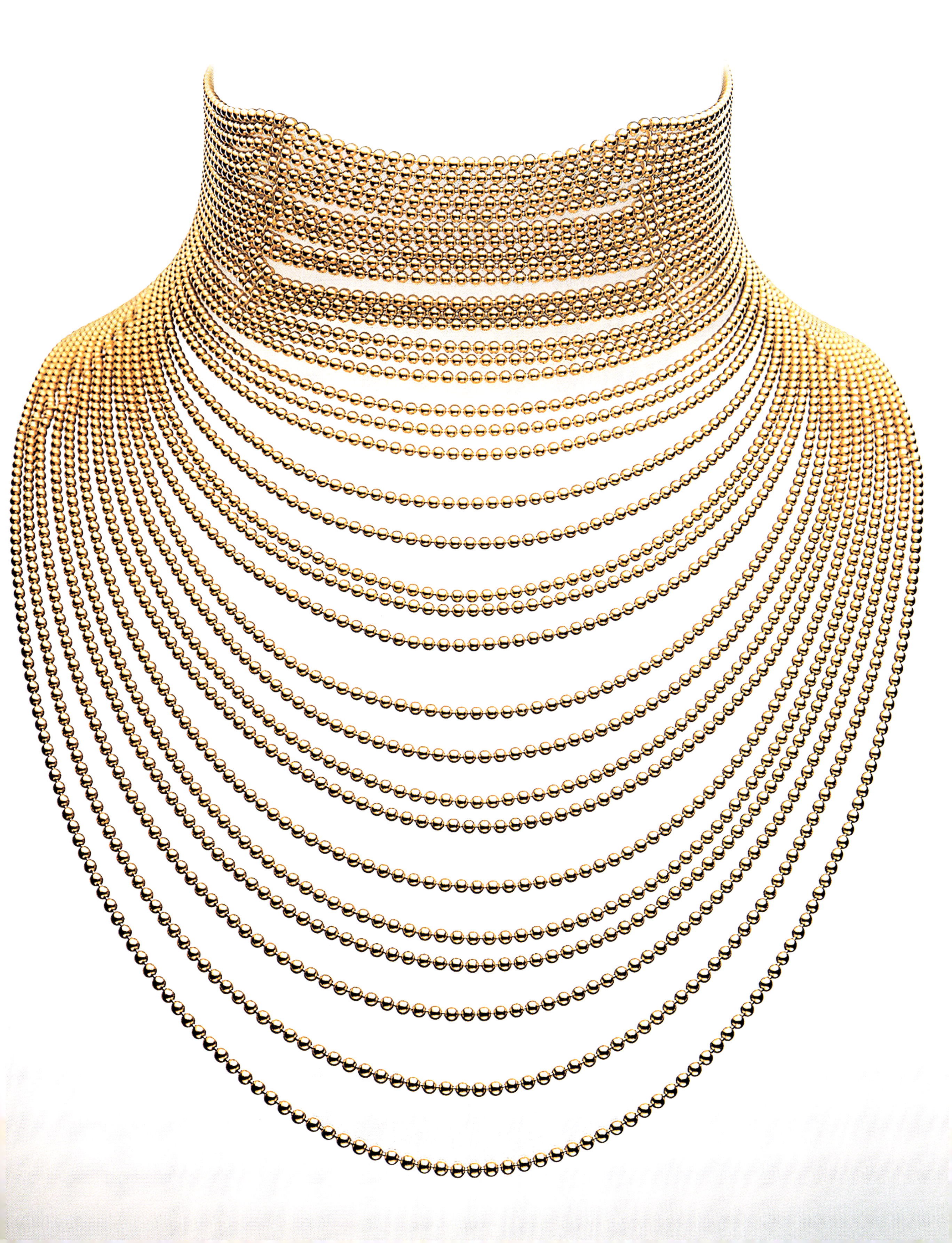

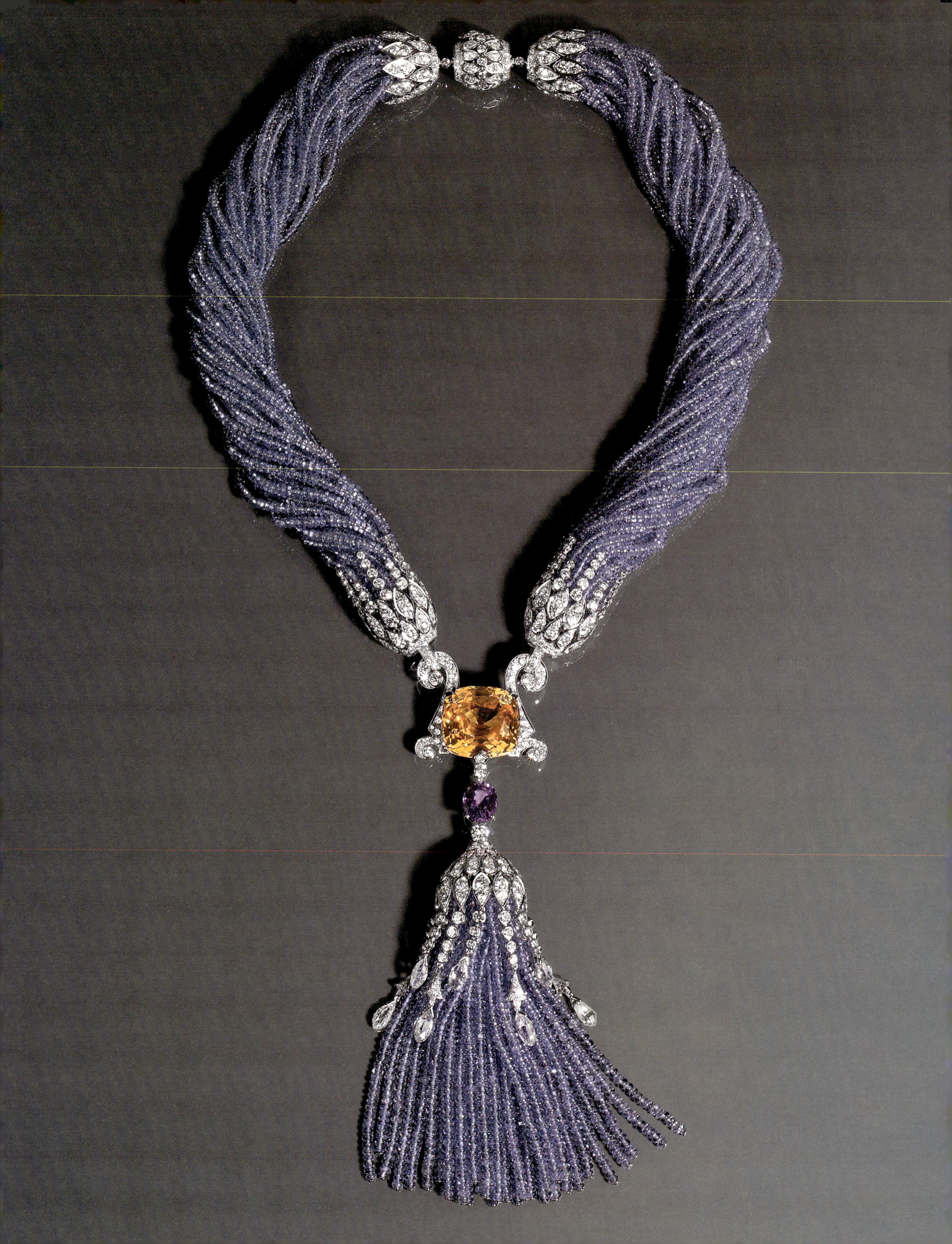

Necklace. Platinum, yellow and bronze-colored briolette-cut diamonds, brilliants, diamond beads, and one rose-cut diamond. *Inde Mystérieuse* collection. Cartier Paris, 2007.

Facing page:
Necklace. Platinum, one 52.23-carat cushion-shaped faceted orange-yellow sapphire, one 4.28-carat oval faceted purple sapphire, briolette-cut diamonds, tanzanite, and brilliants. Cartier Paris, 2006.

Dangling beads and twisting strands

A ring completes this set, a charming jumble of rowdy beads of yellow gold that conveys something generous, warm, and lively thanks to its roundness, color and chaos. Roundness because the circle—and its three-dimensional form, the sphere—symbolizes perfection, totality, eternity. Earth, Sun, and Moon are spheres, as are the human head and human eye. The ritual of whirling dervishes mimics the round dance of planets ringing the sun and the circular shape of earthly Paradise; the sphere is the egg of the universe; the knights seated themselves at a Round Table; finally, the circle is protective, which is why humans invented rings, bracelets, necklaces, belts, and crowns. Just after the Second World War, furniture design also adopted roundness, as tubes often supported shell-like forms. Shells, scallops, cocoons—this inflection in the formal idiom notably sprang from the exploration of new

Brooch. Ten-pointed star with long taper-cut green tourmalines. Gray and yellow gold, brilliant-cut diamonds, and garnet cabochon. Cartier London, 1969.

Facing page: *Caresse d'Orchidées* **necklace.** Platinum, diamonds, fancy yellow diamonds, rose-cut diamonds, briolette-cut diamond beads, briolette-cut yellow diamonds, oval Burmese rubies, and cushion-shaped Burmese rubies. *Caresse d'Orchidées par Cartier* collection. Cartier Paris, 2005.

materials. In the early part of the 1930s Alvar Aalto was using lamellated bentwood, and ten years later Charles and Ray Eames developed molded plywood, followed by molded polyester and, in 1952, by the shell chairs. Soothing curves reigned triumphant. Architects Aalto and Oscar Niemeyer successfully promoted a new vision of functionalism in which arch and wave stood up to right angle, as highways were invaded by little Volkswagen Beetles and, in France, the similarly humpbacked 2CV, cars that eventually became the flower child's vehicle of choice.

In the middle of the 1930s, rings and bracelets were composed of disks and spheres, the latter often encircling the former: lapis lazuli cabochons surround a thick ring of polished gold (1935); two circles of gold beads frame a disk whose shape clearly evokes the Handcuff bracelet (1937); a ring edged with caliber-cut sapphires (1939). These motifs and their variants would extend into the 1940s, a decade that also gave rise to a wide variety of ear clips of polished, twisted, or gadrooned gold, from which usually dangled more or less orderly clusters of gold beads. A 1938 bracelet made in Paris splashed a multitude of increasingly small polished beads on a gold "gas-pipe" ribbon. Rings were large in size in those days, so Cartier favored curves that avoided the masculine look of signet rings. Their ornaments—large half-spheres, sensual pebble and oblong shapes—bowed to the caprices of gold and the setting of stones that evoked a pineapple motif, or a mesh dotted with color, or the black-and-white duet of onyx and brilliants, or ribbed coral highlighted by diamonds, and so on. Three similar rings were sometimes juxtaposed, each set with a cabochon, while crossover rings ended in large gems or a paving of stones. A platinum Boule ring made in Paris in 1941 added four cushion-shaped sapphires to the pavé-set diamonds. The 1950s and 1960s were thick with magnificent, two-hued domes pavé-set with cut stones, or else monochrome and covered with precious beads, discreetly edged with brilliants (models already devised in the 1930s, but of timeless popularity). Rings of yellow gold, like ear clips of similar design, were to be worn during the day, because the Duchess of Windsor, who owned several examples, decreed that after 5 p.m. only platinum could be worn. The ducal decree presumably applied to a superb, round ring with one sapphire

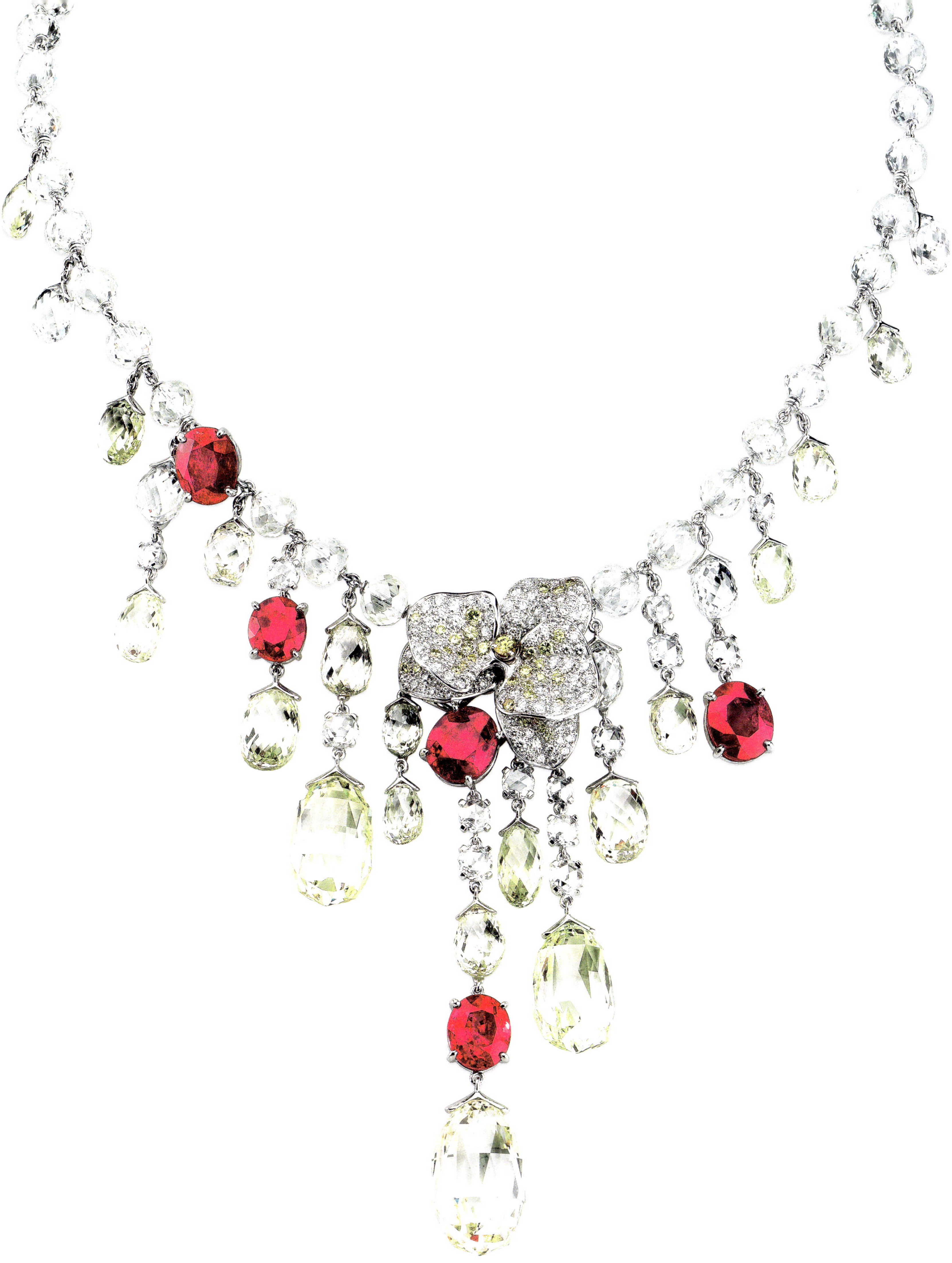

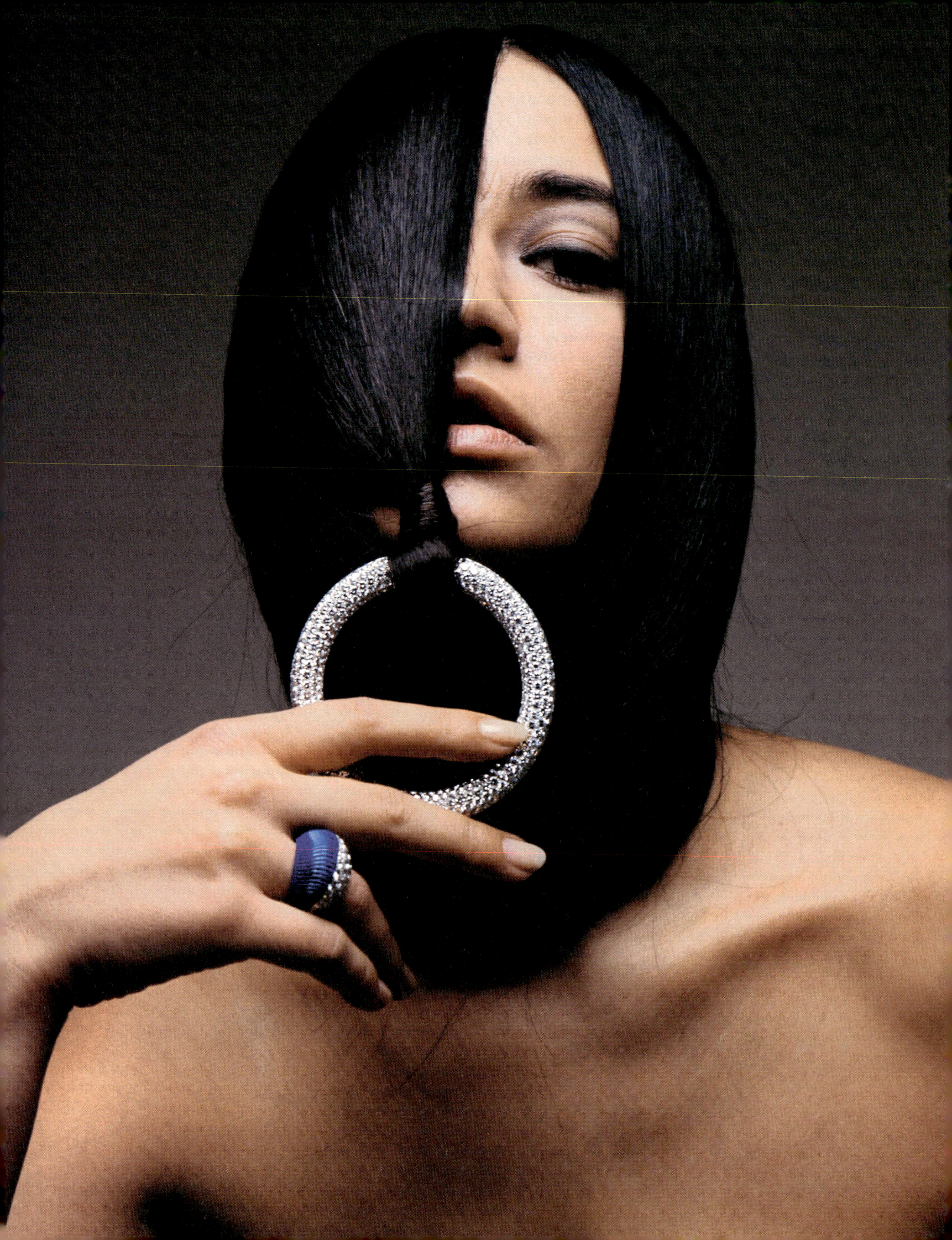

Boule **ring**. Platinum, brilliant-cut diamonds and four cushion-shaped sapphires weighing 18.1 carats in total. Cartier Paris, 1941.

Boule **ring**. Gadrooned platinum, brilliant-cut diamonds, and gadrooned coral. Cartier Paris, 1969.

Ring. Platinum, 463 diamonds weighing 5.05 carats, 68 pink diamonds weighing 1.80 carats, one 4.05-carat ruby, and two faceted rubies weighing 3.1 carats. *Inde Mystérieuse* collection. Cartier Paris, 2007.

Ring. Platinum, twisted and gadrooned gold, brilliant-cut diamonds, and round faceted sapphires. Cartier New York, 1956.

Three-band ring. Platinum, yellow gold, brilliant-cut diamonds, and turquoise cabochons, c. 1950.

Cone-Motif **ring**. White gold, 224 diamonds weighing 3.57 carats, and onyx cones. Cartier Paris, 2003.

Ring. Platinum, brilliant- and baguette-cut diamonds, and one rectangular sapphire with cut corners. Cartier Paris, 1943.

Facing page:
Diamond bangle and ring of diamonds and lapis lazuli. Cartier, 1969. Photo: Bert Stern.

165

Boule **ring**. Platinum, gadrooned gold, brilliant-cut diamonds, and ruby beads. Cartier Paris, 1964.

Ring. Platinum, gold, and brilliant-cut diamonds. Cartier London, 1970.

Wig **ring**. Yellow gold. *Paris Nouvelle Vague Cartier* collection. Cartier Paris, 1999.

Facing page: *Dome* **ring**. Yellow gold, turquoises, and diamonds. Cartier Paris, 1965.

Ring-watch. Platinum, brilliants, sapphires, carved rubies, and carved emeralds. Dial pavé-set with 132 brilliants. Quartz movement, Cartier Paris, 2003.

Ring that becomes a bracelet when its eight hoops are opened up—an unusual transformation for Cartier. Gold, amethyst cabochon, and turquoise cabochons. Cartier London, 1970.

Ring. Platinum, gadrooned gold and gold wire, brilliant-cut diamonds, square faceted emeralds, and coral cabochon. Formerly the collection of the Duchess of Windsor. Cartier Paris, special order, 1947.

Crossover **ring**. Platinum, gadrooned gold, brilliant-cut diamonds, one sugarloaf 3.56-carat sapphire cabochon, round faceted sapphires, and turquoise cabochons. Cartier Paris, 1967.

Ring. Gold, one square step-cut emerald, and eight oval faceted rubies. Cartier Paris, 1945.

Ring. Platinum, one 10.44-carat sapphire, diamonds, and aquamarine. Cartier Paris, 1951.

Ring. Platinum, gadrooned gold, brilliant-cut diamonds, and one 2.95-carat rose-cut ruby. Cartier Paris, 1946.

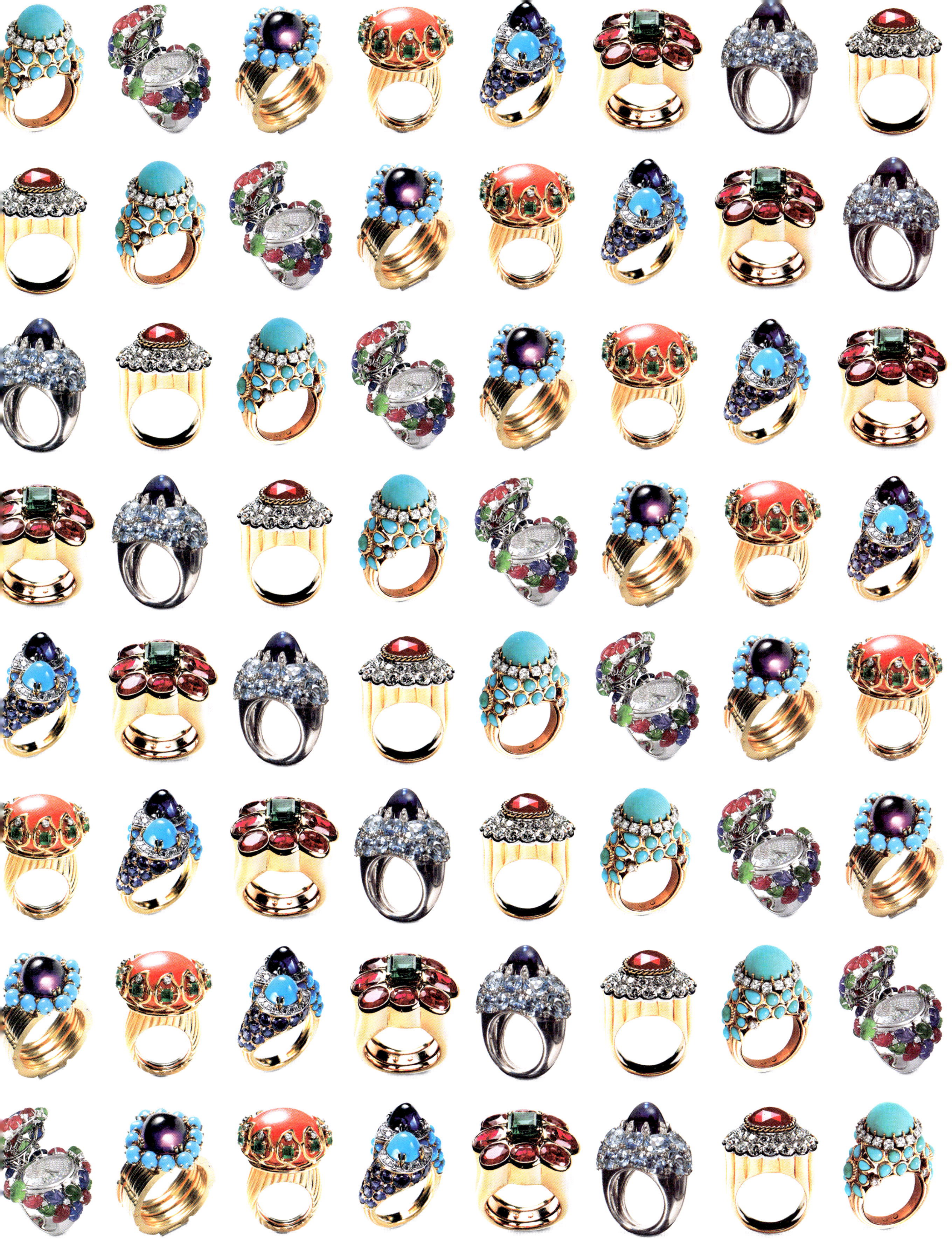

François Kollar, *The Hands of Madame Toussaint, Jewelry Designer*.

Facing page:
Necklace. Strands of diamond beads and brilliant-cut diamonds. Platinum, one 10.55-carat carved yellow sapphire, one 1.54-carat orange diamond, one 6.56-carat briolette-cut diamond, and two rose-cut diamonds weighing 7.06 carats. Cartier Paris, 2005.

sitting on two sapphires, like a globe held by two diamond shoulders (Cartier Paris, 1949). In 1929, Paul Éluard had announced that, "The earth is blue like an orange," a prophetic assertion that came to mind in 1961 along with Yuri Gagarin's words in space and Yves Klein's blue globes. The stars were finally within reach. And then, as the twenty-first century dawned, the Myst ring (2000)—a crystal ball or celestial dome—enclosed a firmament of white diamonds whose sparkle was reflected without end. Fifty years earlier, Sputnik had left the earth to study the sky; a small sphere twenty-three inches (58.4 cm) in diameter with four spiky antenna, it evokes not only a clip brooch of 1937 but also the glitter of the 1950s and 1960s, namely thin shafts of gold tipped with diamonds, poking upward from their spherical base to twinkle like stars or magic mirrors.

In a long article on Jeanne Toussaint in *Le Jardin des Modes* in October 1948, Princess Bibesco wrote, "I knew that a style existed for certain precious objects, wandering stars betrayed by their sparkle, which are recognized throughout the world as jewels by Cartier. But I did not know that they owe their inimitable nature to the mind of a woman." Both women, Toussaint and Bibesco, were society ladies and women with spirit, both sat for portraits by Boldini, and both were later awarded, in their mature years, the red ribbon of France's Légion d'Honneur for their services to art and culture. This tribute is illustrated by a photograph of Toussaint dressed in black, wearing a large brooch on her shoulder and, high on her arm, a 1947 bangle whose heads converge on a precious flower from which dangle four tassels of openwork spheres dotted with emeralds, rubies, and sapphires. Fifteen years later, in one of the many articles celebrating her talent, the frail woman was described in *Réalité Fémina* as wearing a strict suit and "a torrent of pearls" knotted in a cravat attached by a dragon clasp. Jeanne Toussaint was a woman of style, not of passing fashion. The sensual impact of her dangling beads and twisting strands operated in counterpoint to her aesthete's rigor—a moving, generous profusion that expressed every movement as a moment of grace. As Baudelaire wrote in his poem "Jewels," published in *Les Fleurs du mal* (*The Flowers of Evil*) "and I love so wildly things where sound and glitter are one." Which just about says it all.

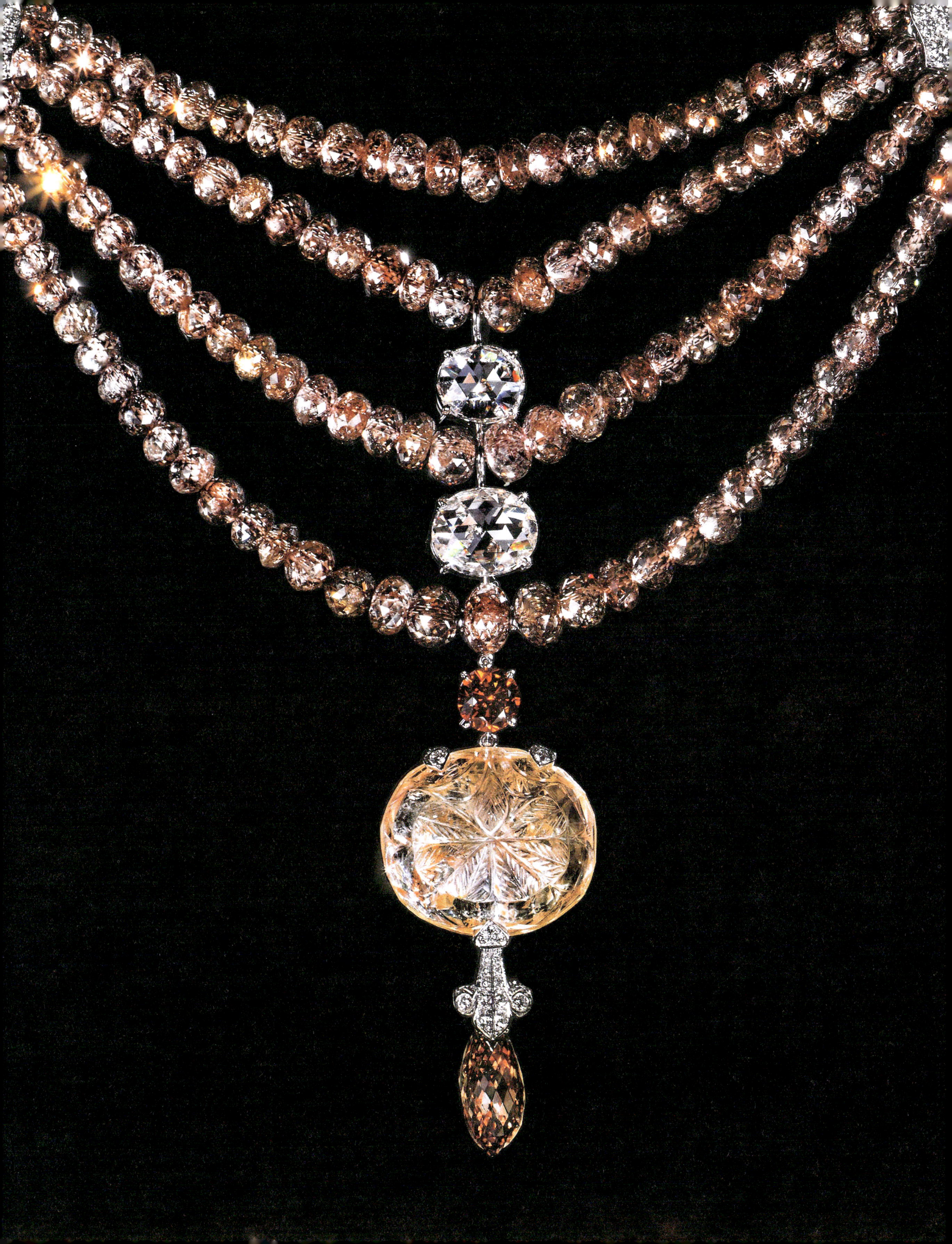

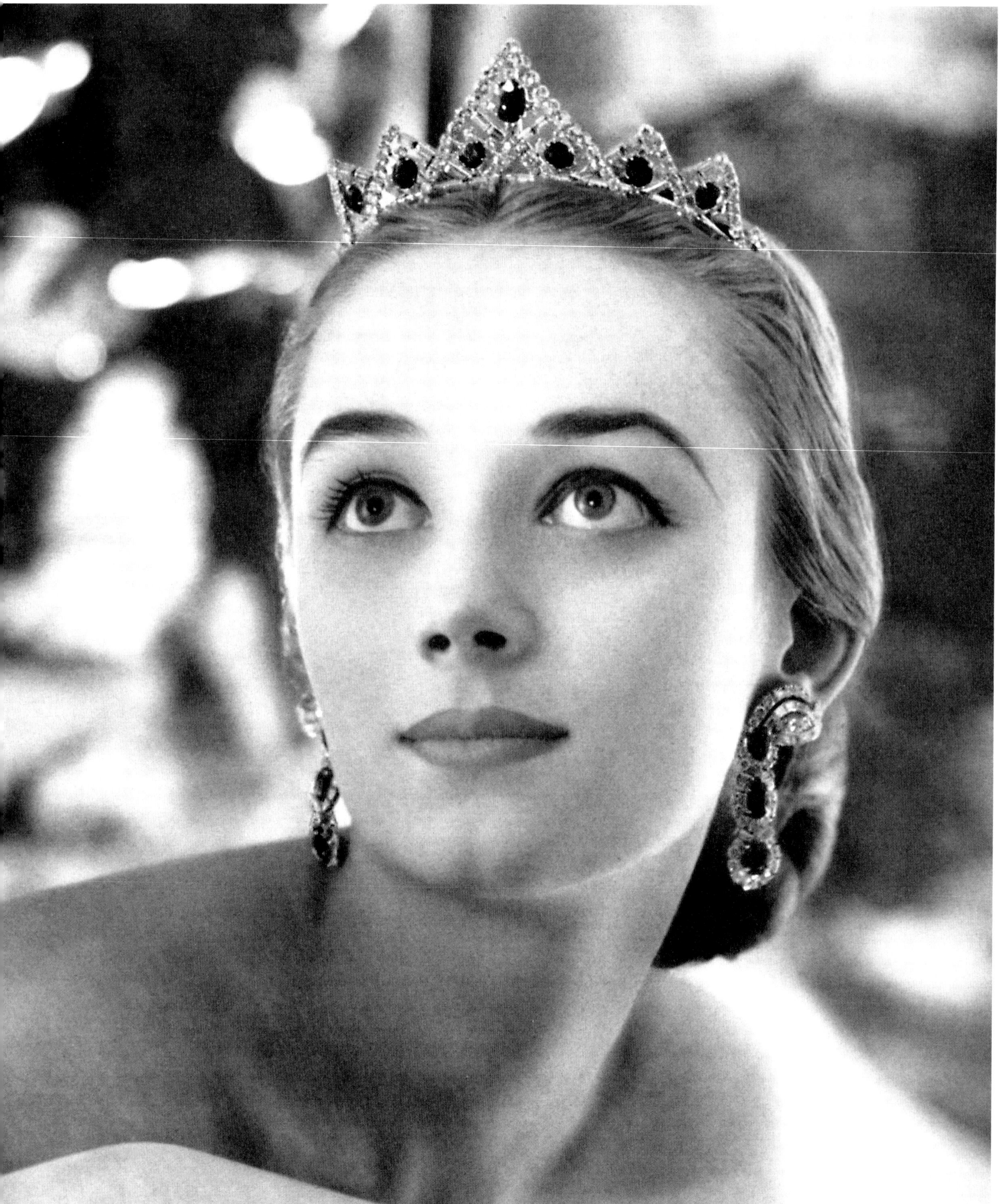

Fishnet **necklace**.
Gold, turquoise,
and lapis lazuli.
Cartier London, 1960.

Facing page:
Vogue magazine,
May 1953.
Photo: Henry Clarke.

As early as 1911 Jacques Cartier traveled to India to meet the maharajas. He reinforced the firm's contacts through exchanges based on reciprocal admiration and curiosity. In those days, westerners could only dream of the glittery splendors of the mysterious east. Fashion designer Paul Poiret invited friends to a magnificent Thousand and Two Nights party whose program, organized by artist Raoul Dufy, explained that, "nothing that exists will exist." Meanwhile, Hindu sovereigns played cricket and were keen to give their gems to Parisian jewelers to be reset, the most spectacular example being Cartier's legendary bib necklace, designed in 1928 for the maharaja of Patiala. Unique in the history of jewelry, associated with the symbolism of a regal neck chain and further magnified by the merger of two cultures, this piece flaunted a pendant that held the De Beers diamond, a yellow stone whose 234.65 carats made it the seventh-largest diamond in the world. Unfortunately, the bib necklace later vanished from sight, along with all the major gems in it; then, seventy years later, Eric Nussbaum of Cartier learned that vestiges of it were to be sold in London. After various complications, Nussbaum managed to buy up what remained, and the Cartier workshops then spent two years reconstructing the necklace, using certain synthetic stones while awaiting worthy replacements for the missing originals. This extraordinary item now enjoys pride of place in the Cartier Collection, and in 2007 Cartier's Inde Mystérieuse collection paid homage to it with a three-strand necklace featuring two stones on either side of a gem-studded hoop, namely a 12.83-carat brilliant and a pear-shaped diamond of 63.66 carats.

Jeanne Toussaint always shared this taste for jewelry of Indian inspiration, notably retaining the appealing use of yellow gold, round or carved stones, and color and volumes that create a three-dimensional effect of space. Such opulence is always tempered, however, by a purely Cartier artistry based on elegance, restraint, and respect for the value of the gems. Endless strands of pearls, rubies, sapphires, or beads of coral, jade, lapis

Torsade **necklace.** Platinum, brilliants, seventeen strands of ruby, sapphire, and emerald beads weighing over 1,100 carats, one 57.27-carat ruby cabochon, and leaf-shaped carved rubies, sapphires, and emeralds. Cartier Paris, 1997.

Bracelet. Gold, turquoises, and twists of faceted amethyst beads. Cartier Paris, 1963.

Bracelet. Platinum, gray gold, silver, round old- and single-cut diamonds, and lapis lazuli beads. Each bead in the central strand is studded with a collet-set diamond. Cartier Paris, 1937.

Bracelet. Gadrooned gold, caliber-cut faceted rubies, and nine twisted strands of ruby beads. Formerly the Rothschild collection. Cartier Paris, 1956.

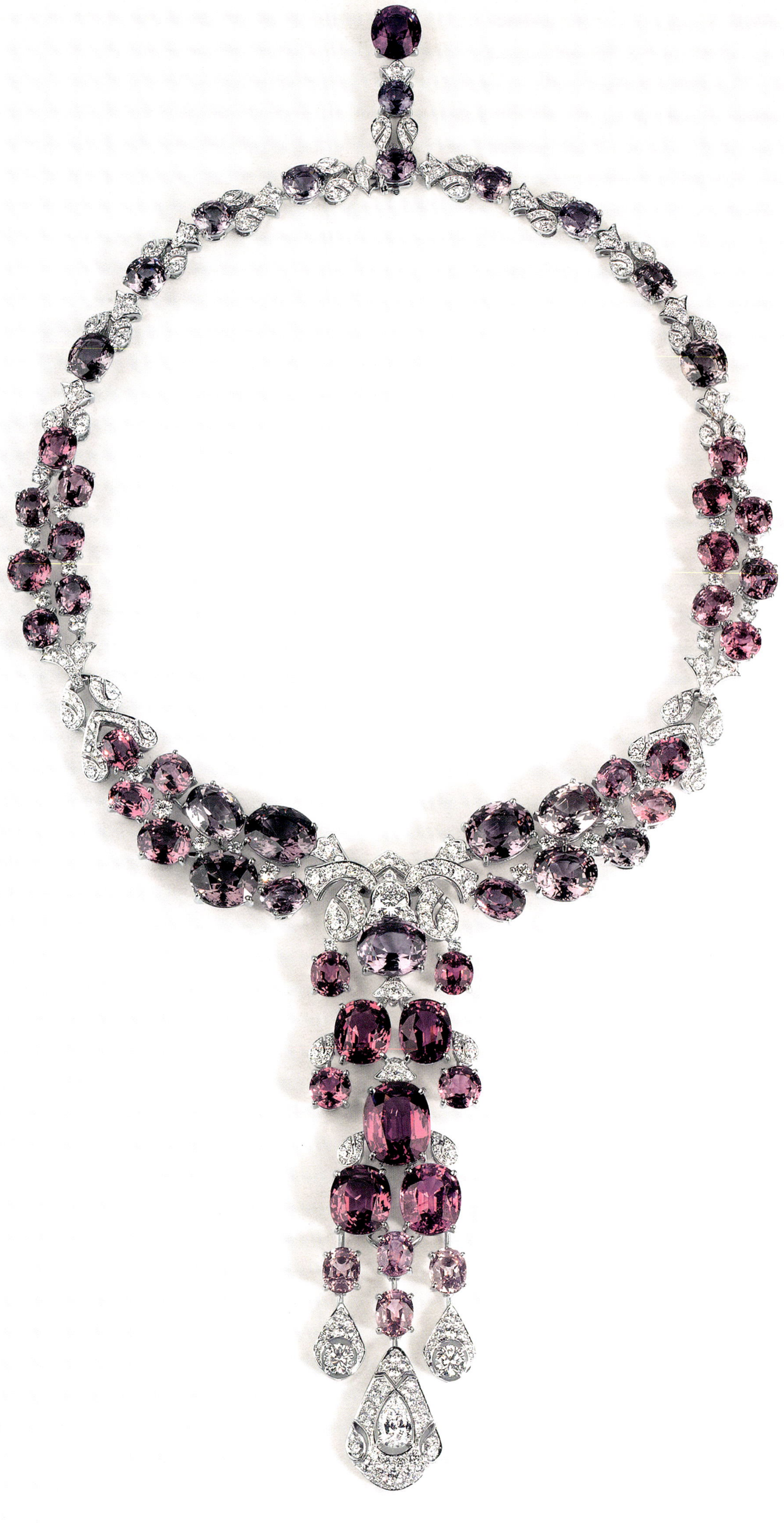

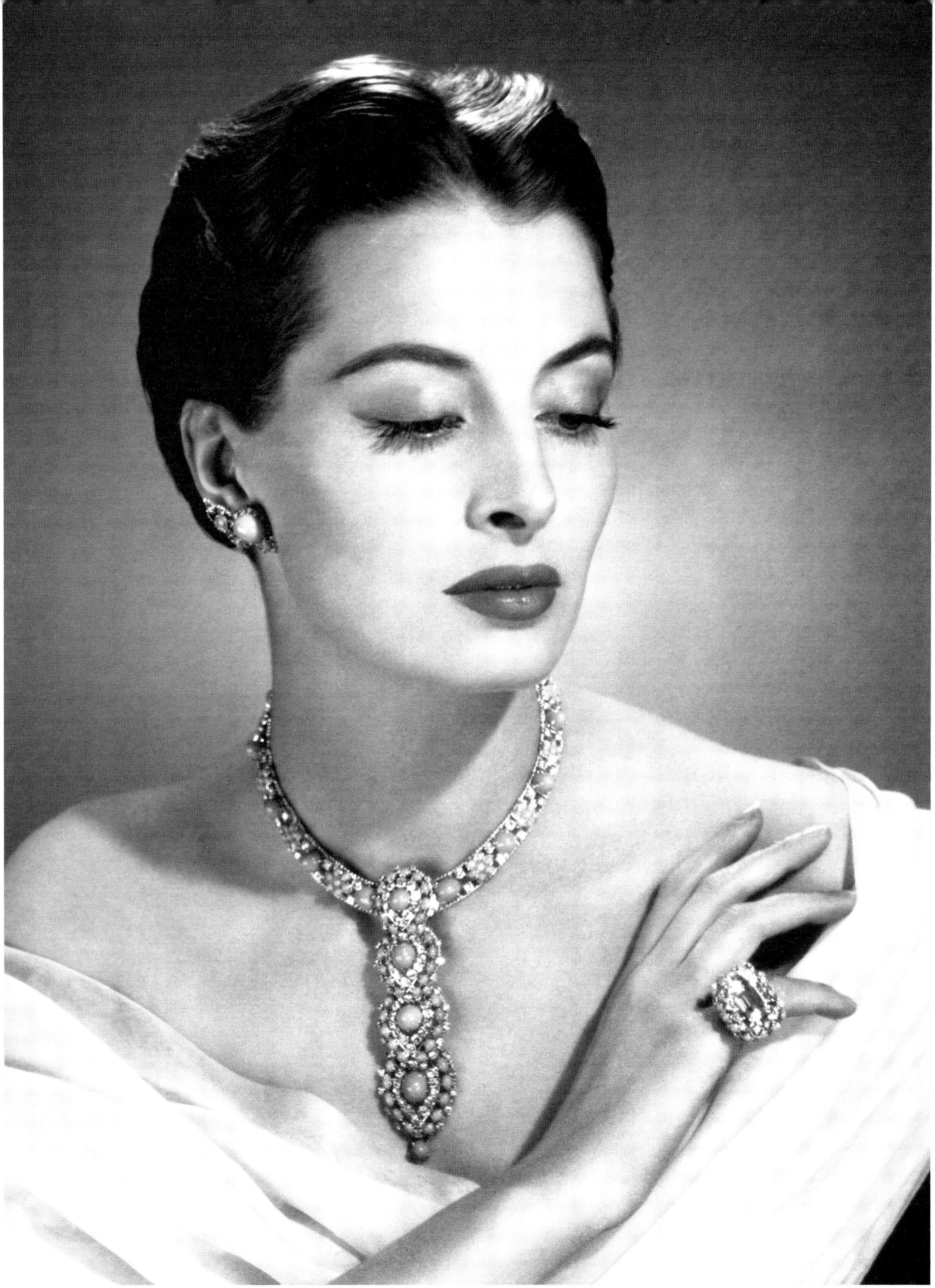

Bracelet. Gold, faceted amethyst beads, clasp of amethyst, diamonds, and turquoises. Cartier Paris, 1963.

Facing page:
Necklace. Plaited gold, faceted amethyst beads, one amethyst cabochon, and turquoise cabochons. Formerly the collection of Daisy Fellowes. Cartier Paris, 1953.

Page 174:
Necklace. Platinum, pink spinels, and diamonds. Cartier Paris, 2006.

Page 175:
Capucine is wearing a parure of turquoises and diamonds. Cartier Paris, 1955. Photo: Dorvyne.

lazuli, amethysts, and so on, gave life over the years to many items of jewelry whose refinement is never devoid of sensuality—the more unruly the combination seems, the more charm its successful marriage exudes. In 1940, a multitude of rubies formed three cones joined at their ends by simple rolled strands of gold. Six years later, the Duchess of Windsor would wear a ruby and sapphire brooch that looks like a bracelet doubled over and quickly tied in order to be dropped into a lady's sewing box alongside embroidery thread—this piece projects the inimitable "chic" of a certain casualness (or at least the appearance of it). And in those years, "chic" was at its height, which probably explains the appeal of supple torsades, or twisted strands that can be casually slung around the neck or wrist, although always boasting a precious clasp of some sort: a sapphire cabochon surrounded by brilliants and leaflike sapphires; a rectangular amethyst stippled with turquoises; a coral rose; an oval turquoise; a multicolored Hindu motif; an engraved emerald; a shell of diamonds. In 1956 a set of three monochrome bracelets—one of sapphires, another of rubies, the third of pearls—featured clasps of six rings of gadrooned gold separated by rows of faceted, caliber-cut stones (provenance: Rothschild family). In 1961 a semirigid model, whose back was pavé-set with diamonds, was composed of a bulky twist of sapphires. In 1973 black and white pearls were combined with coral rings. In 1989 the two ends of a short pearl torsade necklace were joined by shells of gold set with diamonds and, in the middle, a faceted oval yellow sapphire weighing seventy-three carats. And once again the Inde Mystérieuse line, in 2007, featured rows of chrysoberyl beads that first slide to the right side of the neck toward a square of brilliants surrounding a cushion-shaped rubellite, and then fall freely, mingling with lustrous bronze diamonds. There is a seductive appeal to this dishevelment, similar to the appeal of the apparent disorder of two magnificent necklaces made in the 1940s and 1950s: for the Duchess of Windsor, a jumble of sapphire cabochons and diamond points allow a glimpse of a few flowers with diamonds at their center; for Daisy Fellowes, four braids of gold, carefully aligned as far as the clasp—an amethyst cabochon surrounded by turquoise—are then invaded by a clutch of faceted amethyst beads, studded with a jumble of turquoise cabochons.

177

The fall will be
   full of grace…

A "gentle fall" was probably on the mind of Madame Grès, a fashion designer whose first wish had been to devote herself to sculpture, as she draped and molded her full jerseys of plain-colored silk. In 1941 her first collection featured dresses in red, white, and blue, patriotic colors that displeased France's German occupiers, who obliged her to close her atelier. A year later, the fashion house finally opened again at number 1 rue de la Paix, just a few yards from Cartier's little red-white-and-blue sparrow waiting to be freed from its cage. Drape and fall, like tassels and pendants, were expressions of volume and gravity. Jewelers became sculptors, and Cartier excelled in this field. Violette Leduc, one of Jeanne Toussaint's great admirers, evoked the poetic feel of Toussaint's designs by noting that her "favorite jewel is … a bouquet of coral bellflowers, somewhat wilted, in which diamonds are nestled yet visible." Whether figurative or not, the volume and movement of these clusters lend life to inert matter—the languor of this slightly wilted bouquet is precisely what gives it grace.

While the suppleness of these designs—whether sober, sumptuous, or exotic—often tempered the rigor of the chokers when they supplanted long sautoirs, they were also a felicitous solution for other items: a long chain known as a chatelaine (Cartier Paris, 1946) was flanked by two unequal "falls" of openwork balls (these little round cages might also dangle from a plaited gold sautoir or a bracelet and might be dotted with gems); a brooch from 1938, made from older Indian components, combines motifs of gold and enamel set with gems and turquoise with bunches of natural pearls, the shapes and volumes contrasting in an almost baroque way, so irregular and unexpected is the juxtaposition. Tame, in comparison, are the pendants of pearls, gold, and gems that tumble, as from a cornucopia, from enamel domes adorned with Hindu motifs, a superb 1937 example of which are the ones hanging from the ends of a plaited gold tress (allegedly by

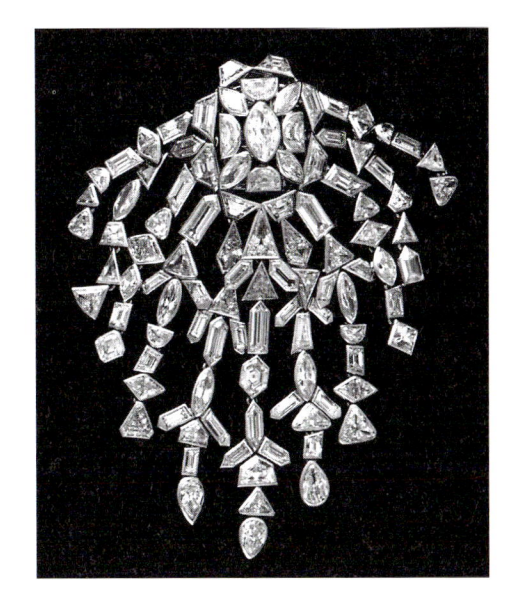

Brooch that can serve as the clasp of a necklace. Platinum and diamonds. Cartier Paris, 1953.

Clip brooch. Cartier London, 1939.

Brooch. Platinum and diamonds. Cartier Paris, 1953.

Clip brooch. Cartier London, 1939.

Clip brooch. Gold, sapphires, and rubies. Formerly the collection of the Duchess of Windsor. Cartier Paris, 1946.

Facing page: *Indian-style* **brooch**. Gold, table-cut diamonds, faceted sapphires, ruby and emerald cabochons, natural round and baroque pearls, turquoise cabochons and beads, and red and green enamel. Brooch made from reused stones. Cartier Paris, 1938.

Pendant ear clips. Platinum, gray gold, sapphires, and diamonds. Cartier Paris, 1941.

Ear pendants. Citrine and diamonds. Cartier London, c. 1950.

Ear pendants. Platinum, pearl, and brilliant- and baguette-cut diamonds. Cartier Paris, 1954.

Earrings. Platinum, diamonds, and two rubellite drops weighing 28.17 carats. *Caresse d'Orchidées par Cartier* collection. Cartier Paris, 2005.

Ear pendants. Platinum, white gold, yellow gold, brilliant-, round old-, single- and rose-cut diamonds, carved emeralds and emerald beads studded with collet-set diamonds, and black enamel. Formerly the collection of Daisy Fellowes and Countess de Casteja. Cartier Paris, special order, 1963.

Snake **earrings.** Platinum, gray gold, yellow diamonds, brilliants, and emeralds. *Les 150 Ans* collection. Cartier Paris, 1997.

Facing page:
Earrings. Lapis lazuli and diamonds. 1965. *Vogue* magazine, June-July 1965. Photo: Helmut Newton.

180

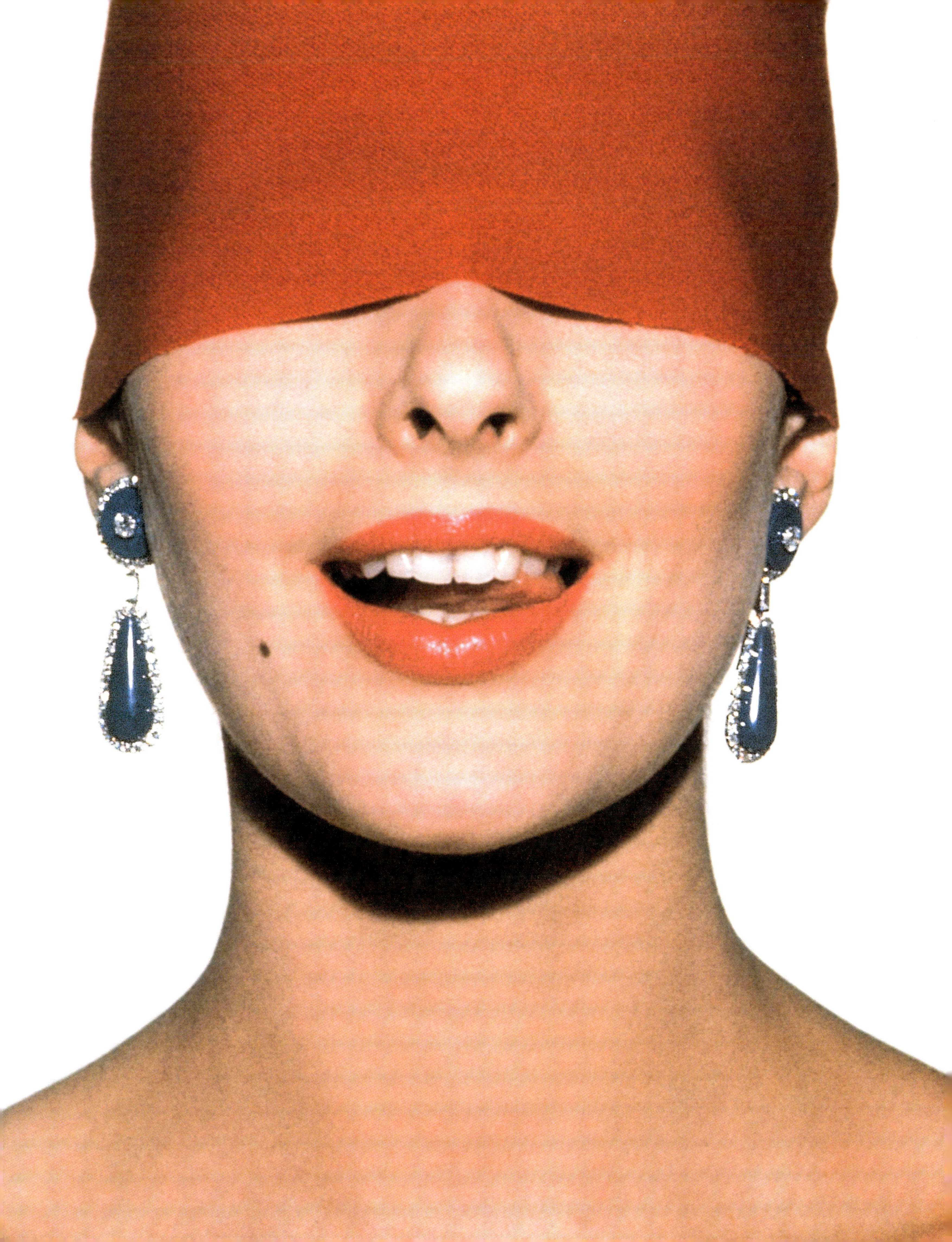

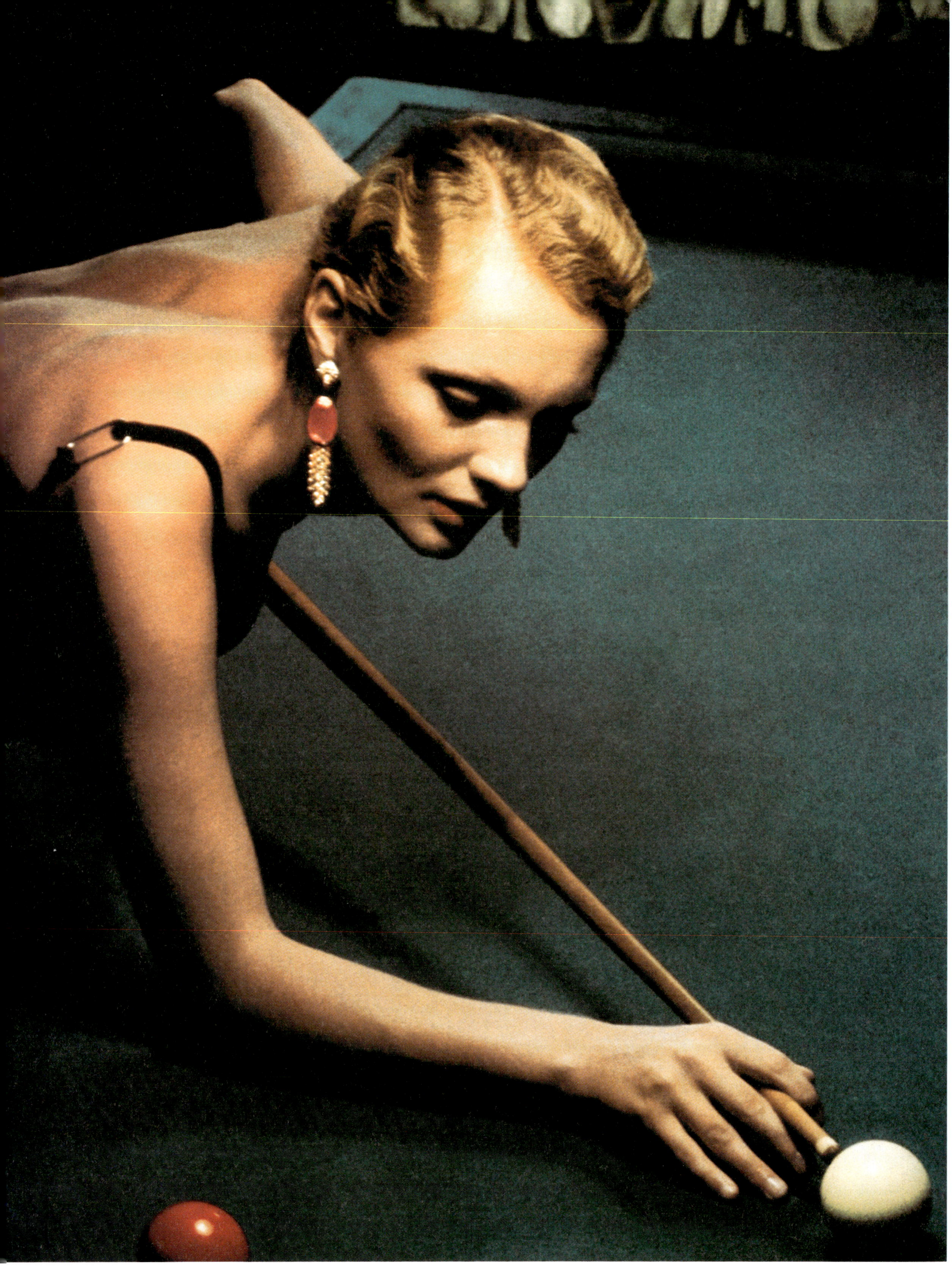

Earrings. Platinum, sixteen briolette-cut diamond beads weighing 14.62 carats, six briolette-cut diamonds weighing 7.99 carats, two rose-cut diamonds weighing 16.74 carats, and two ruby drops weighing 39.72 carats. *Caresse d'Orchidées par Cartier* collection. Cartier Paris, 2005.

Panther-skin **ear pendants.** Gray gold, diamonds, onyx, and six emerald drops. Cartier Paris, 2003.

Earrings. Platinum and diamonds. Cartier Paris, 2003.

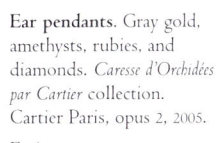

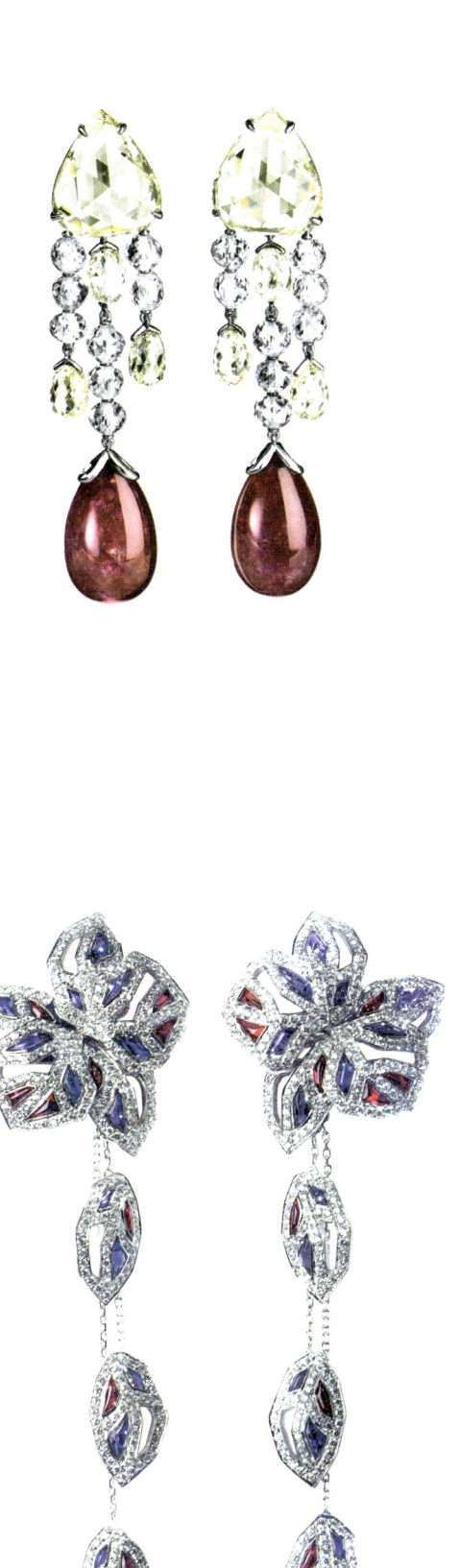

Ear pendants. Gray gold, amethysts, rubies, and diamonds. *Caresse d'Orchidées par Cartier* collection. Cartier Paris, opus 2, 2005.

Facing page:
Vogue magazine,
November 1975.
Photo: Helmut Newton.

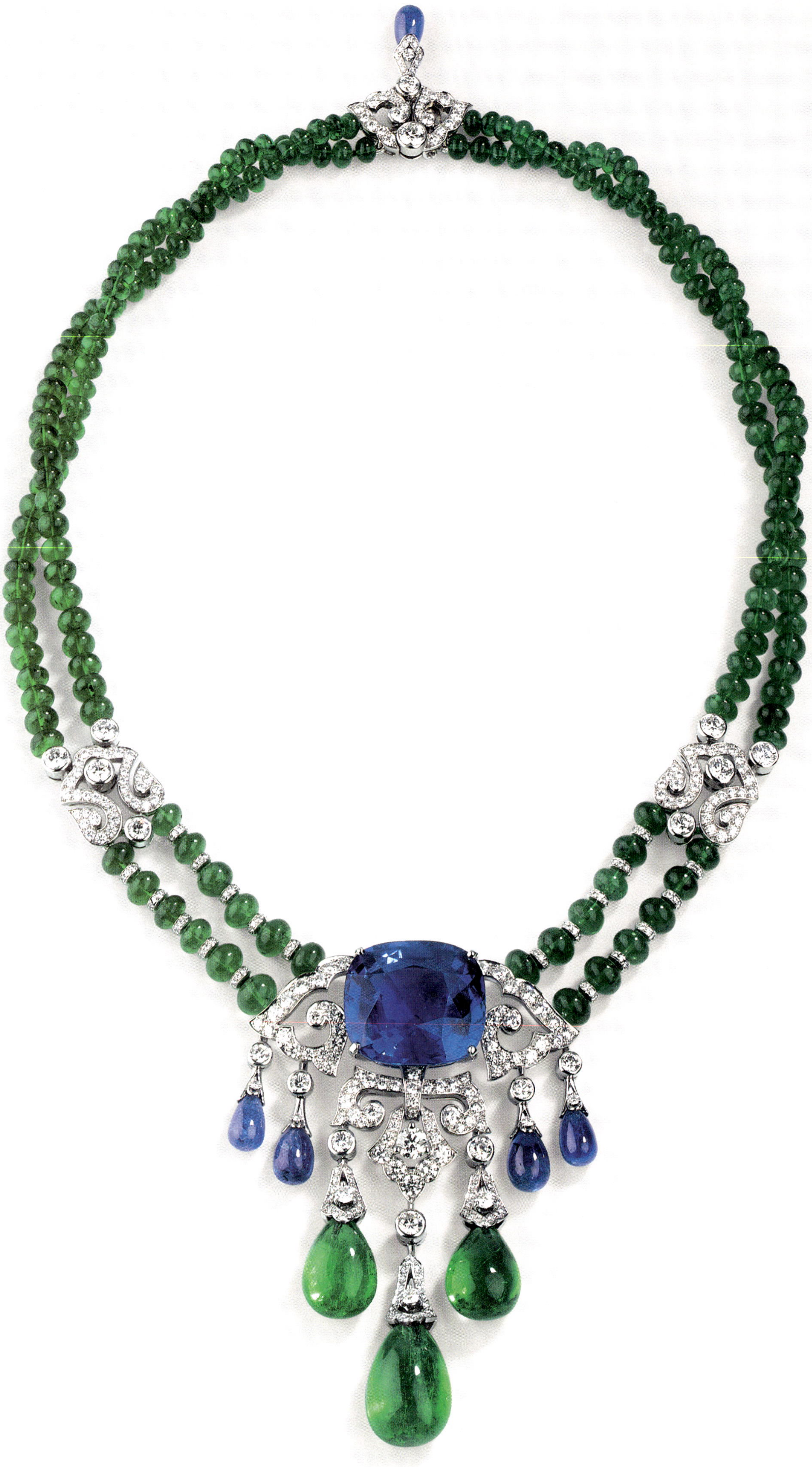

Emerald-cluster **necklace**. Gold, diamonds, and emeralds. Cartier, 1955. *L'Officiel de la couture et de la mode* 405–06 (1955).

Facing page: **Necklace**. Platinum, one 45.81-carat cushion-shaped faceted blue sapphire, three emerald drops weighing 16.77 carats, 11.79 carats, and 9.94 carats, blue sapphire drops, emerald beads, and brilliants. Cartier Paris, 2006.

Toussaint). The so-called Qajar style enjoyed a considerable revival in the 1950s, whose boldness and balance have been perpetuated in cascades of emerald beads studded with rubies, diamonds, and rubellite drops from which emerges an orchid with a flamboyant rubellite at the center (2005), or a cascade of round and briolette-cut white and bronze diamonds whose sparks ignite a carved tourmaline weighing over 136 carats (2007).

Dangling jewels might be less voluminous: a stylish woman of the 1950s, wearing a Jacques Fath mink stole that falls off one shoulder, is shown with a clip brooch of oval, rectangular, and baguette- and marquise-cut diamonds in a rain of light, precious, irregular lines, enlivened by the apparently random arrangement of the stones. In an entirely different aesthetic approach, based on regularity and symmetry, large tassels of pearls dangle from more or less long necklaces that were particularly popular in the 1970s and which came in various color combinations, as noted by the press. A real enthusiasm for the art deco period then arose in fashion, jewelry, and interior decoration, fueled by Jack Clayton's 1974 film of F. Scott Fitzgerald's 1925 novel, *The Great Gatsby*. Cartier was thus able to pay tribute to its own designs of that period. Toussaint was perhaps

A dangling diamond **cluster** worn on a Jacques Fath fur stole, 1954.

Facing page:
Necklace. Platinum and diamonds. Cartier Paris, 1951.

Necklace. Platinum and diamonds. Cartier Paris, 1953.

reminded of a dinner she attended decades earlier with Louis Cartier, F. Scott Fitzgerald, and his wife Zelda; when the latter swooned with admiration for her necklace and vanity case, Toussaint gave them to Zelda. Pearl necklaces and ear pendants streaming with diamonds were worn by Mia Farrow, while Lois Chiles wore a long pearl sautoir dotted with emerald beads and ending in two similar tassels. Much more sober and perfectly classical were the ear pendants of drop pearls and gems that would hang, depending on the period, from knotted ribbons or shells of diamonds—the linear extension gave greater scope, swing, and lightness to a composition whose appeal lay partly in its obvious subjection to the laws of gravity.

Although smaller and somewhat less supple, bib necklaces can be exquisitely refined. A turquoise model in the Cartier Collection is a wonderful example: a hoop of plaited gold from which hang triangular meshes of gold wire, dotted with diamonds, forms the framework. The fall and curve of the mesh wonderfully evoke fabric, and the tips of the two motifs flanking the main, central motif are "turned up," as though pinned in place by a little diamond.

Louis Cartier once recounted that Toussaint, moving a mother-of-pearl plaque from her shoulder to her waist, wondered out loud how it should be employed. "It's too heavy for a brooch, the fabric would be too bunched up and would be damaged." This question recurred to him when, while staying with one of his friends, he noticed a woman "hanging her laundry with a clothespin—and so the principle of a clip that worked in a similar way was born."[21] Like the model just discussed, the Palmette necklaces featured a similar arrangement of five motifs of decreasing size, gem-studded clothespins clipped to an equally precious clothesline. They were often part of a parure, or set that includes bracelet and ear clips (the pendants of which were often detachable). The motifs might be rounder or more pointed, simple or complex, but were usually two-toned (diamonds plus a colored stone), as seen in a magnificent example illustrated in the *Album du Figaro* of 1950, where rubies were ringed by diamonds (worth comparing to one specially ordered by Lady Deterding, wife of the founder of Royal Dutch Shell). Another example illustrated in the press of the 1950s has turquoises and brilliants in a long line that descend from the base of the neck to the bust. Finally, a necklace made for the Duchess of Windsor by the Cartier workshop in 1960 was composed of five similar motifs, this time emeralds ringed by baguette-cut diamonds, underscored by three marquise-cut diamonds, all hanging from a diamond collar.

21. Gautier, *La Saga des Cartier*.

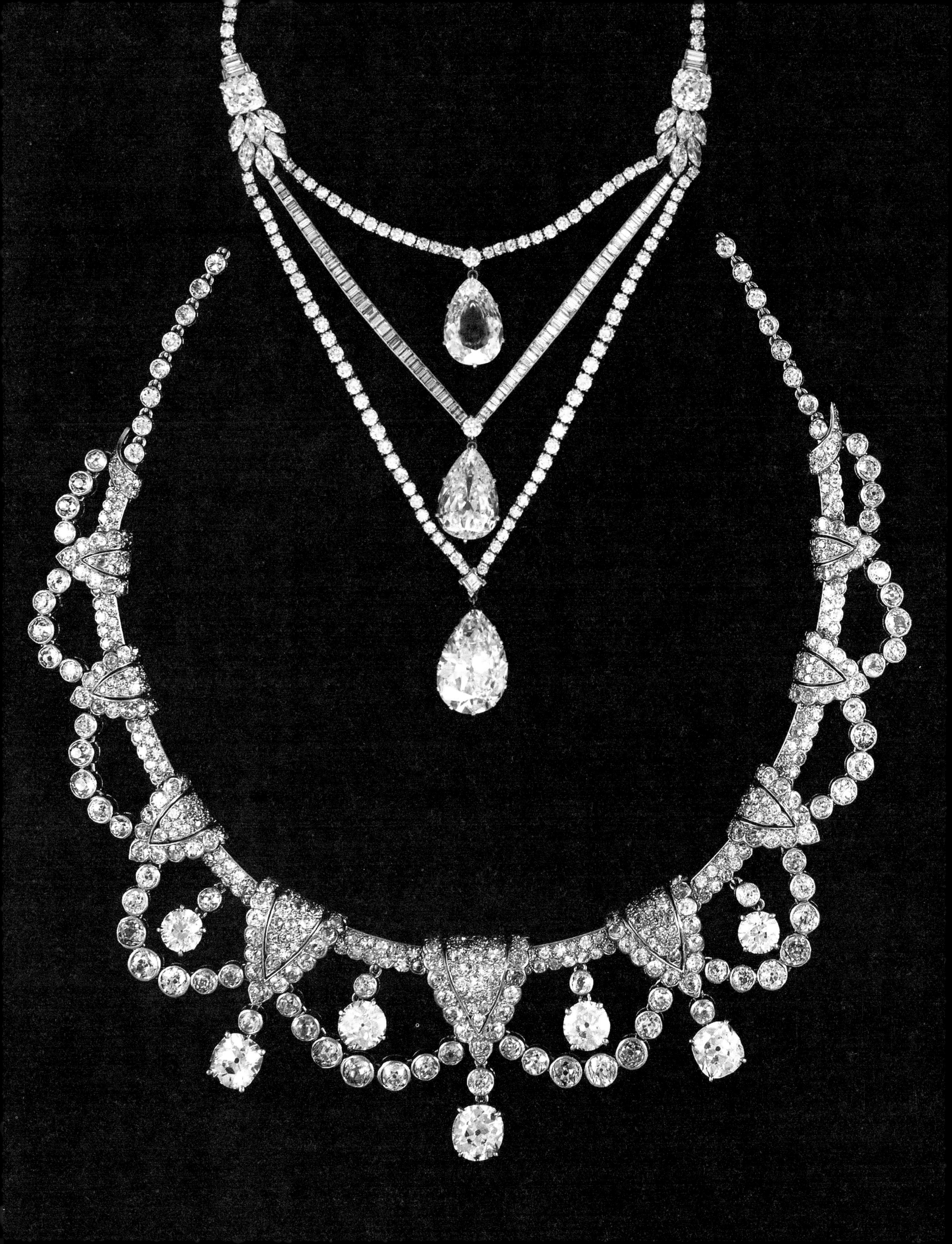

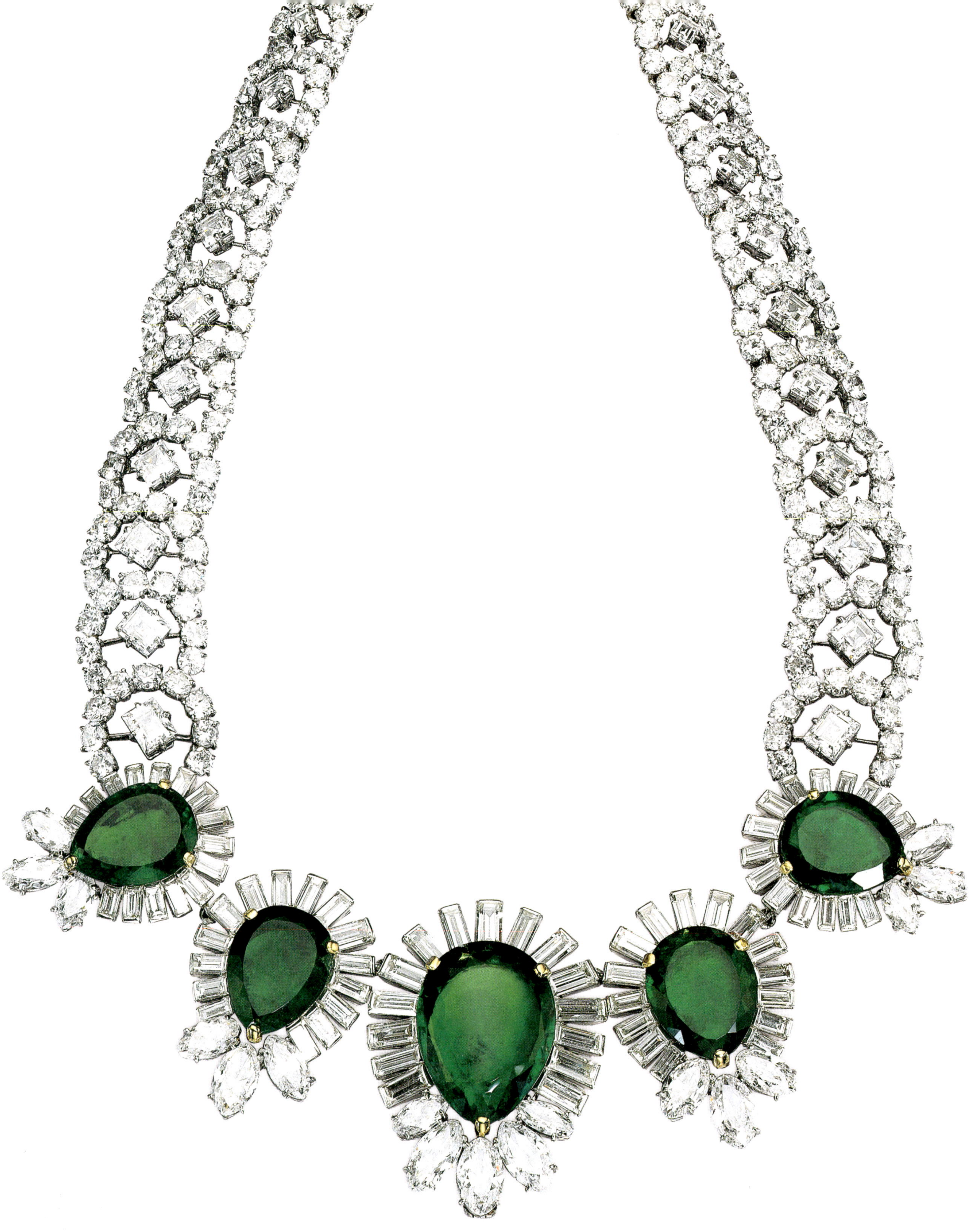

Bangle. Platinum, gray gold, sapphires, and diamonds. Cartier New York, 1937.

Bangle with detachable clip brooches. Platinum, gray and yellow gold, emeralds, and diamonds. Cartier Paris, 1942.

Bracelet. Platinum, diamonds, and sapphires. Cartier Paris, 1948.

Facing page:
Necklace. Diamonds and emeralds. In the center, a 14.61-carat emerald; 110 baguette-cut diamonds weighing 28.01 carats and 170 brilliants weighing 24.76 carats. Formerly the collection of the Duchess of Windsor. Cartier Paris, 1960.

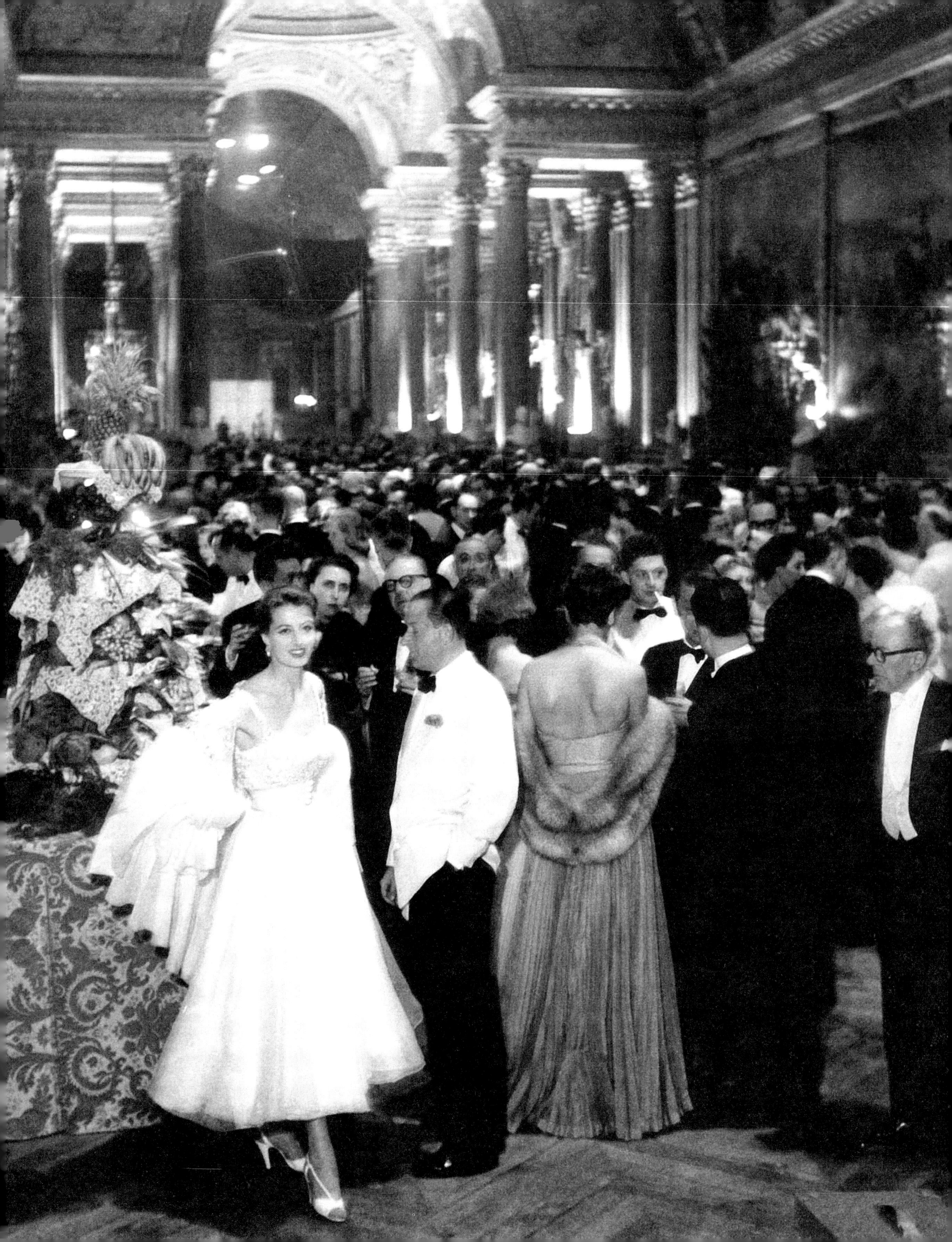

Palmette **necklace.** Gold wire and brilliant- and baguette-cut diamonds. The five motifs can be detached and worn as brooches. Cartier Paris, 1958.

Facing page:
A ball in the Galerie des Batailles at Versailles Chateau on May 25, 1952. Photo: Rue des Archives.

a Bib necklace. Plaited gold and gold wire, brilliant-cut diamonds, and turquoise cabochons. Cartier Paris, 1955.
Facing page: Cartier **parure**. Platinum, gold, rubies, and diamonds, c. 1950. Dior dress. *L'Officiel de la couture et de la mode* 345–46 (1950).

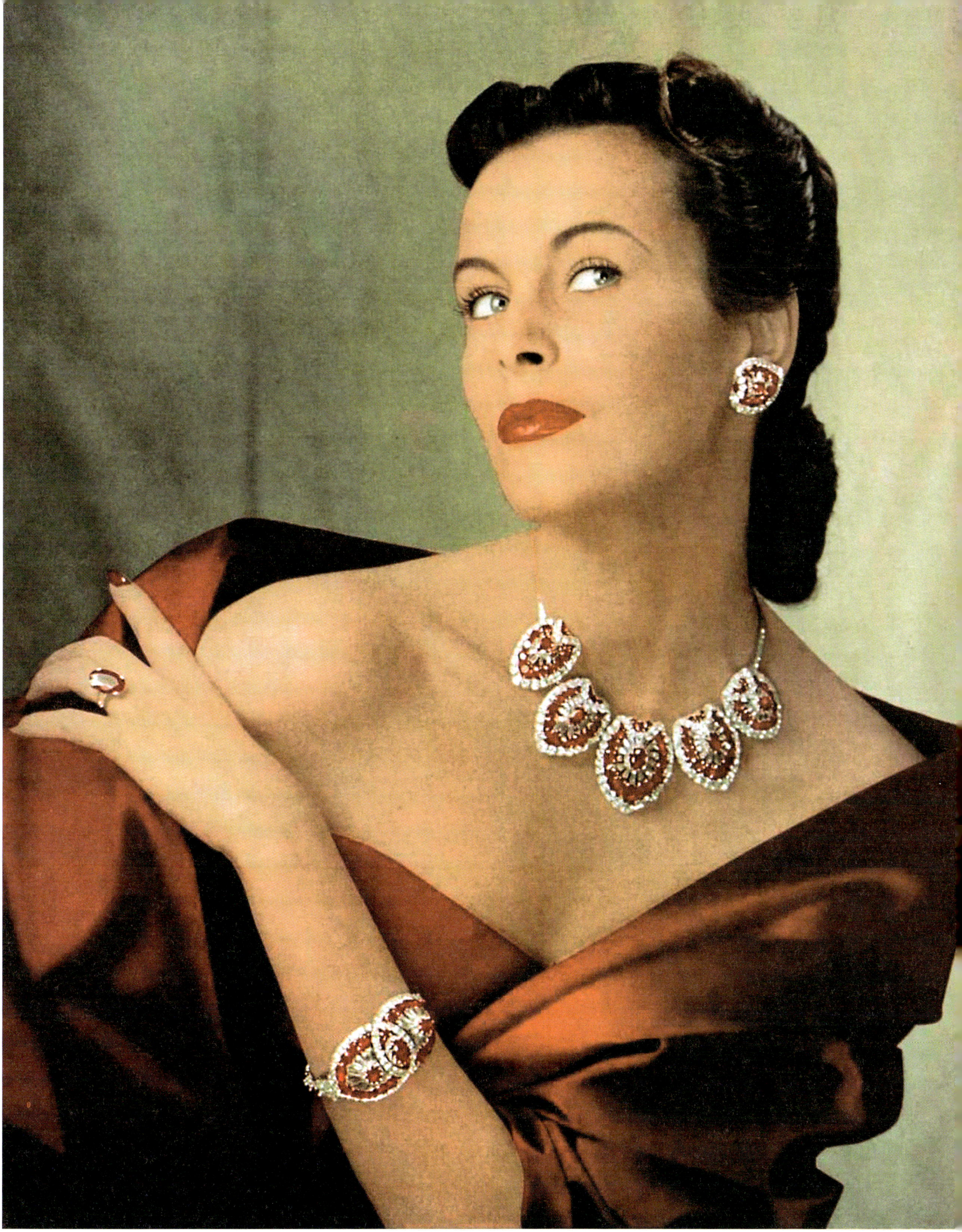

COLOR

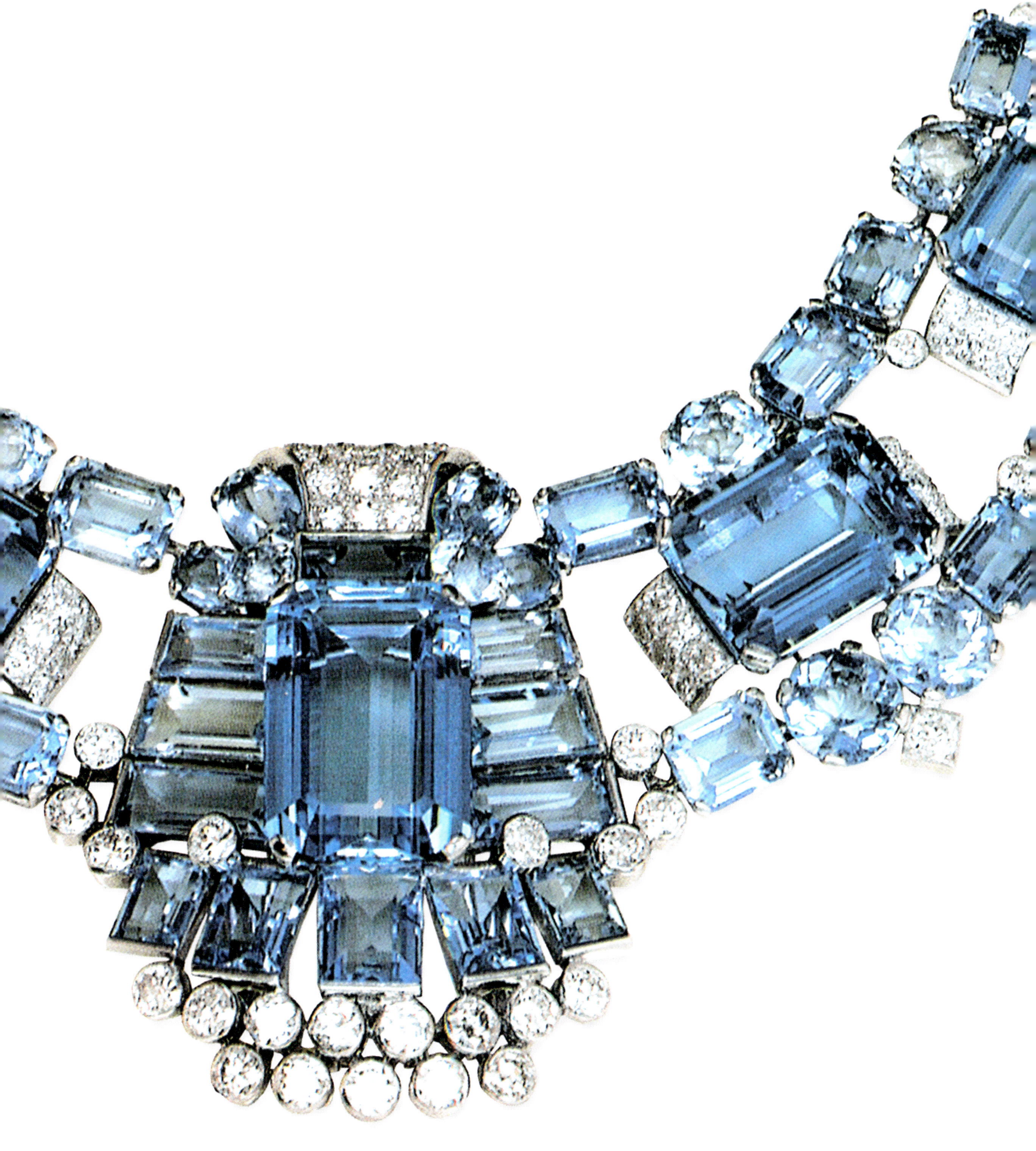

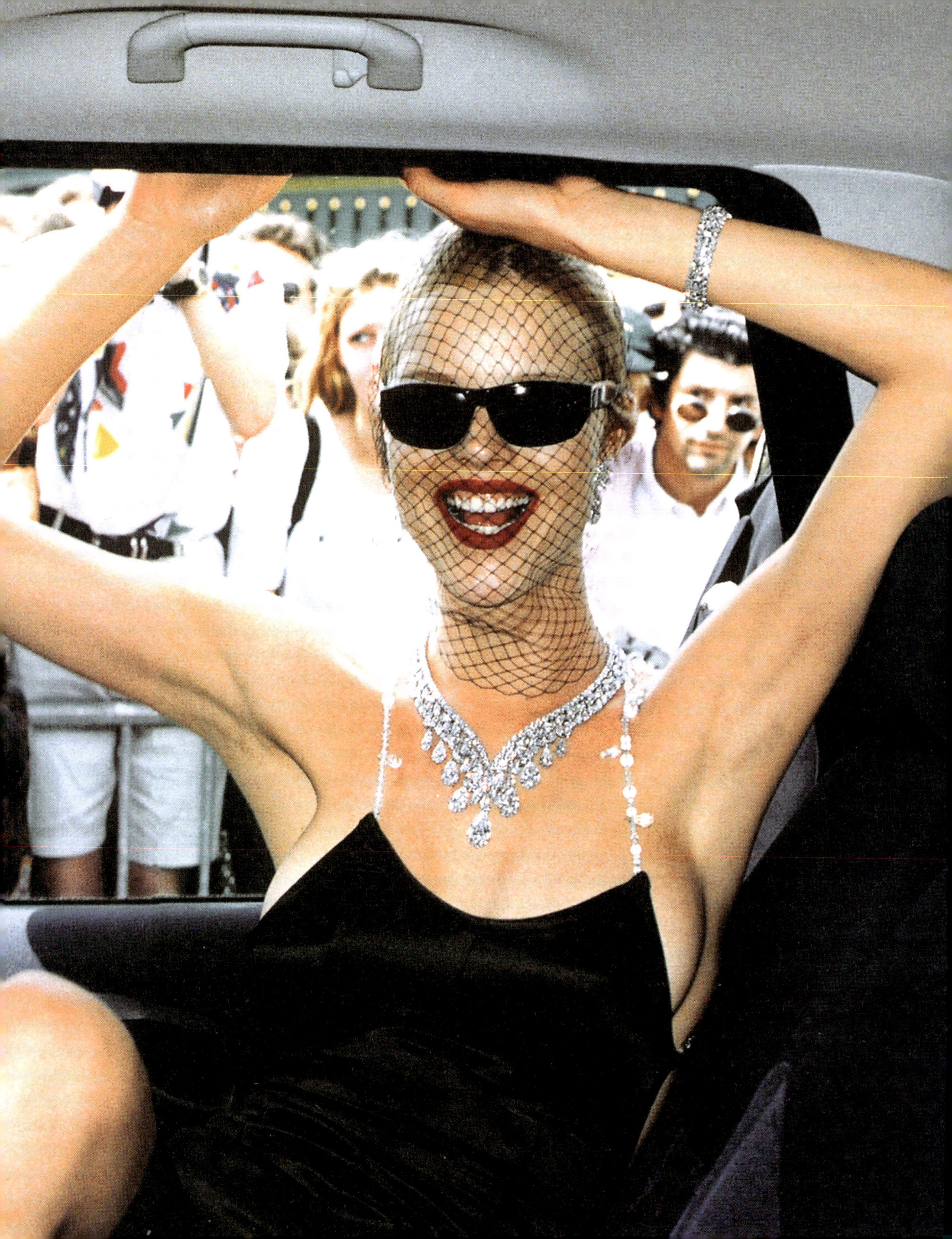

Pages 194–195:
Necklace. Platinum, aquamarines, and diamonds. The central motif can be detached and worn as a brooch. Cartier London, 1940.

Facing page:
Necklace. Platinum and diamonds; in the center a 20.39-carat pear-shaped diamond flanked by two pear-shaped diamonds of 12.04 carats and 10.25 carats. Photo: Helmut Newton, *Paris Match*

Right:
Bracelet. Platinum, six diamonds weighing 26.55 carats, other diamonds. Formerly the collection of the Duchess of Windsor. Cartier Paris, 1956.

Bracelet. Platinum, gold, and round- and baguette-cut diamonds. The two motifs can be detached and worn as brooches. Cartier Paris, 1947.

The duchess of Windsor, who—as we hardly need reminding—paid great attention to the overall harmony as well as the variety of her outfits, asked Hubert de Givenchy to make her a dress that would match her emeralds. To this end Monsieur Sache, who supplied both Givenchy and his friend and mentor Cristóbal Balenciaga with fabrics, created a special "faceted" cloth of a "deep blue-green" color, which rightly won him fame in the trade.[22] Associations between garment and jewelry operate at the level of shapes and colors, the latter certainly being the factor that is the most immediately and intuitively perceived. As artist Eugène Delacroix asserted in the nineteenth century, "color makes no intellectual sense, but is all-powerful when it comes to sensibility." This idea was reiterated in the twentieth century by color theorist Johannes Itten. "The deepest and truest secrets of color effects, I know, are invisible even to the eye and are beheld only by the heart" (*The Art of Color*, 1961). There is a rich symbolism to colors, and even though sometimes contradictory this symbolism retains its power. Colors can be warm, cool, stimulating, soothing; they can be orchestrated in harmonic shades or sharp contrasts, and so on. But whereas painters can achieve an infinite palette of hues by mixing pigments, jewelers have to rely solely on precious materials and the visual effects created by juxtaposing them, enriching these compositions with fine gems whose sparkle can be nuanced through various cutting techniques. Just as artists can be recognized for their palette as much as their draftsmanship, so a jeweler's chromatic compositions function as a signature. Cartier magnifies a gem, exalting sparkle through a velvety setting, or matte effects through light, or color through a shrewd combination—sometimes classic, sometimes bold—that will reveal all its depth, so that the most imposing of diamonds can still display all its grace, the most modest stone all its character.

22. Marie-Andrée Jouve and Jacqueline Demornex, *Balenciaga* (Paris: Éditions du Regard, 1988).

Monochrome
and Rich Harmonies

Ring. Platinum, one 50.41-carat oval-shaped diamond, and brilliants. *Inde Mystérieuse* collection. Cartier Paris, 2007.

Facing page:
Necklace with "Tiger Tears" diamonds (two pear-shaped old-cut diamonds weighing 56.64 and 57.53 carats). Platinum and diamonds. Cartier Paris, 2006.

In a Hitchcock film set in World War II, an ocean liner was torpedoed by a German submarine, and nine passengers found themselves in a lifeboat. They could only avoid starvation by trying to catch fish. But they immediately realized that their efforts would be vain, because they had no bait. Society reporter Constance Porter (played by Tallulah Bankhead), offered up her diamond bracelet. "Sure, we have bait—by Cartier," she says, "I bit on it myself" (*Lifeboat*, Alfred Hitchcock, 1944).

Diamonds are purity and sparkle; their unchanging quality places them at the top of a hierarchy based on strength and power. The etymological root of the word diamond, the Greek *adamas*, means "hardest steel, unbreakable." In France, only objects of worship and crowns were entitled to display this excessively rare gem until the fifteenth century, when Charles VII granted Agnès Sorel, the first woman to be officially considered as a royal "favorite," the right to wear diamonds. Centuries later, in 1969, Richard Burton offered a remarkable diamond to Elizabeth Taylor after their mutual passion had declared itself, like that of Antony and Cleopatra, on the set of Joseph Mankiewicz's *Cleopatra*. The diamond weighed 69.42 carats. When this South African diamond came up for auction, Aristotle Onassis, who had recently married Jacqueline Kennedy, hoped to offer it to her, but Cartier won the bidding at 1,050,000 dollars. The sum went down in history as the first time a diamond cost more than one million dollars. Burton, not to be outdone, immediately bought it from Cartier for an additional 50,000 dollars plus the condition that the stone, henceforth dubbed the Cartier-Burton-Taylor diamond, be displayed on Cartier's Fifth Avenue premises. The American press reported that over six thousand people a day came to look at the Hollywood star's diamond. Taylor wanted to wear it as a pendant, and therefore commissioned Cartier to make a necklace of pear-shaped diamonds that would flank the main diamond on Taylor's breast. (The previous year Burton had given Taylor the Krupp diamond, an emerald-cut stone of over thirty-three carats for which he outbid Harry Winston, and which Cartier set in a ring.) Then in 1972, for Taylor's fortieth birthday, Burton bought from Cartier a yellow, heart-shaped diamond mounted on a pendant that hung from a strand of plaited gold.

Throughout its history, the house of Cartier has had the privilege of seeing some of the most famous and outstanding diamonds pass through its premises in Paris, London, or New York, such as the Indian Briolette, the Star of South Africa, the Star of the East, and the North Star. The Queen of Holland diamond (136.25 carats), set for the maharaja of Nawanagar in 1931 alongside some colored diamonds (including a very rare olive-green stone weighing 12.86 carats), once again passed through the hands of Cartier (London) in 1960. The Jubilee diamond (245.35 carats), which had inaugurated a new style of cutting and owed its name to the fiftieth anniversary, in 1887, of Queen Victoria's accession to the British throne, was sold to Paul-Louis Weiller in 1937, mounted on a brooch evoking a six-pointed star, at Toussaint's suggestion. Later, an absolutely perfect drop of 107.07 carats,[23] whose cutting required months of work, was displayed at Cartier New York in October 1976 and dubbed the "Louis Cartier" diamond in honor of the hundredth anniversary of the birth of the eldest of the "three Cartiers." More recently, the Cartier Tiger Tears, two magnificent, wonderfully clear pear-shaped old-cut diamonds (56.64 and 57.73 carats)—from the legendary, now-abandoned mines at Golconda, where the rarest and most costly diamonds were found—were soberly set on a row of platinum and diamonds. Finally, the Star of the South diamond, whose sparkle is tempered by a nearly pink hue of incomparable softness, earned freedom for the Brazilian slave who found it in the Minas Gerais region in 1853. This raw diamond of 261.24 carats was bought by a syndicate of Paris dealers and was cut in

23. The diamond was certified as D Flawless by the GIA, which is very rare for stones of over one hundred carats.

Bracelet. Gray gold, two round diamonds weighing 4.09 carats, four pear-shaped diamonds weighing 4.87 carats, sixty-eight rose-cut diamonds weighing 54.2 carats, and seven oval-shaped diamonds weighing 16.65 carats. Cartier Paris, 2006.

Facing page:
Necklace. Platinum and diamonds, five of which total 63.04 carats. Cartier London, c. 1954.

Amsterdam by Benjamin Woorzanger of the Martin E. Coster firm, who had cut the Koh-I-Noor diamond. After three months of work, Woorzanger produced a sublime, oblong cushion-shaped stone. Displayed at three Universal Expositions—1855, 1862, and 1867—it was named the "Star of the South" and admired by Emperor Napoleon III and Empress Eugénie. It was then acquired by London jeweler Edward Dresden, who sold it to the gaekwar of Baroda, set in a necklace with the English Dresden diamond, a pear-shaped stone of 78.83 carats. The necklace was worn by Pratap Singh Gaekwar's second wife, the maharani of Baroda, whom the Western press called "the Indian Wallis Simpson" due to her taste for jewels, as immortalized in a photo by Henri Cartier-Bresson.

In 1951, *Vogue* announced that "diamonds are king." This title had never really been disputed, but the return of peace favored the return of white jewels for evening wear. Low-cut dresses by Dior and Balenciaga (whose predilection for tailored black garments was well known) provided perfect settings for gems whose sparkle was enhanced by platinum. Rita Hayworth owned a necklace of thirty-eight round and drop diamonds, while Mona Bismarck (whose collections were sold in 1984 to launch her Paris foundation) wore a bracelet of round diamonds with matching earrings of solitaires. Marlene Dietrich, dressed by Christian Dior for her role in Alfred Hitchcock's *Stage Fright* (1950), wore a choker of diamonds. One very fine choker by Cartier New York, of brilliant-, square-, and baguette-cut diamonds, featured seven pear-shaped stones hanging from squares (78.16 carats, 1941). In 1956 the Duchess of Windsor bought a ravishing bangle with crossover ends made of six rectangular, step-cut diamonds edged with round diamonds, while the back was lined with a simple row of square stones. This elegant sobriety, orchestrated around the alternation of round, square, rectangular, and baguette diamonds, gave way to curvilinear compositions also open to

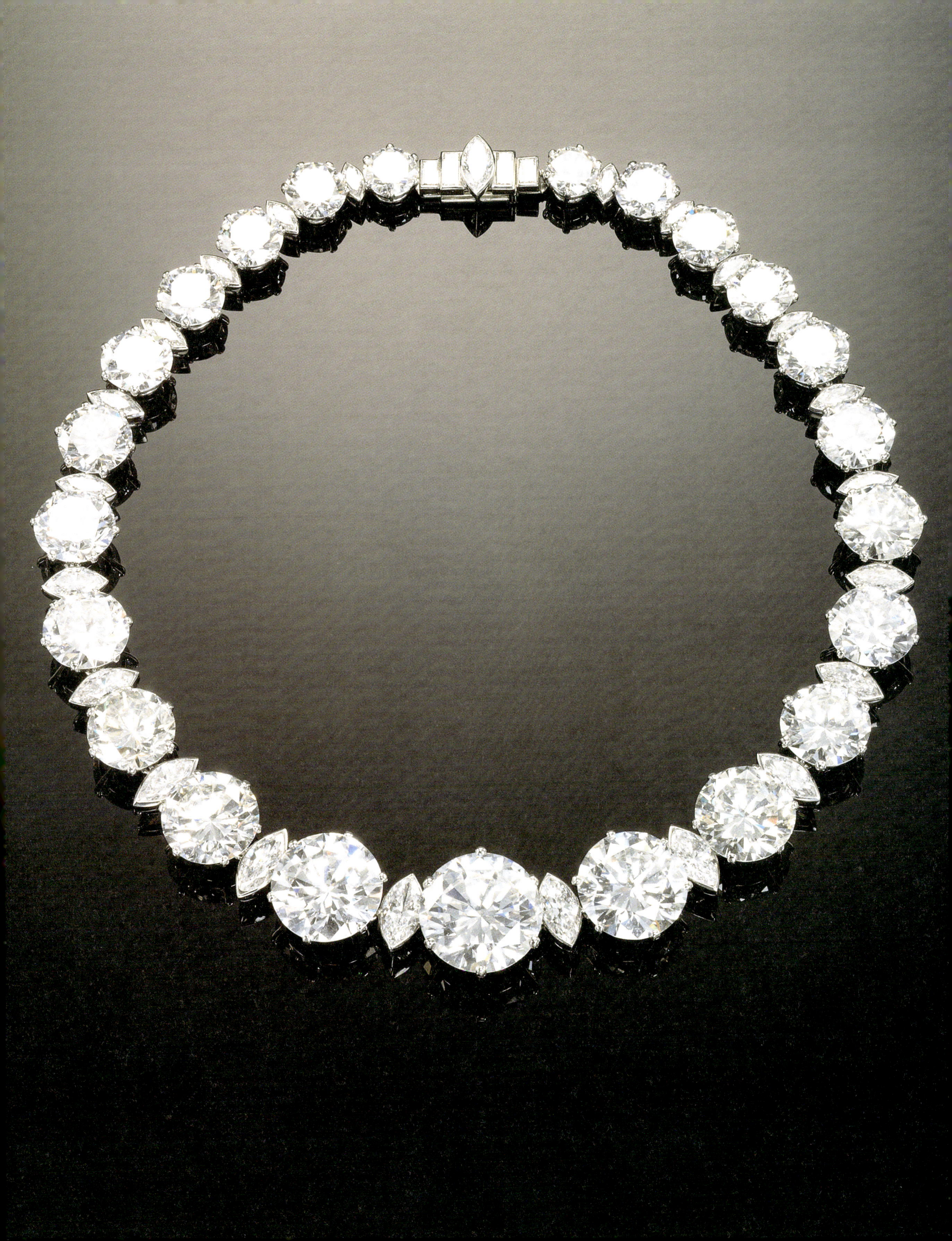

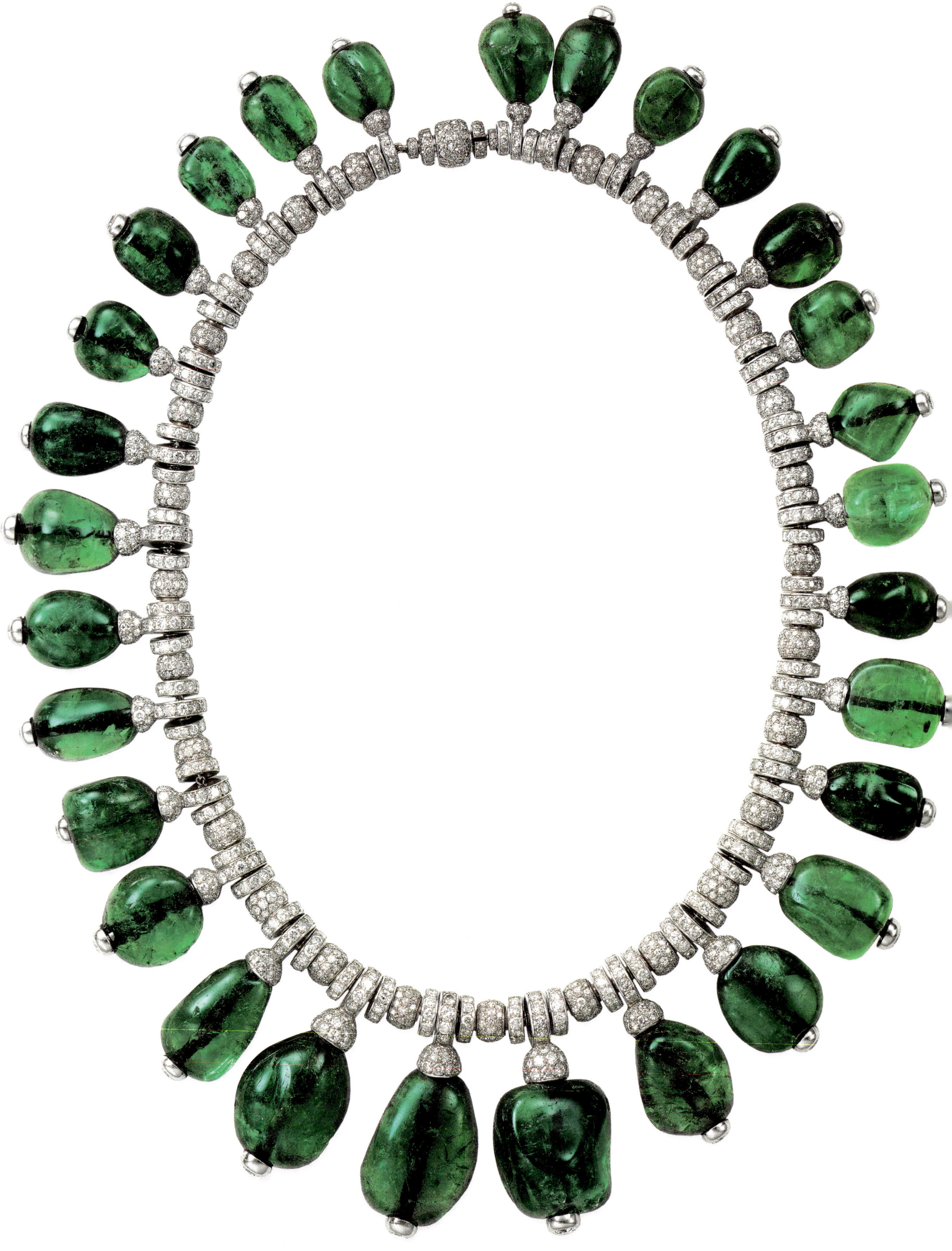

Merle Oberon. Photo: Tony Duquette Estate.

Facing page:
Necklace. Platinum, flexible chain of round diamonds, and twenty-nine graduated emerald cabochons with diamonds at their tips. Specially ordered by Merle Oberon. Cartier London, 1938.

sapphires, rubies, and emeralds, that is to say classic designs that valorized colored stones. Examples include a strand of brilliant- and baguette-cut diamonds on which are affixed three detachable clips of openwork palmettes featuring three step-cut sapphires (1960), a burst of diamonds ringing a rectangular emerald (1961), and a square of marquise-shaped diamonds set around a 37-carat emerald (for Prince Sadruddin Aga Khan in 1960). Emeralds retained their appealing fragility, ranging from a necklace worn by Merle Oberon, composed of twenty-nine baroque pear-shaped emeralds divided by diamond disks (1938) to the Eternity snake set with two Colombian emeralds of 205 and 206 carats, hence exceptional in both size and provenance (1997). Then there were tiaras worn by the Duchess of Windsor (1949) and Barbara Hutton (1947), whose stones had belonged to Maria Pavlovna, wife of Grand Duke Vladimir of Russia, as well as the emeralds of Empress Eugénie, which Cartier bought in 1961 to set as a pendant, not forgetting the trio of emeralds on the Samarkand bracelet (2004). When combined with the color red, emeralds created powerful, luminous harmonies, similar to the ones favored by Fauvist painters. The most vibrant example was owned by the Duchess of Windsor, namely a radiating necklace of gold studded with rubies and emeralds, punctuated with diamonds.

Rubies, identical in nature to sapphires and almost as tough as diamonds, have the privilege of displaying a color that is unusual in the mineral kingdom. Rubies are rarely larger that ten carats—famous rubies such as the Black Prince's ruby and the Côte de Bretagne ruby are in fact spinels—but the maharajas possessed some large Burmese

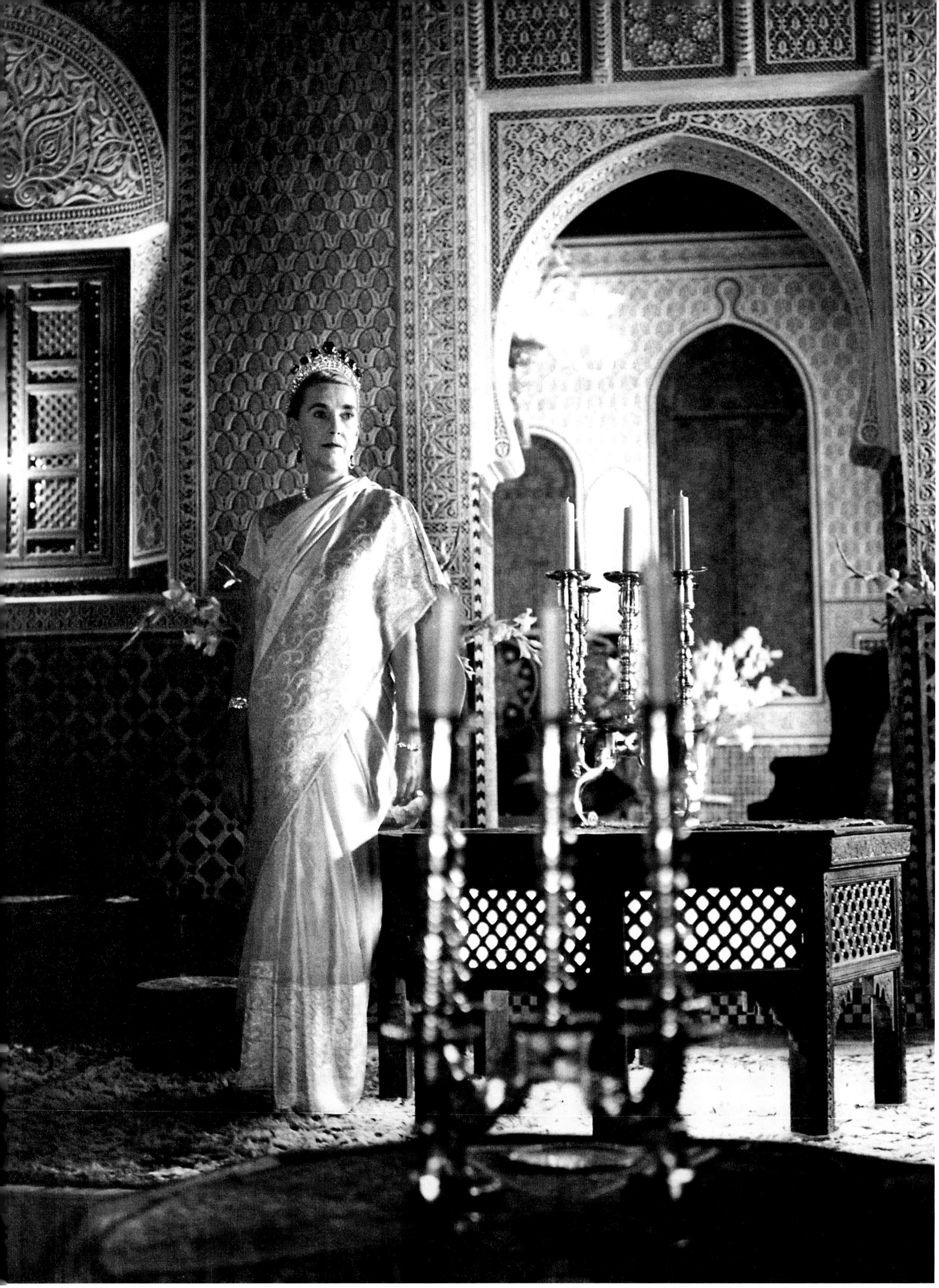

Earrings. Platinum and brilliants. *Inde Mystérieuse* collection. Cartier Paris, 2007.

Necklace that can be worn as a tiara, designed for Barbara Hutton in 1947. The emeralds originally belonged to Maria Pavlovna, consort of Grand Duke Vladimir of Russia.

Facing page:
Barbara Hutton in Tangiers wearing the jewel as a tiara. Photo: Cecil Beaton.

Following pages:
Necklace. Gray gold and 460 brilliants weighing 33 carats in total. Cartier Paris, 1999.

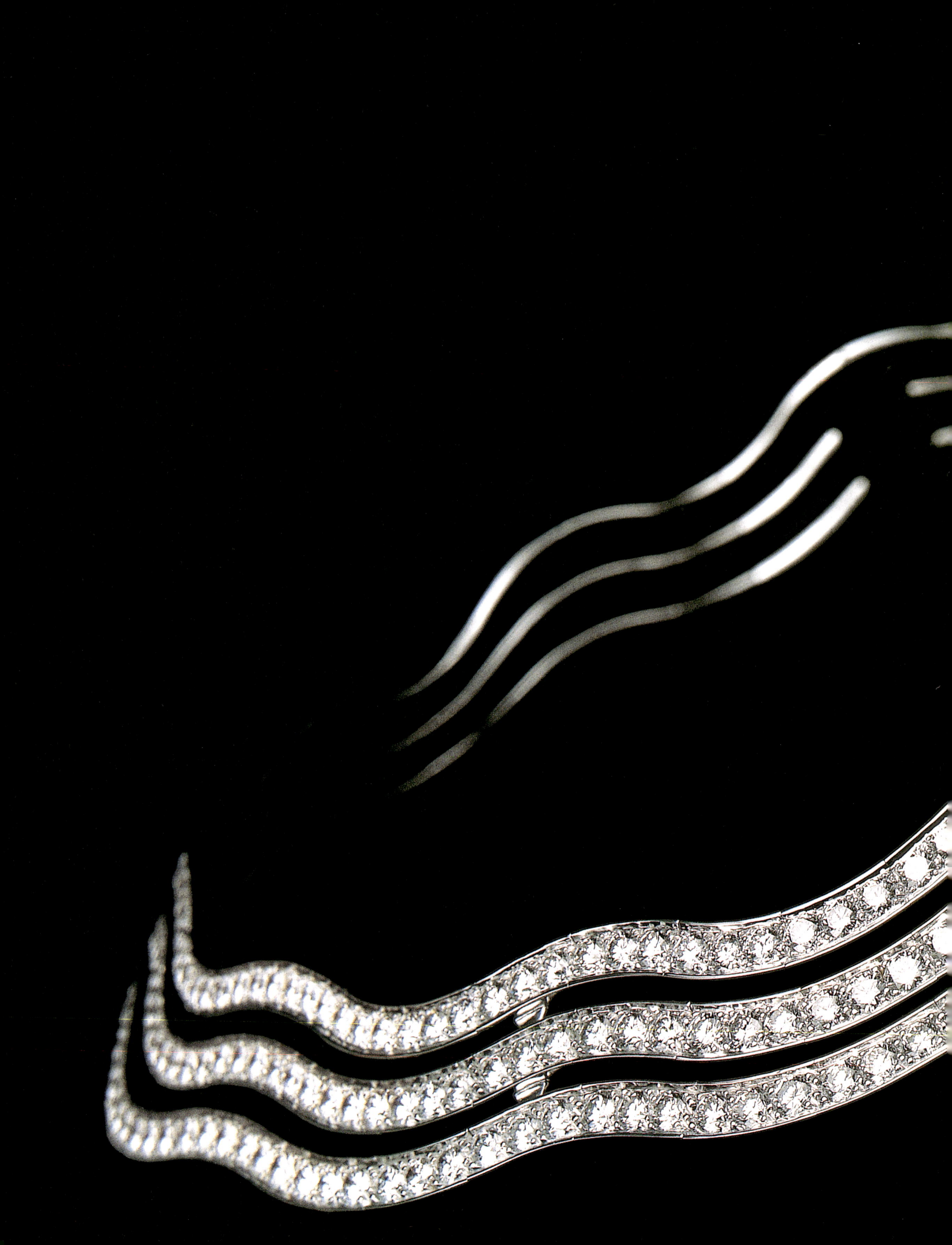

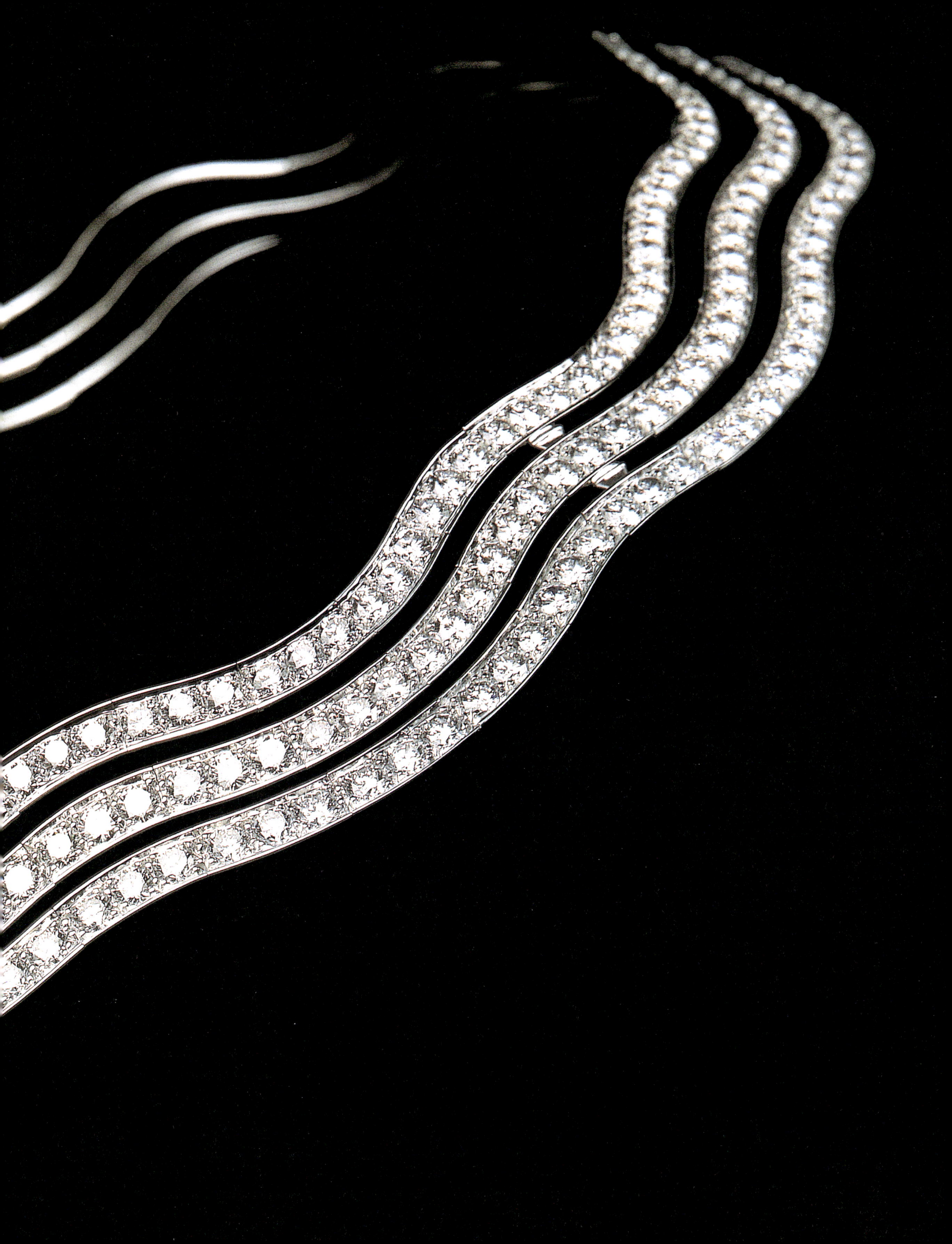

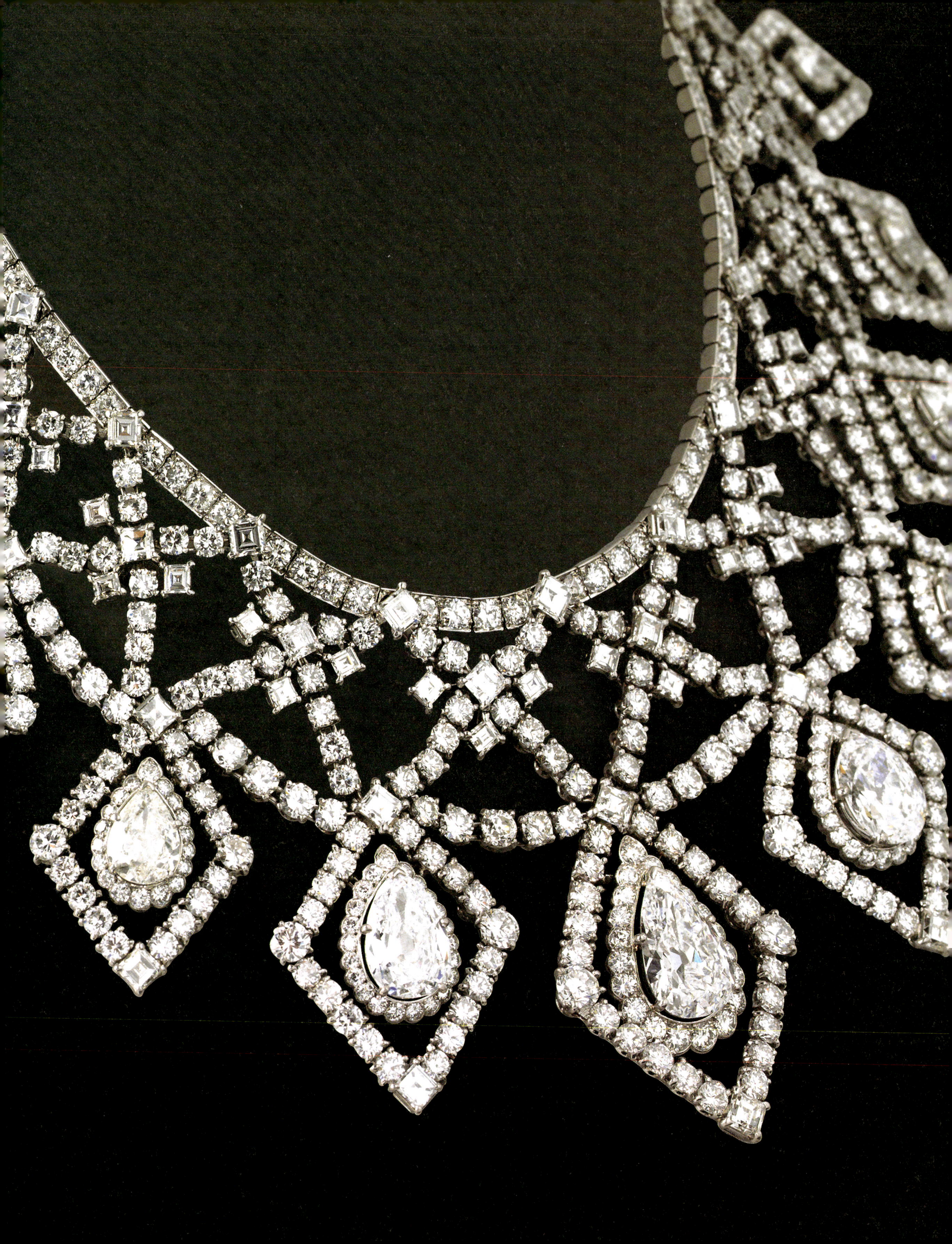

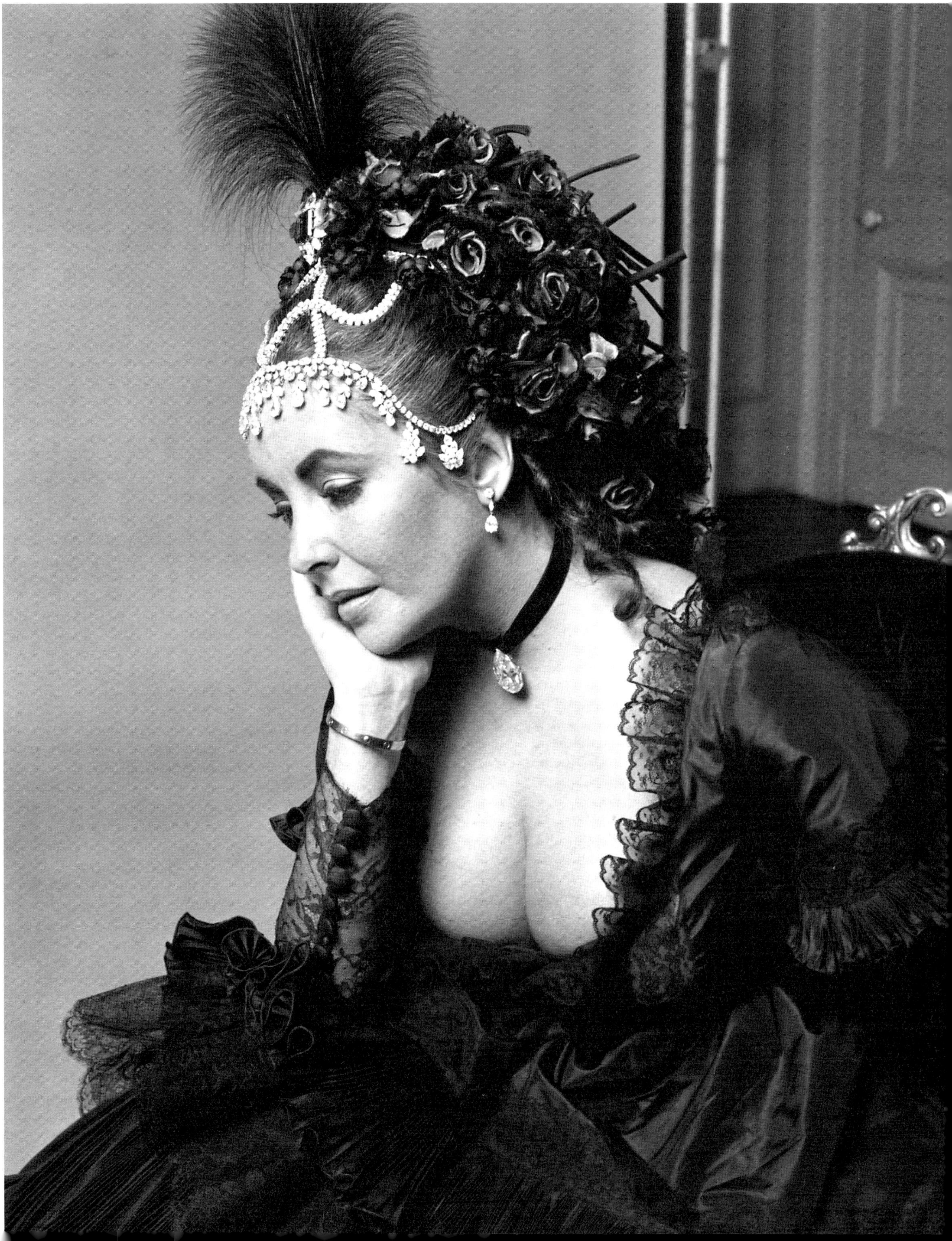

Bracelet. Platinum, diamonds, and eleven marquise-shaped rubies. Cartier Paris, 1948.

Bracelet. Platinum, gold, brilliant-cut diamonds, and faceted and caliber-cut rubies. Cartier Paris, 1955.

Facing page:
Necklace. Platinum, five pear-shaped diamonds weighing, respectively, 10.14, 6.26, 6.17, 5.22, and 5.04 carats, one 4.02-carat cushion-shaped fancy yellow diamond, cushion-shaped diamonds, and brilliants. 2006.

Page 208:
Necklace. Platinum and diamonds. Cartier Paris, 1953.

Page 209:
Elizabeth Taylor at the Proust Ball given by Baron and Baroness de Rothschild in 1972. She is wearing a *Love* bracelet and the Cartier-Burton-Taylor diamond. Photo: Cecil Beaton.

Page 212:
Brooch. Platinum and diamonds. Cartier Paris, 1943.

Brooch. Platinum and diamonds. Cartier Paris, 1951.

Page 213:
Choker and tiara of diamond scrolls. Diamonds on yellow gold. 1953.

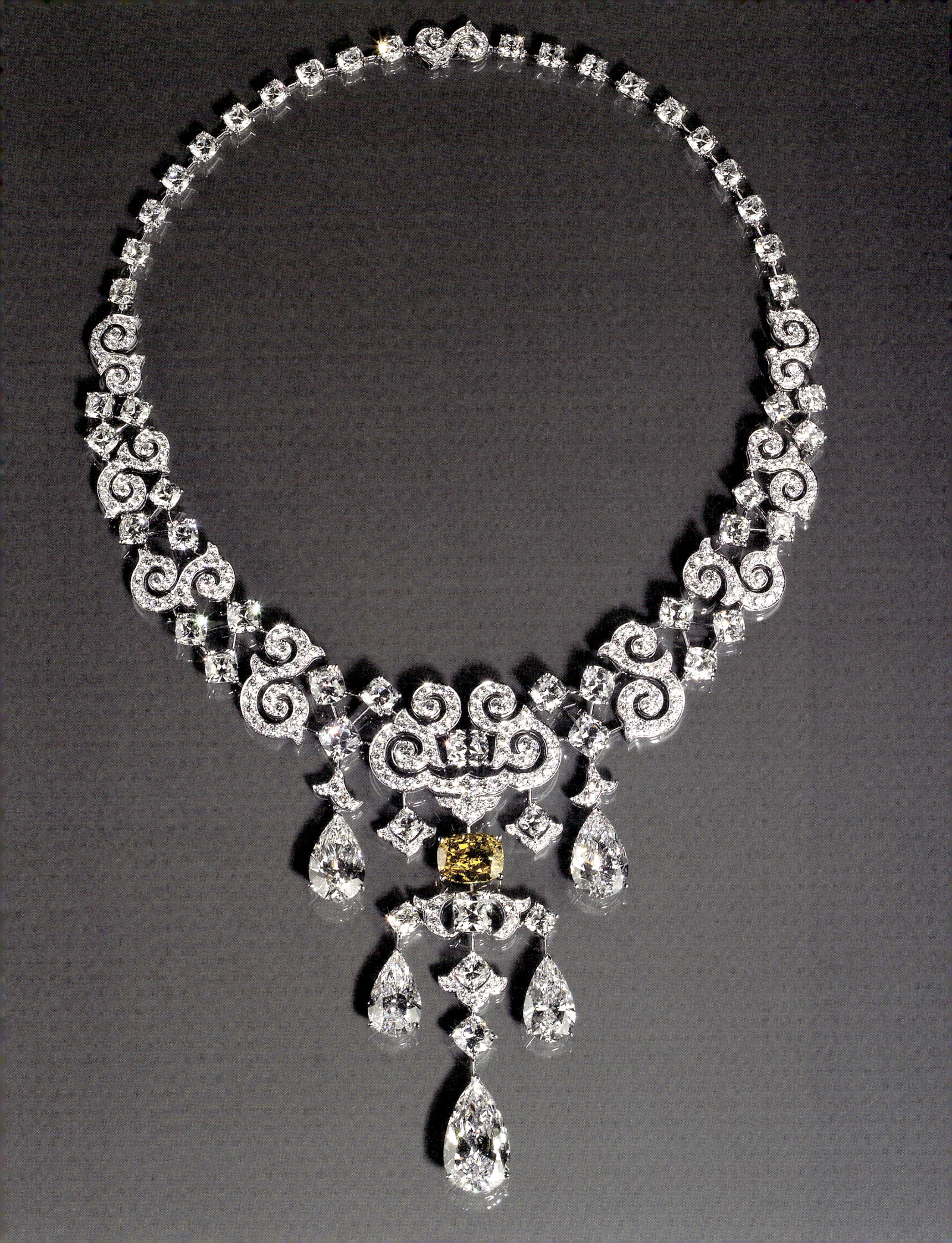

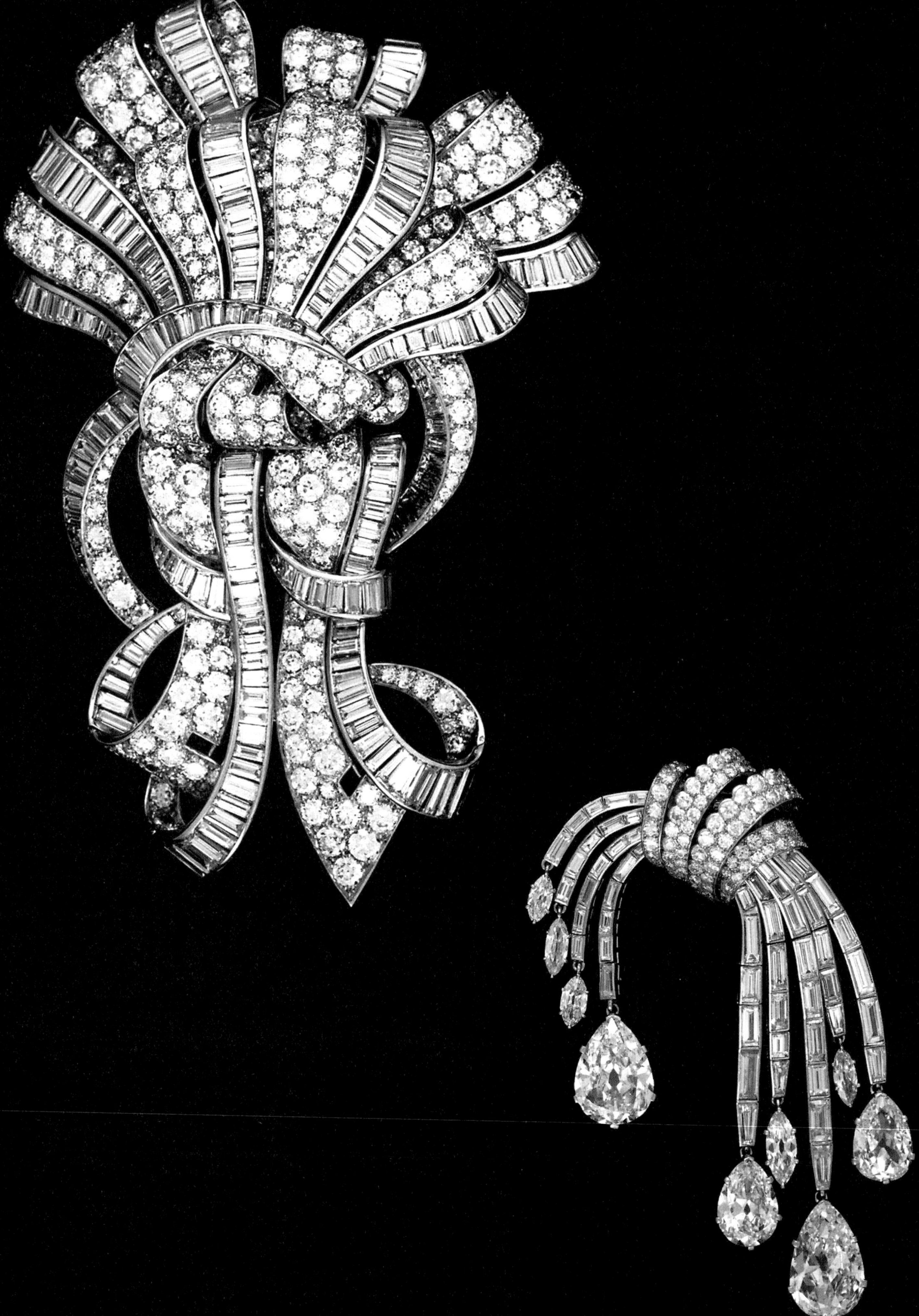

213

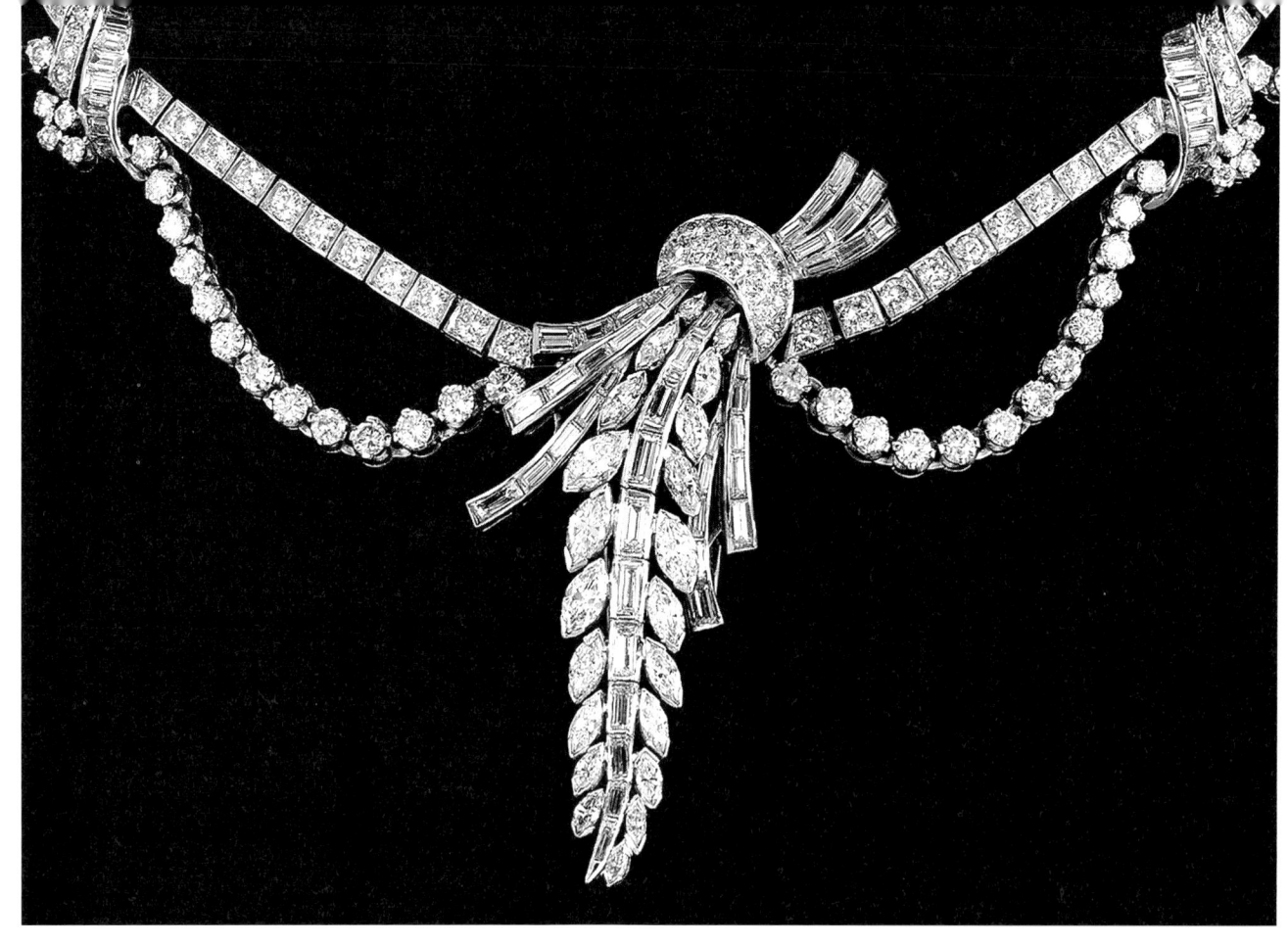

Garland **necklace.**
Platinum and diamonds.
Cartier London, 1959.

Necklace with detachable floral-motif brooches.
Platinum and diamonds.
Cartier London, 1957.

Facing page: **Necklace** with detachable clip brooches.
Platinum and diamonds.
Cartier Paris, 1949.

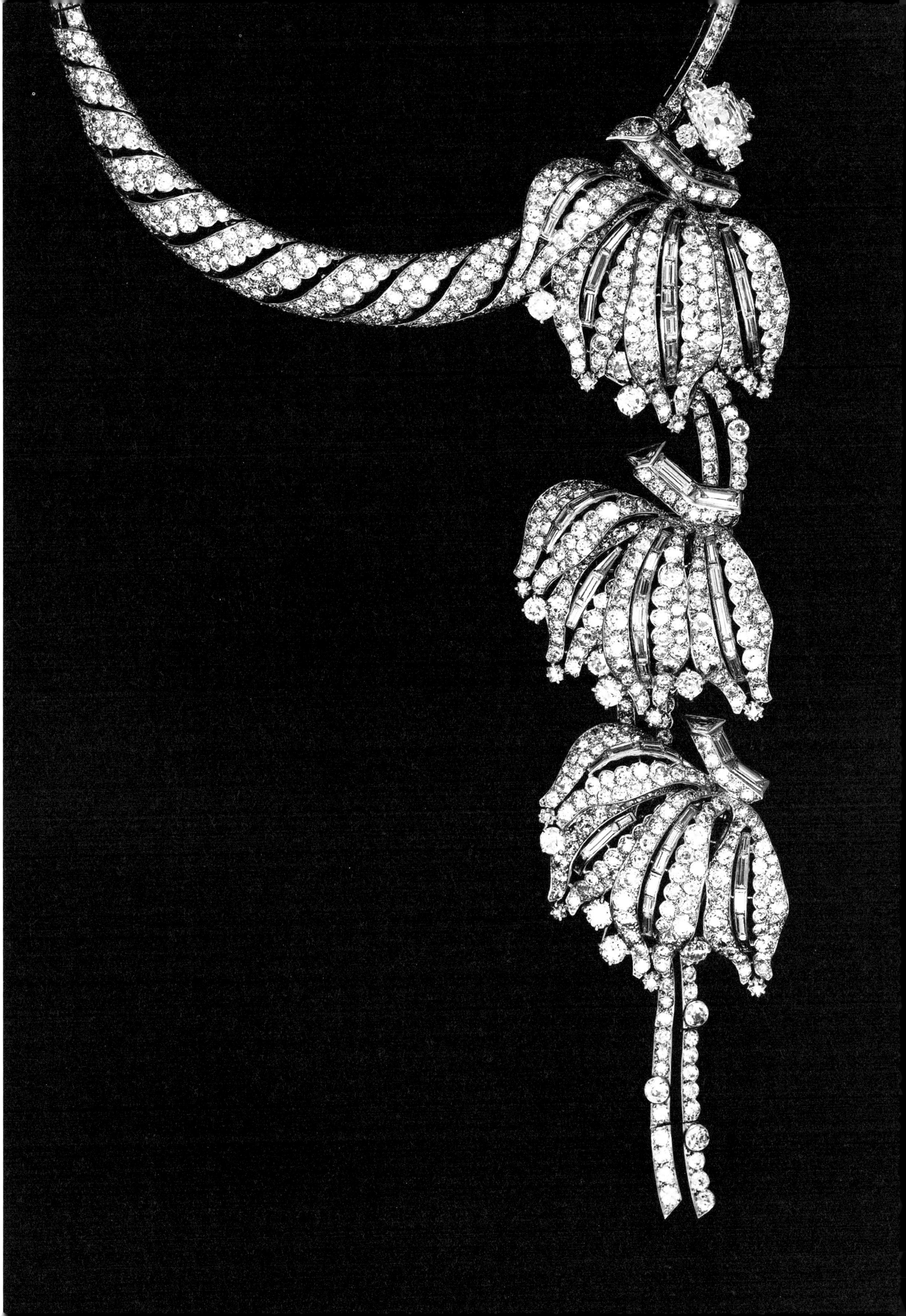

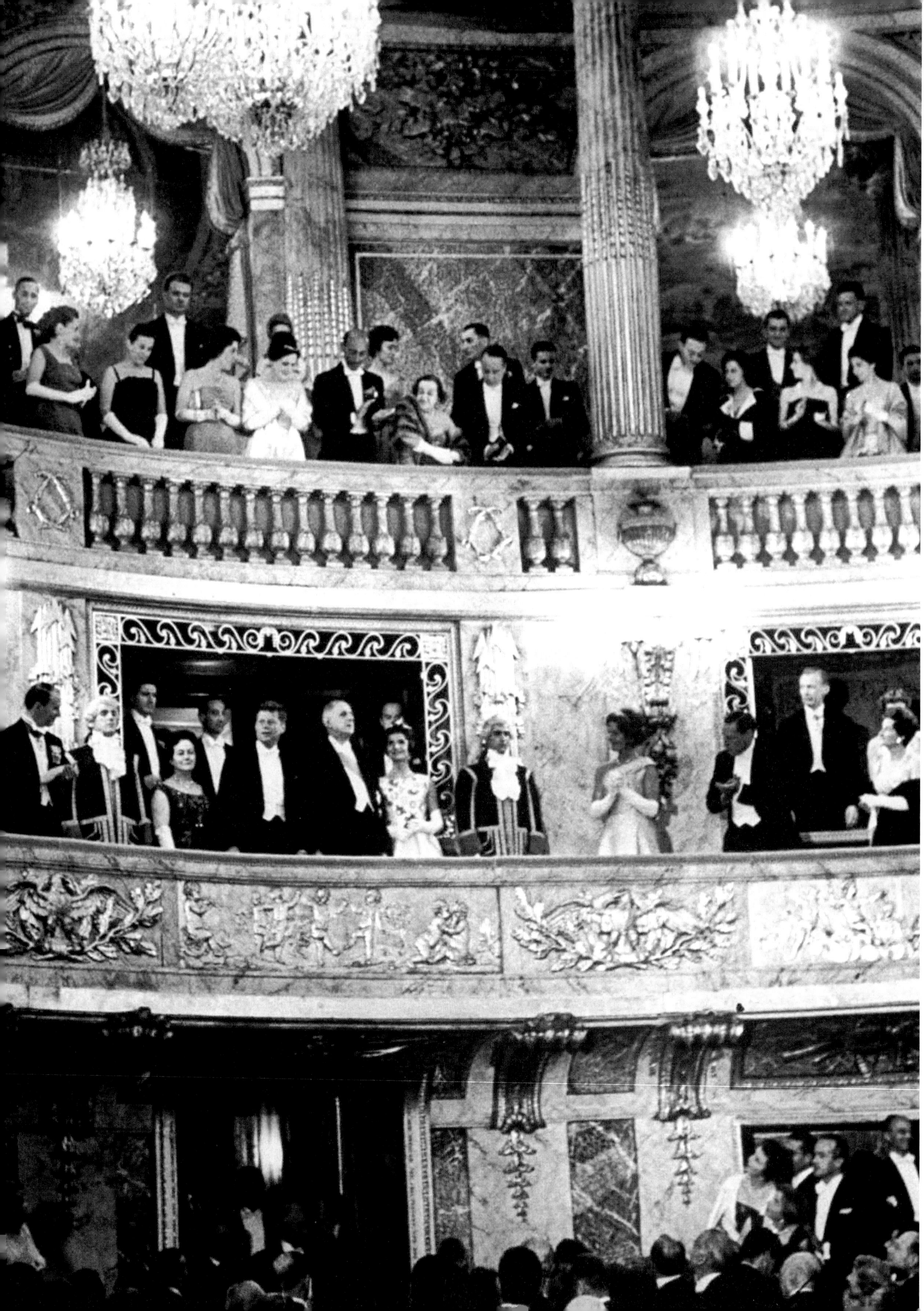

Princess Grace of Monaco
wearing a Cartier diamond
necklace received
as a wedding gift, 1956.
Photo: *Time* magazine.

Facing page:
General de Gaulle flanked
by Jackie and John F.
Kennedy at the Versailles
opera house, 1961.
Photo: *Time Life*.

rubies. When Grace Kelly swapped her Hitchcock costumes for the gown of a fairy-tale princess, she received numerous Cartier gifts, which she would wear for the rest of her life. They included a tiara of rubies and diamonds in the colors of the Principality of Monaco, chosen by the Société des Bains. Similarly, a bracelet in the Cartier Collection (1955) made of round links with brilliant-cut diamonds on the outer surface and faceted rubies on the inner surface is very striking: nothing could be simpler than these straightforward links, but the bright red of the caliber-cut rubies, combined with the contrast underscored by the shape and position of the hoops, lends it surprising volume along with the charm of a deceptive modesty. Yellow gold plays a key part in creating this effect, valorizing the rubies here, just as it underscores the strands of diamonds on a superb necklace that flows from neck to bust, its scintillating threads creating a fishnet of openwork motifs adorned with eleven red cabochons (1975). This is the necklace that prompted Jean Cocteau to write, "Cartier, that subtle magician, who manages to balance the moon, in fragments, on threads of sunlight." White diamonds in the form of faceted balls, yellow diamonds cut in briolettes—whether fragments of the moon or drops of rain—have fallen onto a platinum thread, hanging there in an absence of order or hierarchy that flaunts the most immaterial and most fascinating aspects of the stones. Rubies contribute their warmth and vitality to this impalpable light, while an orchid motif brings freshness to a 2005 creation that includes, among others, five oval and cushion-shaped Burmese rubies (16.44 carats), thirty-eight briolette-cut diamond balls (59.94 carats), and twenty

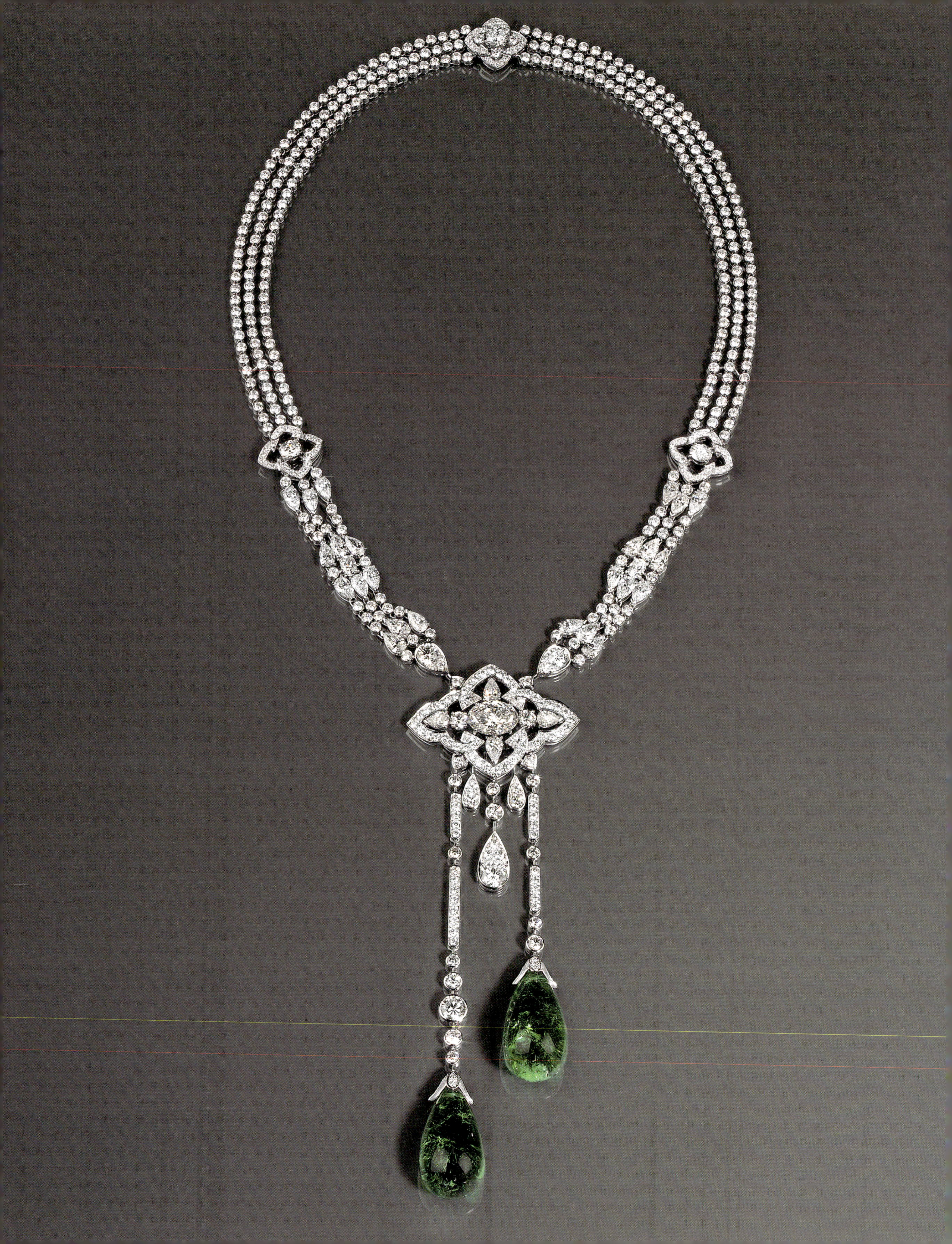

Bracelet. Platinum, gold, emeralds, and baguette- and brilliant-cut diamonds. Cartier Paris, c. 1960.

Bracelet. Gray gold, round brilliants, baguette-cut diamonds, and three cushion-shaped Colombian emeralds weighing, respectively, 50.03, 64.62, and 52.77 carats. Cartier Paris, 2005.

Facing page:
Necklace. Platinum, two emerald drops weighing 31.77 and 33.57 carats, pear- and oval-shaped diamonds, and brilliants. Cartier Paris, 2006.

219

Necklace. Platinum, ribbed emeralds, carved rubies, sapphires and emeralds, sapphire beads, and brilliants. *Inde Mystérieuse* collection. Cartier Paris, 2007.

Hindu **necklace.** Platinum, briolette-cut sapphires, carved sapphires, sapphire beads, carved rubies, ruby beads, ruby cabochons, carved emeralds, fluted and smooth emerald beads, emerald cabochons, and marquise-, baguette-, and round old-cut diamonds. Formerly the collection of Daisy Fellowes and the Countess Casteja. Cartier Paris, special order 1936, altered 1963.

Necklace. Gray gold, emerald cabochon, diamonds, emerald and sapphire beads, and brilliants. *Inde Mystérieuse* collection. Cartier Paris, 2007.

Facing page:
Necklace composed of 162 diamonds weighing 61.49 carats, eleven briolette-cut sapphires weighing 120.43 carats, and twenty-five emerald cabochons weighing 87.42 carats. Cartier Paris, 1997.

yellow briolette-cut diamonds (87.61 carats); yet it seems hard to believe that the design was dictated by the stones—as Cartier philosophy demands—so important is freedom and asymmetry to its overall harmony.

Sapphire—a celestial stone that unites heaven and earth—was traditionally worn by bishops, cardinals, and monarchs. The Duchess of Windsor owned very fine sapphire jewels, some of which have already been cited as remarkable examples of necklace, brooch, ring, or panther, but the sale that dispersed her property in 1987 also brought to light a cushion-shaped sapphire of 206.82 carats, set as a pendant by Cartier in 1951. A long article on the house of Cartier that was published in *Beaux-Arts* in 1989, during the Cartier exhibition at the Petit Palais in Paris, referred to famous auctions where prices attained by Cartier jewels averaged 7.21 times estimate, sometimes climbing to fifty (or even seventy-three) times estimate, whereas the figure for other jewelers was less than three times estimate.[24] A clip brooch of a blue rose (representing an impossible quest, like Citizen Kane's "Rosebud" in Orson Welles's film) is, strangely, one of the few pieces Cartier made with its patented "invisible setting," an almost magical method of juxtaposing stones. The brooch dates from 1959, whereas the patent was filed in March 1933, but the method was immediately dropped because it meant cutting deeply into the underside of a gem in order to slide it onto kind of rail, and Louis Cartier felt that such deep cuts lacked respect for the precious nature of his materials. One wonders what he would have thought of the fate of a Cartier sapphire that was the object of a 1952 trial involving two famous French lawyers, Maurice Garçon (representing the actress Josette Day, who had married a rich Belgian businessman, Maurice Solvay) and René Floriot (representing the defendant). Floriot questioned the Cartier spokesman at the trial—a Mr. Colin—at some length concerning the value of the sixty-carat sapphire, which had been stolen from Josette Day and cut into six smaller stones for easier resale.

24. Isabelle de Wavrin, "Le sacre de Cartier," *Beaux Arts*, special issue (1989).

Bird **brooch.** Platinum, gray gold, one 67.20-carat Burmese sapphire cabochon, emerald cabochons, and round emeralds for the eyes. Cartier Paris, 1999.

Necklace. Platinum, one 117.84 pear-shaped sapphire cabochon, one 29.11-carat carved emerald, brilliant-cut diamonds, and carved sapphire and emerald beads. Cartier Paris, 2005.

Sapphires and diamonds exist in a wide range of colors, from intense red diamonds to the Sri Lankan sapphire known as *padparadsha* ("lotus flower"), whose sublime hue varies from rose to orange according to the light. Such stones are extremely expensive. Rare and magnificent yellow diamonds have passed through Cartier's hands, several of which have already been mentioned, but in the 1960s items set with fancy yellow diamonds (such as tiger-pattern pieces) multiplied. Yellow gold enhances the luminosity of these sun-colored stones, creating handsome harmonies based on contrast with cool emeralds or the smooth yet matte appearance of carved coral. Budding roses, turtles, and parrots joined Cartier's famous reptiles, even as the workshop continued to produce abstract designs of bracelets and necklaces based on a simple row of caliber-cut stones with sparkling tips that "heightened" the tasteful combination of white and bronze-hued diamonds. In 2005 a revamped version of the early twentieth-century diamond sprays and ear pendants with pear-shaped diamonds yielded a demiparure of necklace and earrings that literally dress the earlobe as only Cartier knows how to do, employing a cushion-shaped fancy yellow diamond of over four carats.

Necklace. Platinum, one 123.8-carat carved blue Ceylon sapphire, one cabochon-cut oval blue sapphire, sapphire beads, one natural pearl, and brilliants. Cartier Paris, 2006.

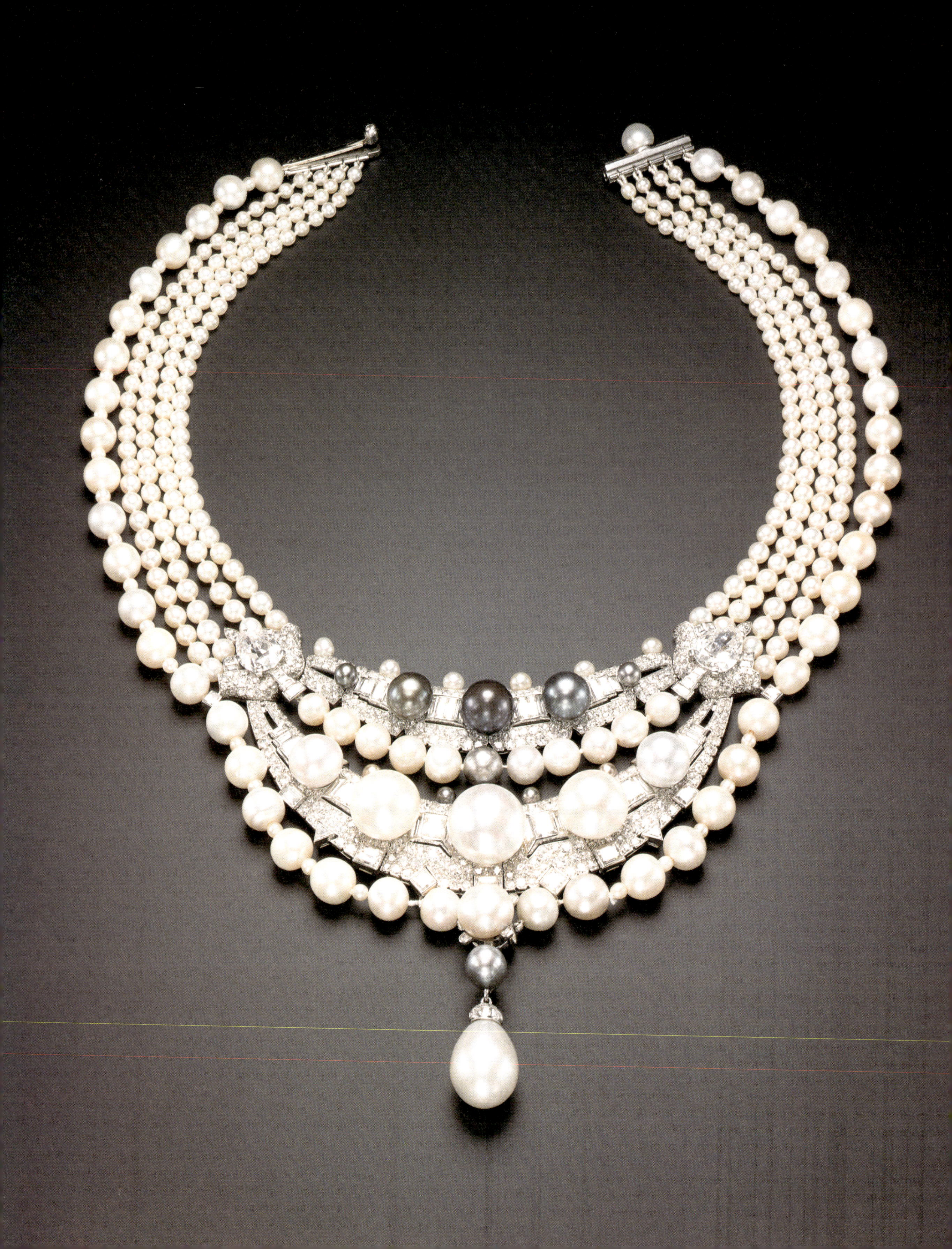

Pearls

Divine **chain necklace** that falls down the back in a cascade of seventy-two natural pearls. The front pendant is a Very Light hexagonal diamond and two natural pearls (gray and pink) framed by two cushion-shaped diamonds; the drop is a natural pearl highlighted by twenty-six brilliants; gold and platinum. Cartier Paris, 1997.

Facing page:
Necklace. Platinum, pearls, and diamonds. Cartier Paris, 1945.

Cleopatra, who wore two large drop-shaped pearls on her ears, told the disbelieving Mark Antony that she could spend over ten million sestertia on a single meal, and then proved it by dissolving one of those pearls in vinegar and drinking it. A more capricious Elizabeth Taylor fed one to her dog: for her thirty-seventh birthday in 1969, Richard Burton gave her an exceptional, mysterious drop-shaped pearl weighing 203.84 grains.[25] Scarcely had it arrived than the pearl vanished. Panic set in until it was discovered, intact, in the mouth of Miss Taylor's Pekinese. Three years later, Cartier designed a remarkable choker of pearls, diamonds, and rubies from which hung a long pendant adorned with a flamboyant motif, leading to the Taylor pearl still held by its original diamond-and-silver bail.

The wild, watery, secret nature of pearls has made them a coveted item since prehistoric times. When the pearls owned by the nizam of Hyderabad were dried in the open air after having been washed by servants, they covered an acre in area. In a wonderful transition, London's late-nineteenth century "pearlies," or costermongers, elected a Pearly King and Queen each year, their outfits being inspired by a street sweeper who, for lack of resources, stitched mother-of-pearl buttons all over his clothes, completely covering them.

By the 1910s Jacques Cartier had become a hunter of pearls in India and the Persian Gulf. Early in the twentieth century pearls were significantly more expensive than diamonds, which had become less rare following the discovery and intensive exploitation of diamond mines in southern Africa. In the 1920s, however, the arrival on the market of Kokichi Mikimoto's cultured pearls,[26] along with economic depression and the steady decline in numbers of pearl divers (who went to work in the oil industry), meant that precious natural pearls suffered. As recounted above, in 1917 Cartier acquired its New York premises in exchange for a natural pearl necklace valued at one million dollars, yet in 1957 this same necklace fetched only 151,000 dollars

[25]. Known as "La Pelegrina or "La Peregrina," the story behind this pearl has always been confused. See Nadelhoffer, *Cartier* 132–33, and n. 22.

[26]. Five cultured pearls experimentally produced by Linnaeus in 1761 are conserved at the Linnean Society of London. Japanese cultured pearls were later joined by pearls from Australia, the South Pacific, and French Polynesia (naturally black with overtones called "flywing," "eggplant," "bronze," etc.)

Necklace of sixty-four natural pearls weighing 634.71 carats and eleven carved baroque emeralds weighing 230.52 carats. The central motif is a 73.31-carat octagonal emerald and a 48.80-carat emerald drop. Additional emerald and ruby beads and cabochons. Cartier Paris, 1997.

Facing page:
Necklace. Yellow gold, cultured pearls, pink tourmaline, and diamonds. Cartier Paris, 1959.

Pages 230–231:
Necklace. Variously colored natural pearls, the Tavernier fancy yellow-brown diamond weighing 56.073 carats, one 32.36-carat cushion-shaped yellow sapphire, and one 4.08-carat cushion-shaped brown diamond. Cartier Paris, 1999.

at auction—a tale that has gone down in the annals of jewelry (and probably in the annals of real estate). Cultured pearls steadily acquired their letters of nobility thanks to the level of quality they reached and their infinitely nuanced range of hues, while natural pearls have become rarities similar to costly antiques.

As a symbol of the moon, pearls are universally associated with femininity. The softness of their highlights and the pleasantness of their touch owe nothing to the human hand. When orchestrated with platinum and diamonds, in which a pearl is the fragile, subtle, iridescent instrument, wonderful harmonies of light are created. Cartier designed torsades, pendants, chokers, and long necklaces worn to one side with the central motif placed on the shoulder. Pearls were considered timeless, ever fashionable, and wearable by day and by night—they went wonderfully with the warm, brown tones of mink fur, whose Oriental appeal was coveted by all elegant women in the postwar period. A very handsome choker (Cartier Paris, 1950) of twenty-eight graduated natural pearls, the largest being nearly 17 millimeters in diameter (1261.33 grains), featured a drop-shaped pearl of 190.6 grains as a pendant, simply linked by a fine line of diamonds that exemplifies the elegance of Cartier's designs, whose subtlety always leads the eye, via some delicate detail, to the true focus represented by the most precious stone or pearl. The effect is evident with a white pearl 18 millimeters in diameter, set in an interlacing pattern of yellow gold and diamonds (Cartier Paris, 1965), a necklace that once belonged to the Duchess of Windsor and was bought in 1987 by Kelly and Calvin Klein, the famous New York fashion designer. One particularly impressive

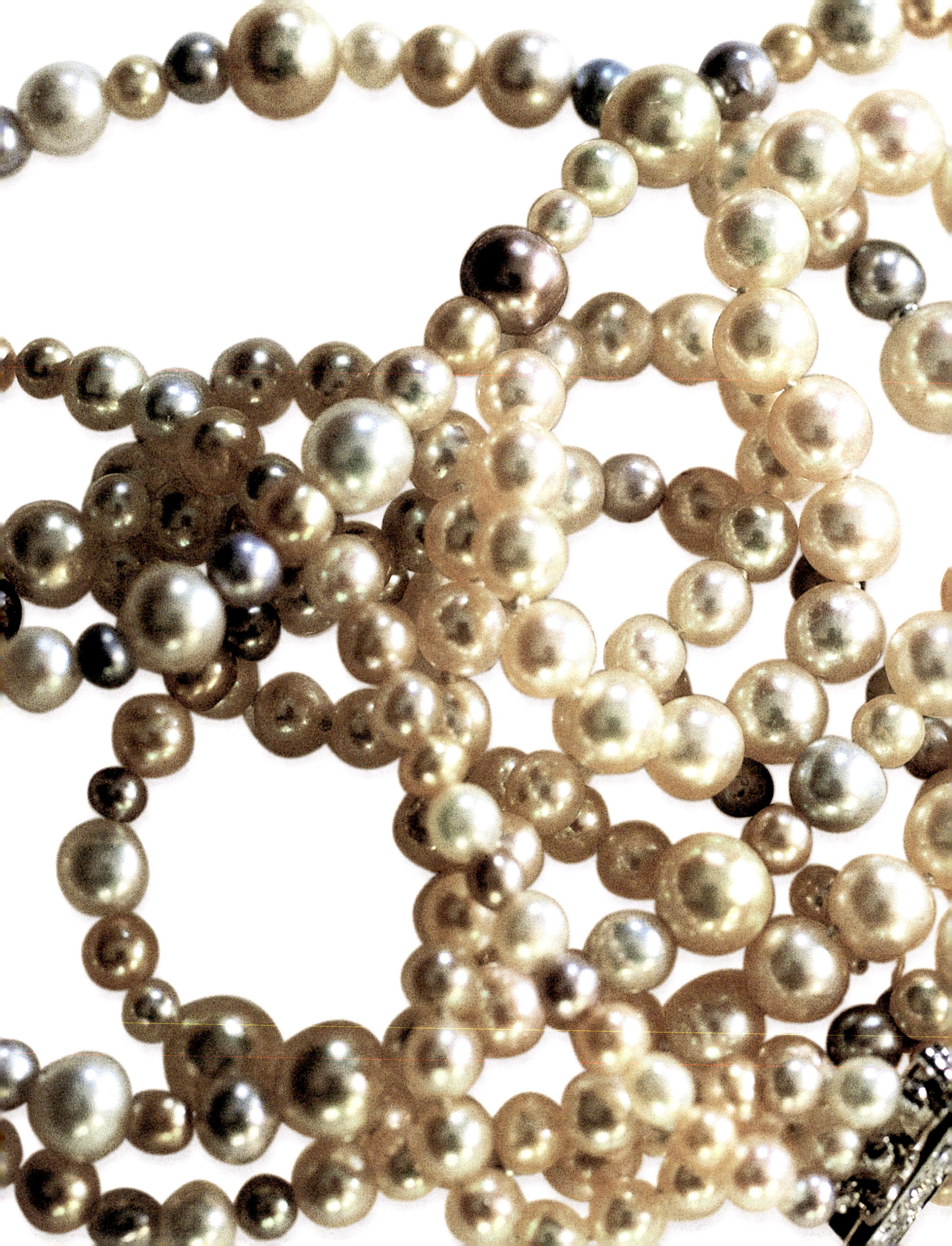

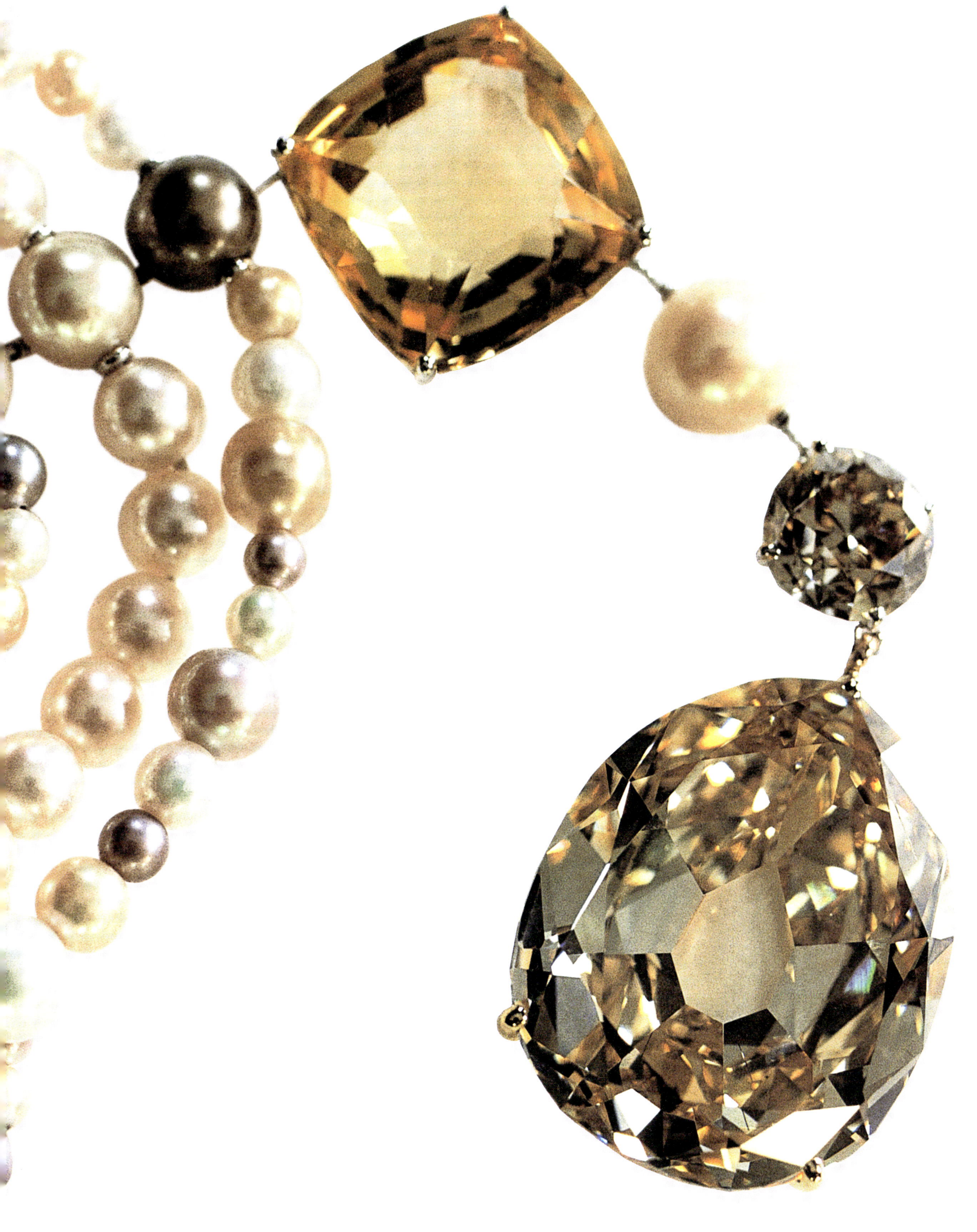

Necklace. Platinum, one 20.34-carat pear-shaped faceted pink sapphire, one heart-shaped diamond, baguette- and brilliant-cut and square-shaped diamonds, and natural pearls. Cartier Paris, 2006.

Facing page:
Necklace. Platinum, round old- and rose-cut diamonds, and natural pearls. Cartier Paris, 1911.

example of a choker was made in Paris in 1945: the center forms a long, biblike crescent combining white, black, gray, and bluish pearls with square-, baguette-, and pear-shaped diamonds; it originally had three pendants of drop-shaped pearls, of which one remains. In 1977 an illustrated article on this choker (which had come up at auction two years earlier) and on Elizabeth Taylor's famous drop-shaped pearl indicated that natural pearls were finally recovering the place they deserved, given their peerless beauty and their investment value.[27] A 1987 Baroda necklace, meanwhile, is a pointed bib of diamonds with a drop-shaped pearl at the end of each point. A 1970s necklace (based on a model from the 1910s), joined together three independent strands of increasing length, thereby setting three pendant pearls on the heart of the breast; it was worn with the deliberately gauzy and soft garments of a decade in search of voluptuousness.

Hippies in those days fueled their angelic mysticism with hallucinogenic substances, asserting that people were made for love; but by the end of the 1970s, punks were piercing their bodies and wearing swastikas, chains, and stud collars. The dream hadn't quite come true.

27. "Les perles, ne pas attendre pour les acheter." *Placements et Investissements* (October 1977).

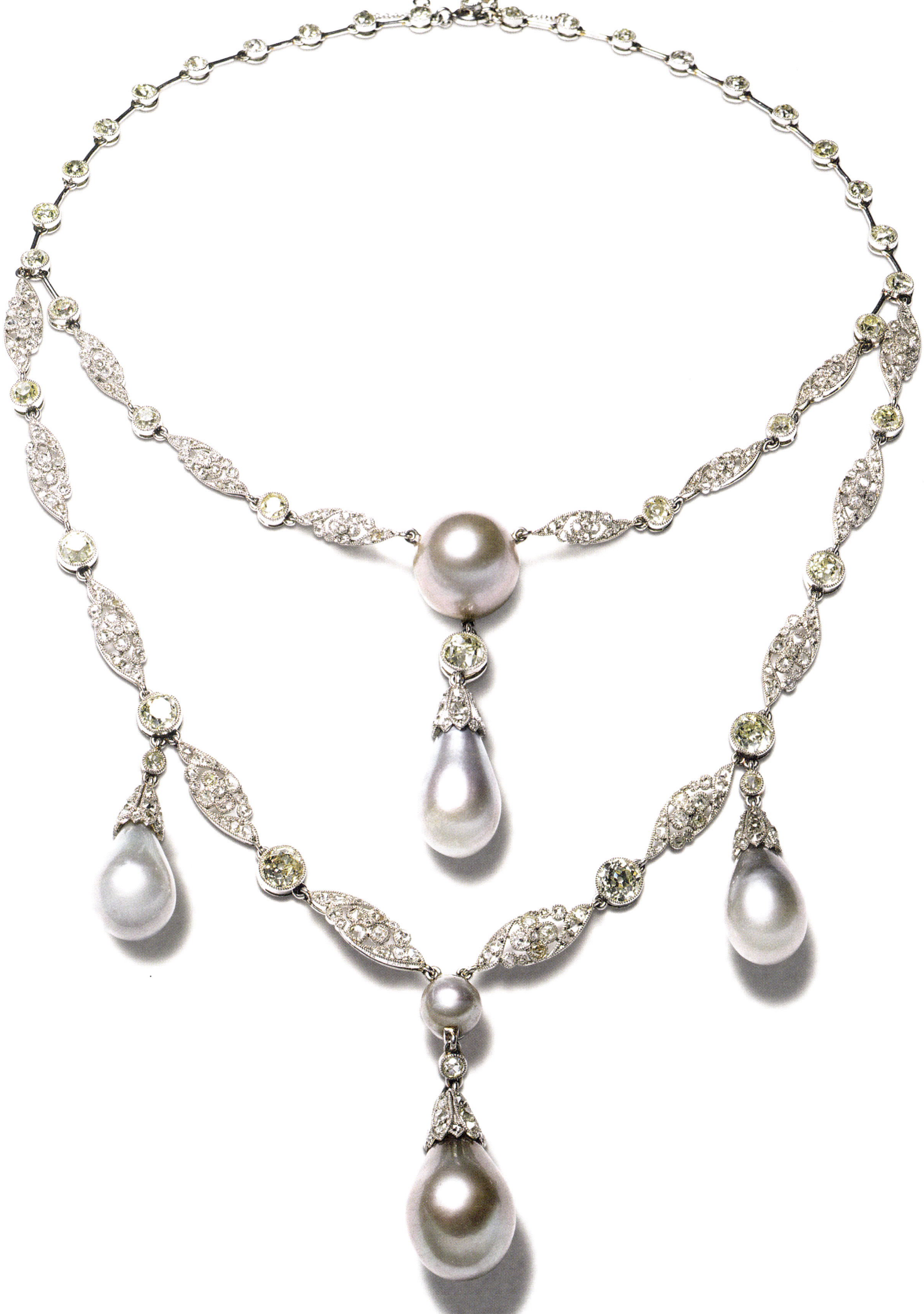

Sophia Loren, at Cartier's, is amazed by a rare, two-hundred-grain pearl. *Paris Match* (March 24, 1956).

Boule earrings. Platinum, yellow gold, seed pearls, and diamonds. Formerly the collection of the Duchess of Windsor. Cartier Paris, 1943.

Facing page:
Necklace of strands of pearls and an emerald twist. 1960. Photo: Horst P. Horst.

The 1980s saw hippies replaced by yuppies whose success, while personal, was certainly not private—success was flaunted to the max until the situation suddenly reversed due to stock-market crashes, wars, and other calamities. In 1991 the novel *American Psycho* by Bret Easton Ellis painted a devastating picture of the times—the protagonist, Patrick Bateman, is a yuppie by day but a cannibal by night. Also in fashion were serial killers. In the latter half of the 1980s, a new generation of designers emerged, including Helmut Lang, the Belgian Groupe des Six, and Martin Margiela, whose designs oscillated between an occasionally disturbing austerity and a great conceptual elegance. Garments slowly became more sober, lines more natural, beauty more interiorized. Hence a necklace of natural pearls made in the 1990s, a pure marvel dubbed "Divine," achieves perfection through carefully balanced chaos: a fine chain is extended on one side by a cascade of seventy-two pearls ranging from strong gray to delicate pink, dispersing then clustering as though a natural avalanche had decided it would be thus; on the other side, a gray drop-shaped pearl is preceded by pearls and diamonds. The Cartier de Lune collection, meanwhile, brought cultured pearls and their harmonic colors back into fashion, while natural pearls continue to yield highly rare items as magnificent as they are delicate: in 2006 an orchid of diamonds with mauve and yellow highlights emerged from a cluster of pink, mauve, pinkish gray, apricot, green-blue, purple, and pinkish cream pearls—it took years to assemble all these pearls, and simply listing them conjures up a dreamlike image.

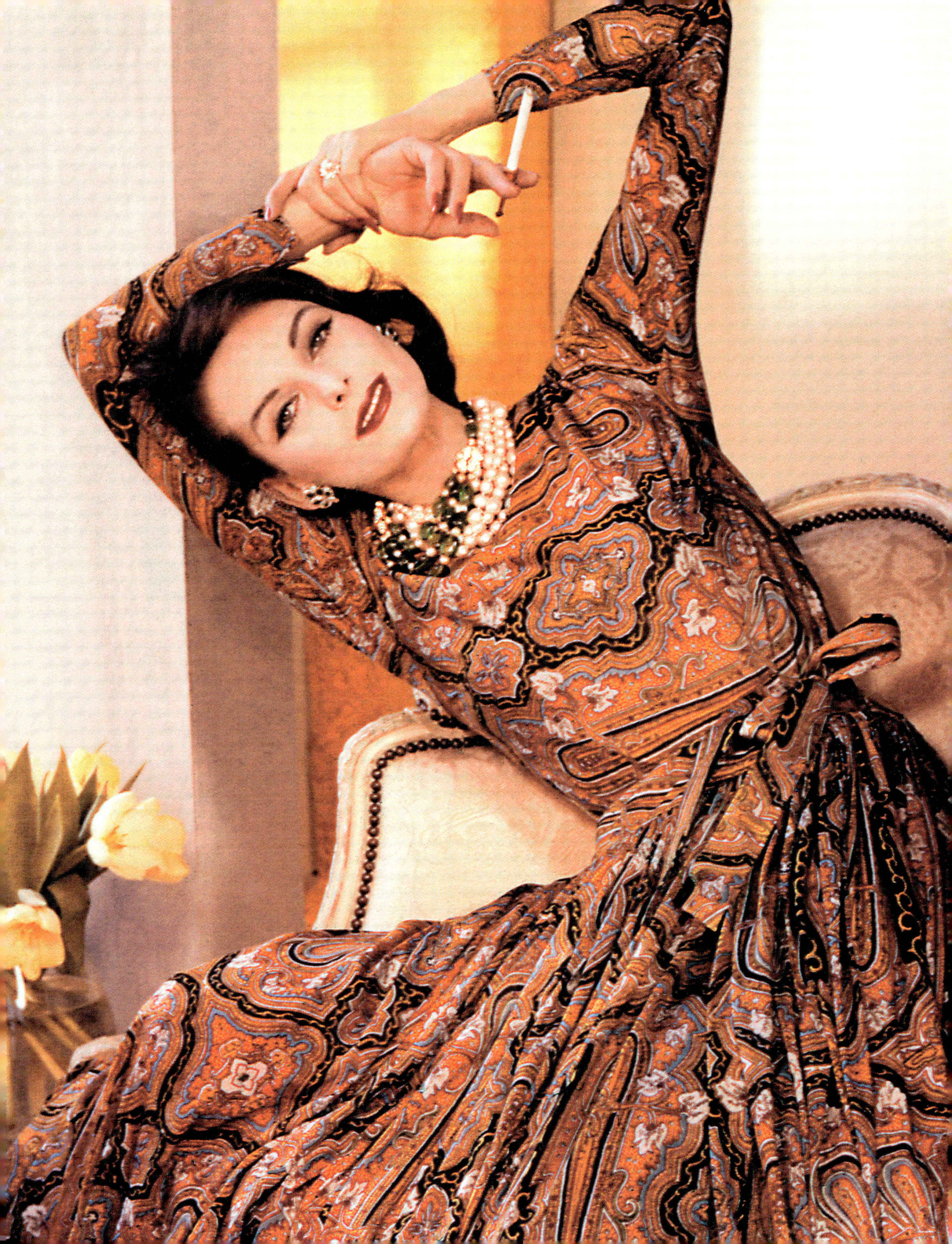

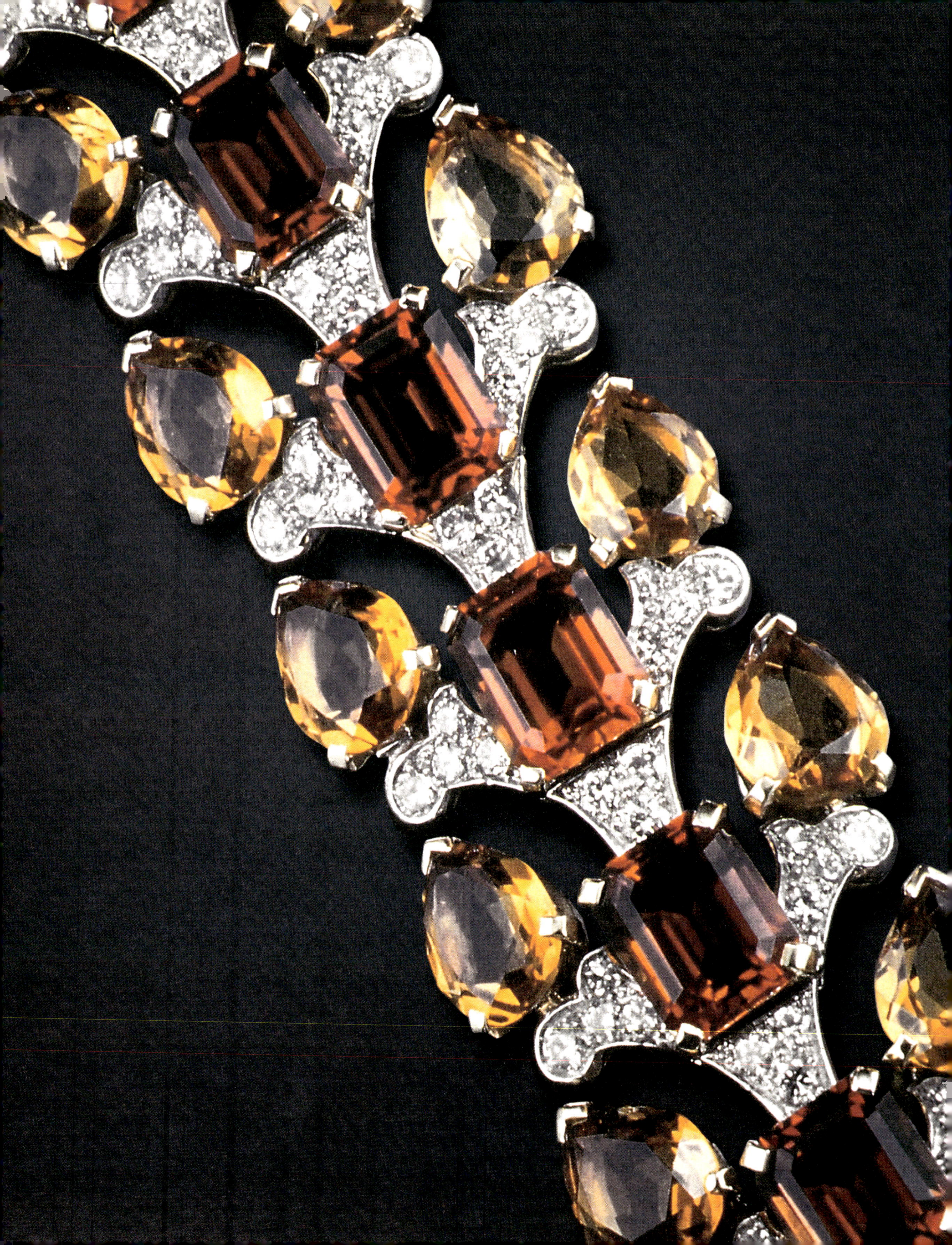

Coral,
Semiprecious Stones,
and Gems

Bracelet. Yellow gold and citrine. Cartier Paris, 1939.

Facing page:
Bracelet, detail. Platinum, citrines, and diamonds. Cartier London.

Cartier's palette has never lacked boldness or brilliance. The combination of blue and green, dubbed "peacock" and probably inspired by Islamic ceramics, appeared in a few pieces as early as 1903 and led to some wonderful work, especially in the 1920s. Placing the blue of sapphires or lapis lazuli against the green of emeralds or jade—judged inappropriate at the time according to conventional attitudes that typically castigate one day what they will hail the next—was one of those Cartier triumphs that stemmed from a spirit and a culture that went far beyond a specific time or place, which is what true innovation requires. During the troubled times that began in the 1930s, semiprecious stones were a remedy for the state of crisis. Less costly yet endowed with shimmering, varied colors, they made it possible to create several spectacular pieces that further enriched Cartier's palette. Handled with the same consideration and discernment as gemstones—with which they were often combined—semiprecious stones led design down the path of greater freedom.

In the 1940s, necklaces, clip brooches, and bracelets appeared in tones both warm and cool, in compositions both sober and geometric, using citrines ranging from pale yellow to dark Madeira set in gold, or aquamarines set in platinum. Two very fine, similar brooches of aquamarine were given to the future Queen Elizabeth by her parents for her eighteenth birthday in 1944. Photos show her wearing them on her lapel—sometimes combined into a single brooch—right into the 1960s.

In 1937 Cartier made an unusual orchid brooch of aquamarines and amethysts set in white gold. This duo seems to prefigure postwar designs with a bite that appealed to the likes of Daisy Fellowes and the Duchess of Windsor. When the duke had a necklace made in 1947 for which he supplied the diamonds and

Bouquet of Violets **brooch.** Pear-shaped amethysts, demantoid garnets, and brilliants. Cartier, c. 1950.

The Duke and Duchess of Windsor at Versailles during a cancer fund-raising event on June 16, 1953. The duchess is wearing her bib necklace.

Facing page:
Bib necklace. Platinum, twisted 18-karat and 20-karat gold, brilliant- and baguette-cut diamonds, one heart-shaped faceted amethyst, twenty-seven step-cut amethysts and one oval faceted amethyst, and turquoise cabochons. Formerly the collection of the Duchess of Windsor. Cartier Paris, special order, 1947.

amethysts, he quite rightly allowed himself to be convinced by Jeanne Toussaint of the need to add turquoises. Sure enough, the overall lines are harmonious, the step-cut amethysts, like the heart-shaped faceted amethyst, are superb, and the diamonds and twisted gold add light and warmth to their mysterious effect, yet it is the cold vivacity of the scattering of turquoise cabochons that transforms this piece of jewelry into a joyous and seductive object. Many other items played on this harmony—parures, torsade bracelets, a 1970 ring whose eight gold rings separate to form a bracelet, and a highly stylized floral brooch that creates a sense of height and volume around a central amethyst (Duchess of Windsor, c. 1950). The same color combination characterized a necklace seen in a 1971 issue of *Vogue* that published a full-page picture of a little girl with hair as "frothy" as her apricot-colored Sonia Rykiel bolero; everything about the photo testifies to the gulf separating the postwar fashion from the 1970s—everything, that is, except the color of the necklace.

Turquoise gained appreciation in Europe in the nineteenth century for its "forget-me-not" color. It can be used in tone-on-tone combinations with lapis lazuli or sapphires. A necklace for the Duchess of Bedford (c. 1950)

238

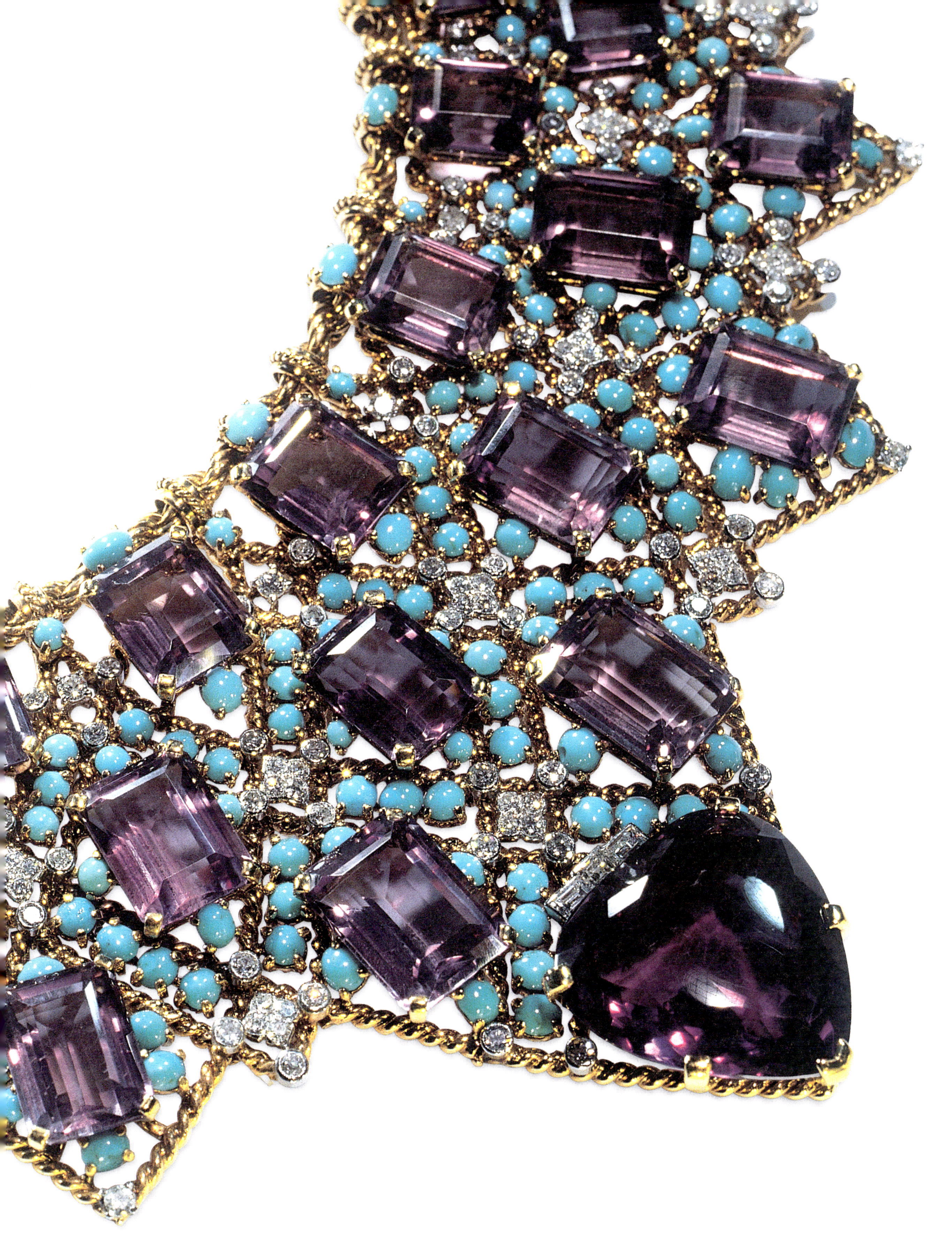

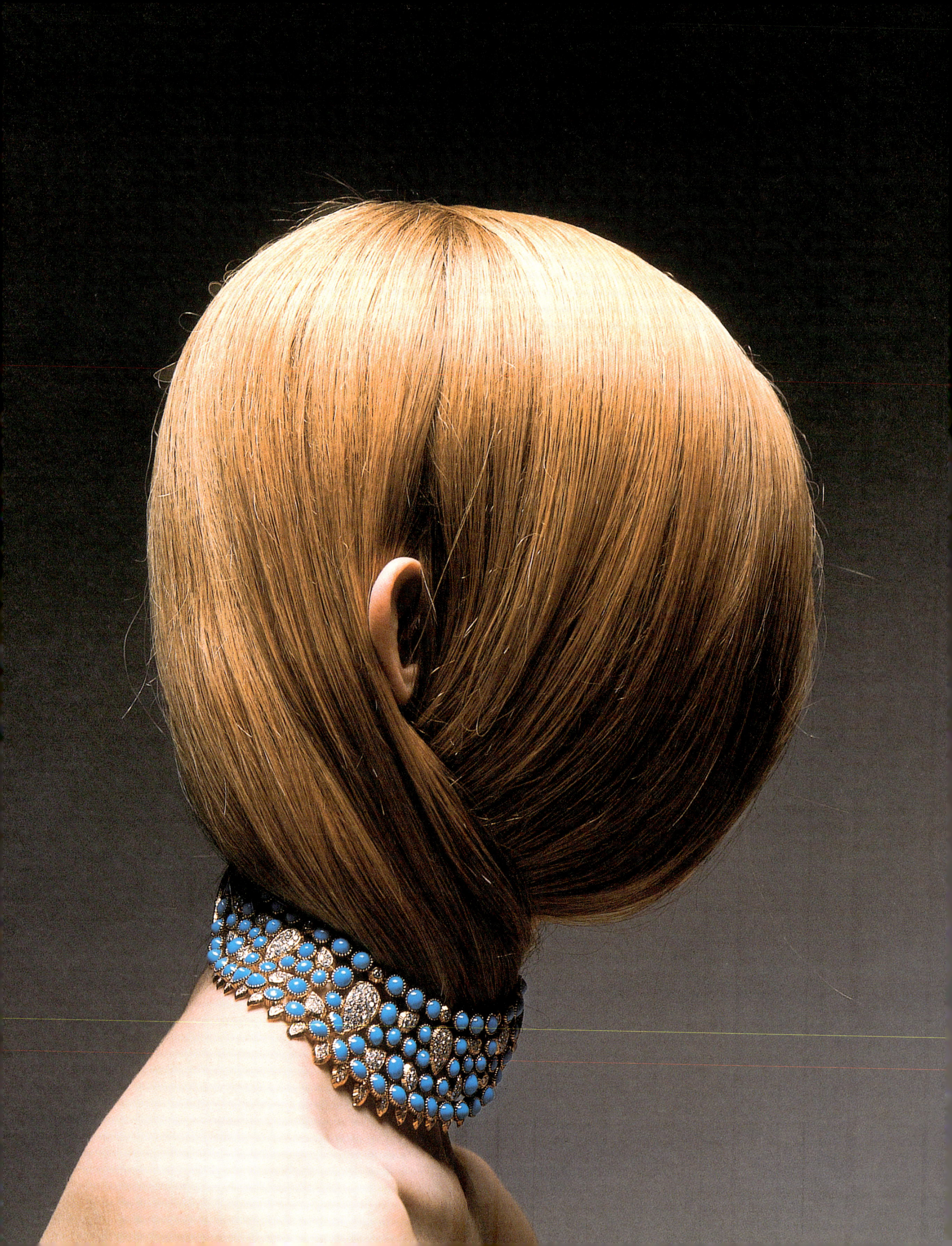

Bracelet. Turquoises and diamonds. Cartier Paris, 1958.

Facing page:
Bert Stern. *Vogue*, 1969.

242

Necklace. Beads of amethyst and fluted coral and diamonds on yellow gold, 2003.

Facing page: **Necklace.** Platinum, pink and purple spinels, cushion-shaped diamonds, natural pearls, and brilliants. Cartier Paris, 2006.

featured blue and green turquoises clustered with sapphires and diamonds. But the 1950s also produced many examples that combined gold, turquoise, and diamonds, such as a necklace forming a mesh of strands of gold dotted with brilliants and large blue cabochons (Cartier Paris, 1950).

In 1975 Guy Bourdin photographed a young woman wearing an airy silk dress by Yves Saint Laurent along with a similarly airy necklace of diamond-and-coral mesh, plus matching ring and bracelet. Ten years earlier, on the theme of wild beasts and coral, *Vogue* featured sandals by Mario Valentino and Roger Vivier alongside jewelry by Cartier; this time Bourdin's photograph showed only part of the model's body, whom the beholder imagines—the bust not being visible—wearing a monokini (a term barely one year old at the time): on her feet are sandals beaded with coral, on her finger a charming Cartier emerald and coral turtle, and on her wrist a strand of ribbed coral beads with a diamond clasp (a simple hook and loop dating from 1947, the year of the New Look, with which it shares the name). The cover of the trade magazine *L'Officiel de la couture et de la mode* showed a woman wearing a Grès white dress with asymmetrical neckline, lips painted the same coral red as her jewelry; her wrist is wrapped in three turns of coral and diamonds, her neck has a multistrand twist of pearls adorned with a bunch of red and white bellflowers. Coral—a strange animal once thought to be a petrified tree—has long been a rich source of inspiration to Cartier, and the 1920s saw the emergence of lasting combinations with black (onyx, enamel, jet), green (emerald), orange, and the white diamonds without which no composition would be complete. Black and orange are wonderfully elegant, enhancing the green light of

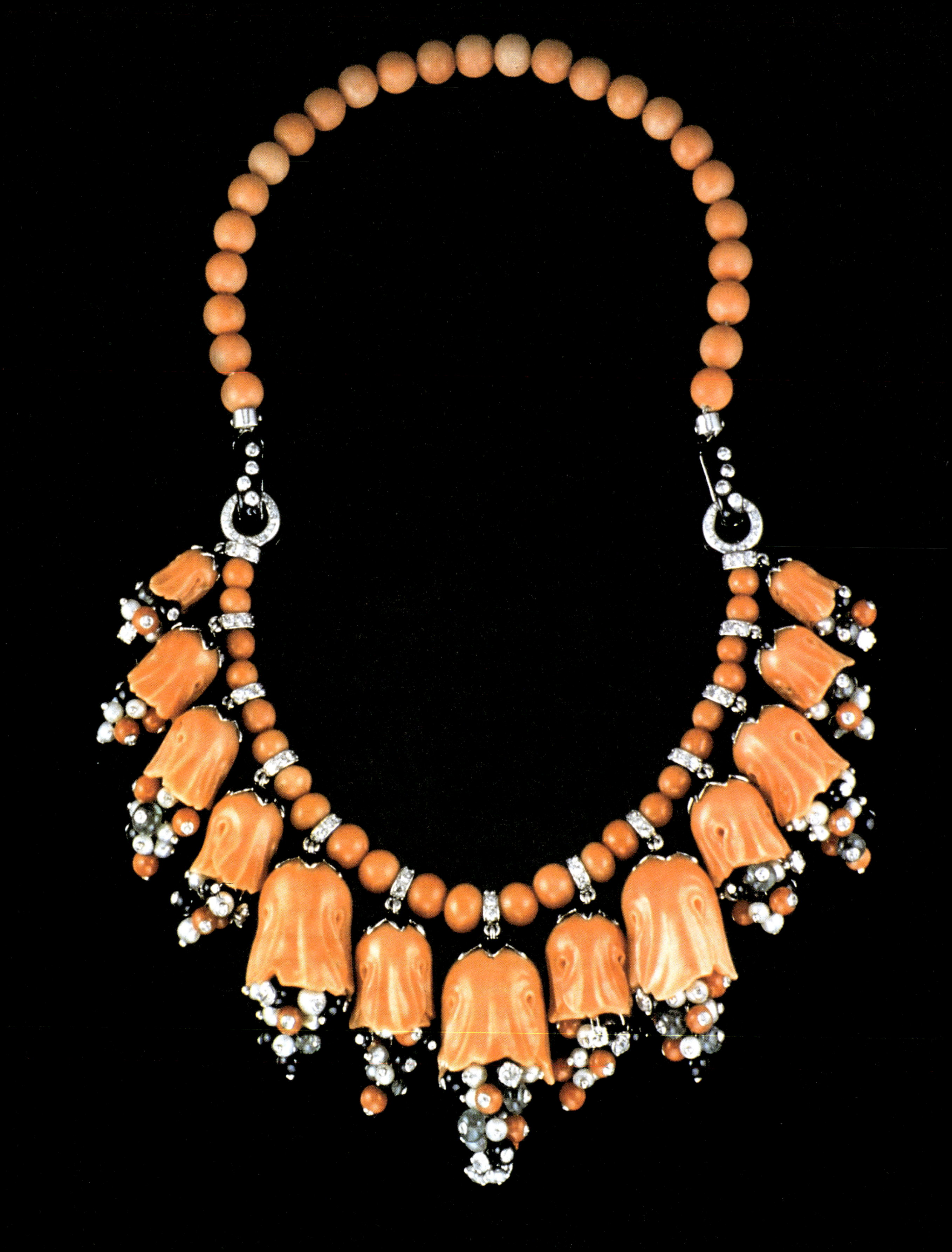

Brooch. Gold, diamonds, and coral. Cartier Paris, c. 1960.

Flower **brooch.** Yellow gold and platinum, spiraling bouquet of diamonds, leaves of gold, and rods of coral. Cartier Paris, 1970.

Flower **brooch.** Coral and brilliant-cut diamond, quivering leaves of engine-turned gold. Cartier Paris, 1960.

Facing page:
Necklace. String of coral beads, black enamel, and diamonds, from which hang thirteen carved coral bellflowers with clusters of coral, onyx, and emeralds. Formerly the collection of María Félix. Cartier Paris, 1934.

Turtle-Chimera **clock**. Chinese nineteenth-century carved coral figurine, diamonds, black enamel, white onyx, emeralds, and platinum. Cartier Paris, 1943.

Facing page:
Parure of coral, pearls, and diamonds. Cartier, 1954. Dress by Grès. *L'Officiel de la couture et de la mode* 393–94 (1954).

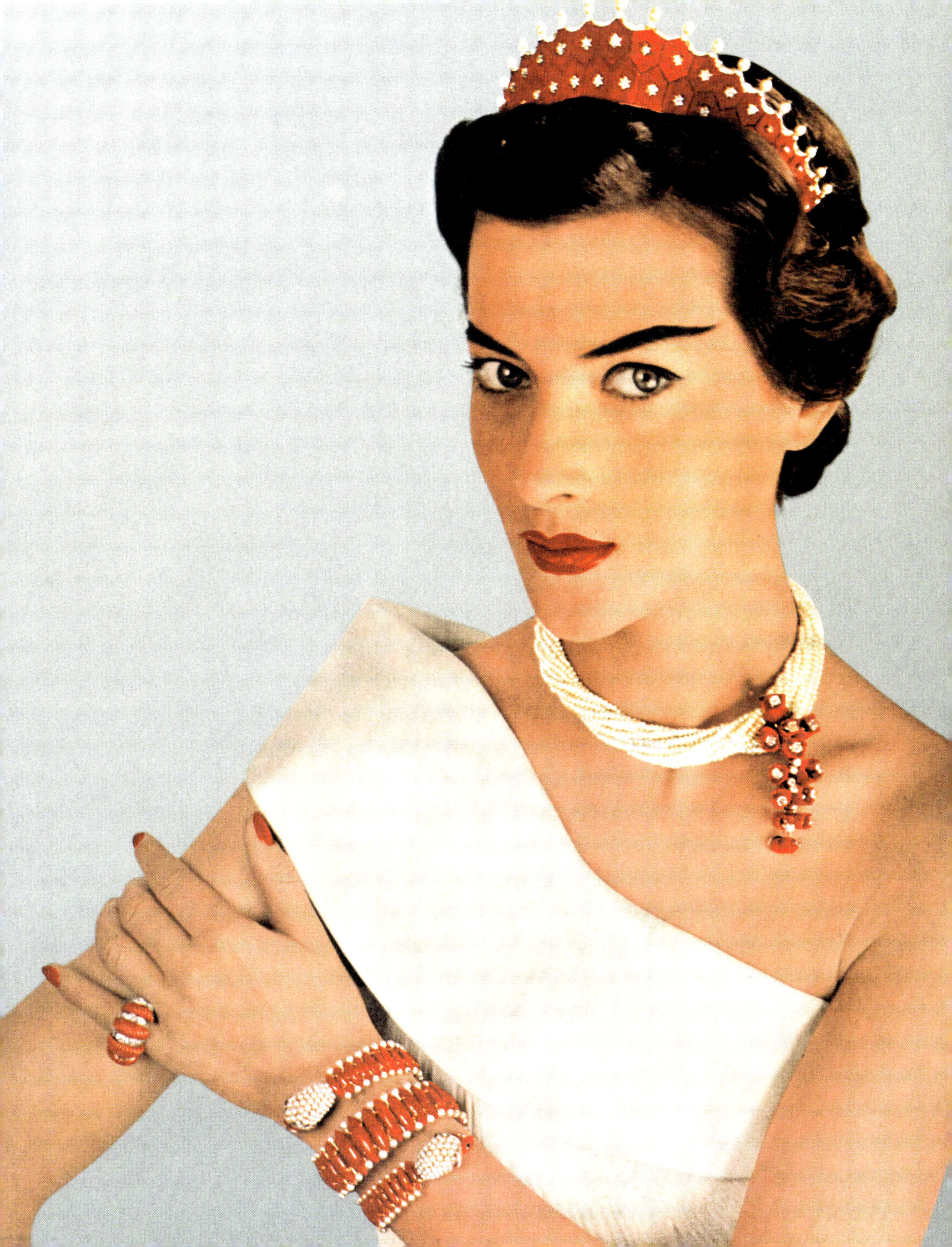

Bib necklace. Plaited gold, turquoise, and diamonds. Cartier Paris, 1956.

Snake **earrings**. Yellow and pink gold, rose-cut diamonds, rubies, and turquoise-colored enamel. Specially ordered by María Félix. Cartier Paris, 1971.

Bangle. Twisted yellow gold, yellow gold wire and polished yellow gold, white gold, brilliant-cut diamonds, and turquoise cabochons. The bracelet opens on a hinge. Cartier Paris, 1953.

emeralds all the more. In 1955 María Félix bought a necklace of coral beads and carved bellflowers from which there fell clusters of onyx and emeralds studded with diamonds; ten years later she bought earrings of upside-down crescents set with diamonds and emeralds. Right from the early 1930s, a bracelet featuring the famous panther motif was composed of three strands of ribbed coral beads, the middle one being higher than the other two and studded with collet-set diamonds. Over the years many precious clasps, both abstract and figurative, would enrich this particular model with swirls of diamonds or chimera heads.

Color is now enjoying its heyday, able to range from subtle harmonies to bold contrasts, from monochrome to combinations, from tradition to invention. Pearls, semiprecious stones, and fine gems offer an infinite range of hues, suggesting the work of a painter more than a jeweler when we contemplate an orchid or other piece. Petals, with their amazingly realistic modeling, are spangled with touches of color, from the palest to the darkest green, from pink to deepest garnet, from orange to light brown; this pointillist painting—or pixelated image—can be composed of spinels, demantoid garnets, or mandarin garnets. The strong but now timeless accents of the "peacock" look, Tutti Frutti compositions, and the tiger-skin pattern henceforth reign alongside the hues of a new spirit nourished by the power of a style constantly challenged yet always respected.

"If anything can save us, it's beauty," concluded the introduction to the catalog of the exhibition of *Cartier Design Viewed by Ettore Sottsass*. All dreams are still possible.

Bibliography

Amic, Yolande. *Intérieurs: Le Mobilier français, 1945–1964.* Paris: Éditions du Regard, 1983.

Anargyros, Sophie. *Intérieurs: Le Mobilier français, 1980.* Paris: Éditions du Regard, 1983.

Balfour, Ian. *Famous Diamonds.* Christie's, 1987.

Bari, Hubert, and Violaine Sautter. *Diamants.* Paris: Muséum national d'histoire naturelle / Adam Biro, 2001.

Barracca, Jader, Giampiero Negretti, and Franco Nencini. *Le Temps de Cartier.* Milan: Wrist International, 1989.

Beaton, Cecil. With a preface by Christian Dior. *Cinquante ans d'élégance et d'art de vivre.* Paris: Amiot-Dumont, 1954.

Beaud, Marie-Claude, Jean de Loisy, and Hervé Chandès. *Fondation Cartier pour l'art contemporain.* Arles: Cartier / Acte Sud, 2004.

Bennett, David, and Daniela Maschetti. *Understanding Jewelry.* London: Antique Collectors' Club, 1989, 1996.

Bieler, Rüdiger, Benett Bronson, Paula M. Mikkelen, and Neil H. Landman. *Pearls: A Natural History.* New York: American Museum of Natural History / Harry N Abrams, Inc., 2001.

Bollon, Patrice. With illustrations by Stefano Canulli. *Précis d'extravagance.* Paris: Éditions du Regard, 1995.

Bony, Anne. *Les Années 40.* Paris: Éditions du Regard, 1985.

Brunhammer, Yvonne. *Le Mobilier français: 1930–1960.* Paris: Massin, 1997.

Bure, Gilles de. *Intérieurs, Le Mobilier français: 1965–1979.* Paris: Éditions du Regard, 1983.

Cartier: L'Album. Paris: Éditions du Regard, 2003.

Cartlidge, Barbara. *Les Bijoux au XX siècle.* Paris: Éditions Payot, 1986.

Cerval, Marguerite de, ed. *Dictionnaire international du bijou.* Paris: Éditions du Regard, 1998.

Cerval, Marguerite de. *Mauboussin.* Paris: Éditions du Regard, 1992.

Chaille, François, and Eric Nussbaum. *The Cartier Collection: Jewelry.* Paris: Flammarion, 2004.

Chaille, François, and Franco Cologni. *The Cartier Collection: Timepieces.* Paris: Flammarion, 2006.

Chaille, François. *Cartier: Creative Writing.* Paris: Flammarion, 2000.

Chaille, François. *Cartier: Innovation through the Twentieth Century.* Paris: Flammarion, 2007.

Chazal, Gilles. *L'Art de Cartier.* Exh. cat. Paris: Musée du Petit Palais, 1989.

Cologni, Franco. *Cartier: The Tank Watch.* Paris: Flammarion, 1998.

Cologni, Franco, and Ettore Mocchetti. *L'Objet Cartier: 150 ans de tradition et d'innovation.* Lausanne: Bibliothèque des arts, 1992.

Cologni, Franco, and Eric Nussbaum. *Cartier: Le joaillier du platine.* Lausanne: Bibliothèque des arts, 1995.

Cologni, Franco, and Eric Nussbaum. *Cartier: Splendeurs de la joaillerie.* Paris: Bibliothèque des arts, 1996.

Culme, John, and Nicholas Rayner. *The Jewels of the Duchess of Windsor.* New York: Rizzoli International Publications, 1987.

Daufresne, Jean-Claude. *Fêtes à Paris au XX siècle: Architectures éphémères de 1919 à 1989.* Belgium: Mardaga, 2001.

Demornex, Jacqueline, and Marie-Andrée Jouve. *Cristobal Balenciaga.* Paris: Éditions du Regard, 1988.

Destino, Ralph. *Rétrospective Louis Cartier.* Cartier, 1976.

Edkins, Diana, and Ki Hackney. *People & Pearls.* London: Aurum Press, 2000.

Epées de joaillier. Cartier, 1972.

Face à l'histoire 1933–1996. Exh.cat. Paris: Centre Georges Pompidou, 1996.

Fasel, Marion, Debra Healy, and Penny Proddow. *Hollywood Jewels: Movies, Jewelry, Stars.* New York: Abradale / Harry N. Abrams, Inc., 1996.

Fasel, Marion, and Penny Proddow. *Diamonds, a Century of Spectacular Jewels.* New York: Harry N. Abrams, Inc., 1996.

Fasel, Marion, and Penny Proddow. *With this Ring: The Ultimate Guide to Wedding Jewelry.* New York: Bulfinch Press, 2004.

Field, Leslie. *The Queen's Jewels: The Personal Collection of Elizabeth II.* London: Guild Publishing, 1987.

Gabardi, Melissa. *Les Bijoux des années 1950.* Paris: Éditions de l'Amateur, 1987.

Gabardi, Melissa, and Solange Schnall. *Bijoux de l'Art Déco aux années 1940.* Paris: Éditions de l'Amateur, 1986.

Gautier, Gilberte. *La Saga des Cartier: 1847–1988.* Paris: Éditions Michel Lafon, 1988.

Gidel, Henry. *Cocteau.* Paris: Flammarion, 1998.

Giroud, Françoise. *Dior.* Paris: Éditions du Regard, 1987.

Hue-Williams, Sarah. *Guide de la joaillerie.* Paris: Christie's / Assouline, Paris, 2001.

Jean Cocteau sur le fils du siècle. Exh. cat. Paris: Centre Georges Pompidou, 2004.

The Jewels of the Duchess of Windsor. Sotheby's Geneva, April 2–3, 1987.

Jullian, Philippe. *Les Styles.* Paris: Plon, 1961.

Lasowski, Patrick Wald, and Anne-Marie Clais. *Boucheron: La Capture de l'éclat.* Paris: Éditions Cercle d'art, 2005.

Lemaire, Gérard-Georges. *Les Cafés littéraires.* Paris: Éditions de la Différence, 1997.

Mascetti, Daniela, and Amanda Triossi. *Earrings: From Antiquity to the Present,* London: Thames & Hudson, 1991.

Mascetti, Daniela, and Amanda Triossi. *The Necklace: From Antiquity to the Present.* London: Thames & Hudson, 1997.

Nadelhoffer, Hans. *Cartier.* Paris: Éditions du Regard, 1984, 2007. London: Thames & Hudson, 1984, 2007.

Papi, Stefano, and Alexandra Rhodes. *Les plus belles collections de bijoux.* Paris: Bibliothèque des arts, 1999.

Raulet, Sylvie. *Bijoux des années 1940–1950.* Paris: Éditions du Regard, 1987.

Raulet, Sylvie. *Van Cleef & Arpels.* Paris: Éditions du Regard, 1986.

Sottsass, Ettore. *Le design Cartier vu par Ettore Sottsass.* Paris: Skira / Le Seuil, 2002.

Tennenbaum, Suzanne, and Janet Zapata. *The Jeweled Garden.* New York: Vendome Press, 2006.

Tennenbaum, Suzanne, and Janet Zapata. *The Jeweled Menagerie.* London: Thames & Hudson, 2001.

Vachaudez, Christophe. *Bijoux des reines et princesses de Belgique.* Brussels: Racine, 2004.

Ward, Anne, John Cherry, Charlotte Gere, and Barbara Cartlidge. *La Bague de l'Antiquité à nos jours.* Paris: Bibliothèque des arts, 1981.

Zapata, Janet, Ulysses Dietz, and Zette Emmons. *Gems from the East and West: The Doris Duke Jewelry Collection.* New York: Doris Duke Charitable Connection, 2003.

Photographic Credits

P. 2: Thierry Malty © Cartier. **P. 4:** Thierry Malty © Cartier. **P. 6:** Tim Griffiths © Cartier. **P. 8:** Archives Cartier © Cartier. **P. 10:** From left to right: Mary of England, © Collection C. Boulay. Easter egg, © Courtesy Metropolitan Museum of Art, New York. Louis Cartier, Photo Nadar, Archives Cartier © Cartier. Grand Duchess Maria Pavlovna, © Collection C. Boulay. Jacques Cartier, Archives Cartier © Cartier. Corsage ornament, Archives Cartier © Cartier. **P. 11:** From left to right: Pierre Cartier, All rights reserved, Brooch, Archives Cartier © Cartier. Consuelo Vanderbilt, Archives Cartier © Cartier. Corsage ornament, Archives Cartier © Cartier. Grand Duchess Olga, Archives Cartier © Cartier. **PP. 12–13:** Archives Cartier © Cartier. **P. 14:** From left to right: Bib necklace, Archives Cartier © Cartier. Mystery clock, Collection Cartier, photo Nick Welsh © Cartier. Jeanne Toussaint, Archives Cartier © Cartier. The Begum, photo Fayer of Vienna © Illustrated London News Picture Library. **P. 15:** From left to right: Queen Mary of Romania, Archives Cartier © Cartier. Maharajah Sir Yadavindra Singh, © Courtesy John Fasal Collection. Powder compact and lipstick holder, Collection Cartier, photo Nick Welsh © Cartier. Shoulder ornament *Bérénice*, Archives Cartier © Cartier. *Tutti frutti* necklace, Collection Cartier, photo Nick Welsh © Cartier. **P. 16:** From left to right: Cartier boutique, New York, Archives Cartier © Cartier. Lady Mendl, photo François Kollar / RMN. *Chimera* mystery clock, Collection Cartier, photo Nick Welsh © Cartier. Barbara Hutton, © Cecil Beaton photograph. **P. 17:** From left to right: *Bow-knot* brooch, Archives Cartier © Cartier. Mrs Carl Bendix, Archives Cartier © Cartier. Lipstick holder and powder compact brooch Collection Cartier, photo Nick Welsh © Cartier. Horst P. Horst for © *Vogue* / Condé Nast Publications Inc. Courtesy *Vogue* US. Brooch, Collection Cartier, photo Nick Welsh © Cartier. **P. 18:** From left to right: Brooch, Collection Cartier, photo Nick Welsh © Cartier. Horst P. Horst for *Vogue*, © *Vogue* / Condé Nast Publications Inc., courtesy *Vogue* US. Ear pendants, Collection Cartier, photo Nick Welsh © Cartier. Diamond necklace, George Hoyningen-Huene for *Vogue Studio* Paris, © *Vogue* / Condé Nast Publications Inc. Courtesy *Vogue* US. Cartier boutique, London, Archives Cartier © Cartier. Fibula brooch, Collection Cartier, photo Nick Welsh © Cartier. **P. 19:** From left to right: Vase brooch, Collection Cartier, photo Nick Welsh © Cartier. *Allegory of America*, © María Félix / A. Tzapoff. *Drawings of the Third Days*, Fondation Cartier for l'art contemporain, photo Florian Kleinefenn. **P. 20:** Photo Eyedea / Keystone France. **PP. 22–23:** From left to right: Collection Cartier, photo Nick Welsh © Cartier. Courtesy Sotheby's © Photo Sotheby's. Collection Cartier, photo Nick Welsh © Cartier. Courtesy Sotheby's © Photo Sotheby's. Collection Cartier, photo Nick Welsh © Cartier. **P. 24:** *Oiseau libéré*, Collection Cartier, photo Nick Welsh © Cartier. *Bird's nest*, Collection Cartier, photo Nick Welsh © Cartier. *Bird brooch*, courtesy Etude Tajan, photo Philippe Sebert. **P. 25:** Courtesy Sotheby's © Photo Sotheby's. **P. 26:** © Bettmann / Corbis. **P. 27:** Photo Louis Tirilly © Cartier. **P. 28:** From left to right: Courtesy Sotheby's © Photo Sotheby's. © Cartier. Courtesy Sotheby's © Photo Sotheby's. Courtesy Christie's © Photo Christie's. Courtesy Sotheby's © Photo Sotheby's. Bottom: Courtesy Sotheby's, photo Sotheby's. **P. 29:** Photo André Ostier. **P. 30:** Archives Cartier © Cartier. **P. 31:** From top to bottom: Collection Cartier, photo Nick Welsh © Cartier. © Cartier. Collection Cartier, photo Nick Welsh © Cartier. **P. 32:** From left to right: Collection Cartier, photo Nick Welsh. © Cartier. © Cartier. Courtesy Christie's © Photo Christie's. Bottom: Courtesy Sotheby's © Photo Sotheby's. **P. 33:** Two *Parrots*: Courtesy Sotheby's © Photo Sotheby's. Bottom: Photo Katel Riou © Cartier. **P. 34:** © Ateliers ABC / Cartier. **P. 35:** From top to bottom: Courtesy Pierre Bergé & Associés, photo Philippe Sebert. Courtesy Christie's © Photo Christie's. © Cartier. **P. 36:** *Cowboy duck*, © Cartier. *Duck*, © Cartier. T*wo ducks*, Collection Cartier, photo Nick Welsh © Cartier. *Clip brooch*, Courtesy Etude Beaussant-Lefèvre. *Three ducks*, Courtesy Sotheby's © Photo Sotheby's. *Duck head*, Collection Cartier, photo Nick Welsh © Cartier. **P. 37:** From left to right: Courtesy Christie's © Photo Christie's. Courtesy Sotheby's © Photo Sotheby's. **P. 38:** From left to right: Courtesy Christie's © Photo Christie's. Courtesy Sotheby's © Photo Sotheby's. **P. 39:** Private collection, photo Tino Hammid / GIA. **P. 40:** Archives Cartier © Cartier. **P. 41:** From left to right: Photo Daniel Podva © Cartier. © Cartier. **P. 42:** From left to right: Courtesy Pierre Bergé & Associés, photo Philippe Sebert. Archives Cartier © Cartier. Courtesy Sotheby's © Photo Sotheby's. **P. 43:** Courtesy Sotheby's, photo Sotheby's. **P. 44:** Photo Tino Hammid / GIA. **P. 45:** *Ladybird* brooch, private collection, photo Jean-Michel Tardy. *Ladybirds* broochs, Courtesy Etude Tajan, photo Philippe Sebert. *Clip brooch* and *Earrings*, Collection Cartier, photo Nick Welsh © Cartier. **P. 46:** From top to bottom: Collection Cartier, photo Nick Welsh © Cartier. Courtesy Sotheby's, photo Sotheby's. © Cartier. Collection Cartier, photo Nick Welsh © Cartier. **P. 47:** Irving Penn, *Model with Dragonfly by Cartier on her Face*. New York, 1966.© 1966. Condé Nast Publications Inc. **P. 48:** Collection Cartier, photo Nick Welsh © Cartier. **P. 49:** Courtesy Pierre Bergé & Associés, photo Philippe Sebert. **P. 50:** From left to right: Courtesy Artcurial, All rights reserved Photo Jean-Michel Tardy. 3-private collection. Courtesy Sotheby's © Photo Sotheby's. **P. 51:** From left to right: Collection Cartier. © Cartier. Collection Cartier, photo Nick Welsh © Cartier. Collection Cartier, photo Nick Welsh © Cartier. **P. 52:** Top: Collection Cartier, photo Nick Welsh © Cartier. Bottom: Courtesy Etude Tajan, photo Philippe Sebert. **P. 53:** © Cartier. **P. 54:** From left to right, top: Collection Cartier, photo Nick Welsh © Cartier. © Cartier. © Cartier. Collection Cartier, photo Nick Welsh © Cartier. Bottom: Collection Cartier, photo Nick Welsh © Cartier. **P. 55:** Collection Cartier, photo Nick Welsh © Cartier. **P. 56:** Courtesy Cartier, All rights reserved **P 57:** From top to bottom: Archives Cartier © Cartier. Photo Luc Fournol © Cartier. **P. 58:** From top to bottom: Photo Katel Riou © Cartier. Photo Roger-Viollet. Photo Katel Riou © Cartier. **P. 59:** Top: Courtesy Etude Tajan, photo Philippe Sebert. Bottom: All rights reserved **P. 60:** Top: © Cartier. Bottom: Collection Cartier, photo Nick Welsh © Cartier. **P. 61:** Archives Cartier © Cartier. **P. 62:** Collection Cartier, photo Nick Welsh © Cartier. **P. 63:** Collection Cartier, photo Nick Welsh © Cartier. **P. 64:** Photo Katel Riou © Cartier. **P. 65:** Photo Philippe Massard © Éditions Assouline. **P. 66:** Brooch: Collection Cartier, photo Nick Welsh © Cartier. Poster: D. R. **P. 67:** Courtesy Sotheby's, photo Sotheby's. **P. 68:** Photo Katel Riou © Cartier. **P. 69:** Photo Jacques Boulay © Cartier. **P. 70:** © Cartier. **P. 71:** From top to bottom: Courtesy Sotheby's, photo Sotheby's, Genève. Photo Louis Tirilly © Cartier. Courtesy Artcurial, photo Philippe Sebert. **P. 72:** Bracelets: © Cartier. Bag: Collection Cartier, photo Nick Welsh © Cartier. **P. 73:** Collection Cartier, photo Nick Welsh © Cartier. **P. 74:** From top to bottom: Collection Cartier, photo Nick Welsh © Cartier. Photo Jon Brenneis / Time Life Pictures © Getty Images. **P. 75:** E. Sottsass © Sottsass Associati / Cartier. **P. 76:** From left to right: Photo Laurent Tirilly © Cartier. Courtesy Sotheby's, photo Sotheby's. Bottom: Courtesy Pierre Bergé & Associés, photo Philippe Sebert. **P. 77:** From left to right: © Courtesy Sotheby's, photo Sotheby's. Guy Bouchet © Cartier. Bottom: Cartier. **P. 78:** Collection Cartier, photo Nick Welsh © Cartier. **P. 79:** Collection Cartier, photo Nick Welsh © Cartier. **P. 80:** Private collection, © Cartier, All rights reserved **P. 81:** From top to bottom: Fondation Pierre Cartier, Geneva, photo M. Kuchen, © ADAGP Paris, 2008. Collection Cartier, photo Nick Welsh © Cartier. **P. 82:** From top to bottom: Collection Cartier, photo Nick Welsh © Cartier. Bottom: © Cartier. **P. 83:** From top to bottom: Collection Cartier, photo Nick Welsh © Cartier. © Cartier, All rights reserved **P. 84:** From top to bottom: Courtesy Christie's, photo Christie's. Collection Cartier, photo Nick Welsh © Cartier. **P. 85:** Cartier Paris, 2005, photo Katel Riou © Cartier. **P. 86:** Collection Cartier, photo Nick Welsh © Cartier. **P. 87:** Archives Cartier © Cartier. **PP. 88–89:** Collection Cartier, photo Patricia Canino © Éditions du Regard. **P. 90:** Collection Cartier, photo Nick Welsh © Cartier. **P. 91:** Photo Mitchell Feinberg © Cartier. **P. 92:** Collection Cartier, photo Nick Welsh © Cartier. **P. 93:** From top to bottom: Photo Katel Riou © Cartier. Photo Mitchell Feinberg © Cartier. **P. 94:** From left to right: Courtesy Sotheby's, photo Sotheby's. Collection Cartier, photo Nick Welsh © Cartier. Courtesy Christie's, photo Christie's. Courtesy Christie's, photo Christie's. **P. 95:** © Cartier. *Giraffe*: Photo A. Savitch © Cartier. **P. 96:** From left to right: © Cartier. © Cartier. Courtesy Primavera Gallery, New York. Bottom: All rights reserved **P. 97:** From top to bottom: Cartier. Collection Cartier, photo Nick Welsh © Cartier. **P. 98:** Courtesy Sotheby's, photo Sotheby's. **P. 99:** From left to right: Collection Cartier, photo Nick Welsh © Cartier. © Cartier. Collection Cartier, photo Nick Welsh © Cartier. Courtesy Christie's, photo Christie's. **P. 100:** Courtesy Pierre Bergé & Associés, photo Philippe Sebert. **P. 101:** Top: © Cartier. Bottom (3 photos): Collection Cartier, photo Nick Welsh © Cartier. **P. 102:** © Marcus Adams / Cartier. Archives Cartier © Cartier. **P. 103:** From left to right: Courtesy Sotheby's, photo Sotheby's. Courtesy Christie's, photo Christie's. Courtesy Christie's, photo Christie's. **P. 104:** *Coral flower brooch:* Courtesy Etude Tajan, photo Philippe Sebert. Dessins: Archives Cartier © Cartier. *Flower brooch:* Courtesy Christie's, photo Christie's. **P. 105:** From top to bottom: Photo Horst P. Horst / Courtesy *Vogue* © 1942. Archives Cartier © Cartier. Two bottom pictures: Courtesy Sotheby's, photo Sotheby's. **P. 106:** Top: © Cartier. Other photos: Collection Cartier, photo Nick Welsh © Cartier. **P. 107:** Courtesy Christie's, photo Christie's. **P. 108:** Archives Cartier © Cartier. **P. 109:** Photo A. Durst. ©Vogue / Condé-Nast. **P. 110:** Courtesy Sotheby's, photo Sotheby's. **P. 111:** From top to bottom: Courtesy Sotheby's, photo Sotheby's. Courtesy Antiquorum, All rights reserved Photo Nick Welsh © Cartier. **P. 112:** Archives Cartier © Cartier. **P. 113:** © *L'Officiel de la couture et de la mode.* **P. 114:** Photo R. Rutledge © Vogue / Condé Nast. **P. 115:** From left to right, top: Collection Cartier, photo Nick Welsh © Cartier. © Cartier. © Cartier. Courtesy Sotheby's, photo Sotheby's. Bottom: © Cartier. **P. 116:** © Cartier. **P. 117:** Top: Collection Cartier, photo Nick Welsh © Cartier. Bottom, from left to right: Archives Cartier © Cartier. Archives Cartier © Cartier. Courtesy Etude Couteau-Bégarie. Archives Cartier © Cartier. **P. 118:** From left to right, first line: Courtesy Christie's, photo Christie's. Archives Cartier © Cartier. Collection Cartier, photo Nick Welsh © Cartier. All other pictures: Archives Cartier © Cartier. **P. 119:** Archives Cartier © Cartier. **P. 120:** Archives Cartier © Cartier. **P. 121:** From top to bottom: © Cartier. Collection Cartier, photo Nick Welsh © Cartier. © Cartier. © Cartier. Collection Cartier, photo Nick Welsh © Cartier. **P. 122:** From top to bottom: Collection Cartier, photo Nick Welsh © Cartier. Courtesy Sotheby's, photo Sotheby's. © Cartier. **P. 123:** From top to bottom: Photo Katel Riou © Cartier. Courtesy Christie's, photo Christie's. Collection Cartier, photo Nick Welsh © Cartier. Courtesy Sotheby's, photo Sotheby's. **P. 124:** Collection Cartier, photo Nick Welsh © Cartier. **P. 125:** Photo Katel Riou © Cartier. **P. 126:** Photo Katel Riou © Cartier. **P. 127:** Photo Katel Riou © Cartier. **P. 128:** © Cartier, photo Jean-Michel Tardy. **P. 130:** Courtesy Sotheby's, photo Sotheby's. **P. 131:** Collection Cartier, photo Nick Welsh © Cartier. **P. 132:** Collection Cartier, photo Nick Welsh © Cartier. **P. 133:** Collection Cartier, photo Nick Welsh © Cartier. **P. 134:** Courtesy Christie's, photo Christie's. **P. 135:** All rights reserved **P. 136:** From top to bottom: Courtesy Sotheby's, photo Sotheby's. Collection Cartier, photo Nick Welsh © Cartier. Courtesy Sotheby's, photo Sotheby's. **P. 137:** Courtesy Sotheby's, photo Sotheby's. **P. 138:** Courtesy Sotheby's, photo Sotheby's. **P. 139:** From top to bottom: Courtesy Sotheby's, photo Sotheby's. © Cartier. **P. 140:** Top: Archives Cartier © Cartier. Bottom: © Cartier. **P. 141:** © *L'Officiel de la couture et de la mode.* **P. 142:** © Cartier. **P. 143:** Photo Michel Feinberg © Cartier. **P. 144:** Courtesy Siegelson, New York. **P. 145:** Courtesy Sotheby's, photo Sotheby's. **P. 146:** From top to bottom: Courtesy Sotheby's, photo Sotheby's. © Cartier. **P. 147:** Courtesy Sotheby's, photo Sotheby's. **P. 148:** © Cartier. **P. 149:** Top: © Cartier. Bottom: Courtesy Sotheby's, photo Sotheby's. **P. 150:** Collection Cartier, photo Nick Welsh © Cartier. **P. 151:** From top to bottom: © *L'Officiel de la couture et de la mode.* Collection Cartier, photo Nick Welsh © Cartier. © Cartier. **P. 152:** From top to bottom: Courtesy Tajan, photo Philippe Sebert. Courtesy Sotheby's, photo Sotheby's. **P. 153:** © Cartier. **P. 155:** © Cartier, photo Jean-Michel Tardy. **P. 156:** Collection Cartier, photo Nick Welsh © Cartier. **P. 157:** Photo Mitchell Feinberg © Cartier. **P. 158:** Collection Cartier, photo Nick Welsh © Cartier. **P. 159:** © Cartier, photo Mitchell Feinberg. **P. 160:** Photo Katel Riou © Cartier. **P. 161:** Photo Jacques Boulay © Cartier. **P. 162:** Courtesy Artcurial, All rights reserved **P. 163:** © Cartier, photo Katel Riou. **P. 164:** Photo Bert Stern © Condé Nast Publications. **P. 165:** From top to bottom, from left to right: Collection Cartier, photo Nick Welsh © Cartier. Collection Cartier, photo Nick Welsh © Cartier. Photo Katel Riou © Cartier. Collection Cartier, photo Nick Welsh © Cartier. Courtesy Pierre Bergé & Associés, photo Philippe Sebert. Photo Katel Riou © Cartier. Collection Cartier, photo Nick Welsh © Cartier. **P. 166:** From top to bottom: Collection Cartier, photo Nick Welsh © Cartier. Collection Cartier, photo Nick Welsh © Cartier. Photo Mitchell Feinberg © Cartier. **P. 167:** From left to right: © Cartier, photo E. Sauvage © Cartier. Collection Cartier, photo Nick Welsh © Cartier. Collection Cartier, photo Nick Welsh © Cartier. Collection Cartier, photo Nick Welsh © Cartier. Collection Cartier, photo Nick Welsh © Cartier. Courtesy Sotheby's, photo Sotheby's. Collection Cartier, photo Nick Welsh © Cartier. **P. 168:** © Photo François Kollar / RMN. **P. 169:** Photo Katel Riou © Cartier. **P. 170:** Photo Henry Clarke, © *Vogue* / Condé-Nast. **P. 171:** Archives Cartier © Cartier. **P. 172:** Photo Mitchell Feinberg © Cartier. **P. 173:** From top to bottom: Courtesy Pierre Bergé & Associés, photo Philippe Sebert. Collection Cartier, photo Nick Welsh © Cartier. Collection Cartier, photo Nick Welsh © Cartier. **P. 174:** Photo Katel Riou © Cartier. **P. 175:** Photo Dorvyne © Cartier. **P. 176:** Courtesy Pierre Bergé & Associés, photo Philippe Sebert. **P. 177:** Collection Cartier, photo Nick Welsh © Cartier. **P. 178:** Collection Cartier, photo Nick Welsh © Cartier. **P. 179:** All photos: Archives Cartier © Cartier. Except, bottom: Courtesy Sotheby's, photo Sotheby's. **P. 180:** From top to bottom, from left to right: © Cartier. Courtesy Christie's, photo Christie's. Courtesy Sotheby's, photo Sotheby's. Photo Katel Riou © Cartier. Collection Cartier, photo Nick Welsh © Cartier. © Cartier, All rights reserved **P. 181:** Photo Helmut Newton, © *Vogue* / Condé-Nast. **P. 182:** Photo Helmut Newton, © *Vogue* / Condé-Nast. **P. 183:** All photos: Katel Riou © Cartier. Except, bottom right: Photo F. Dieleman © Cartier. **P. 184:** Photo Katel Riou © Cartier. **P. 185:** © *L'Officiel de la couture et de la mode.* **P. 186:** Archives Cartier © Cartier. **P. 187:** Archives Cartier © Cartier. **P. 188:** Courtesy Sotheby's, photo Sotheby's. **P. 189:** © Cartier. **P. 190:** Photo Rue des Archives. **P. 191:** Collection Cartier, photo Nick Welsh © Cartier. **P. 192:** Collection Cartier, photo Nick Welsh © Cartier. **P. 193:** © *L'Officiel de la couture et de la mode.* **PP. 194–195:** Courtesy Antiquorum, All rights reserved **P. 196:** Photo Helmut Newton for *Paris Match*. **P. 197:** Courtesy Sotheby's, photo Sotheby's. **P. 198:** © Cartier, photo Jacques Boulay. **P. 199:** © Cartier, photo Katel Riou. **P. 200:** Photo Katel Riou © Cartier. **P. 201:** Courtesy Sotheby's, photo Sotheby's. **P. 202:** Archives Cartier © Cartier. **P. 203:** Photo Tony Duquette Estate. **P. 204:** © Photo Cecil Beaton, courtesy Sotheby's London. **P. 205:** From top to bottom: Photo Jacques Boulay © Cartier. Archives Cartier © Cartier. **P. 206-207:** Photo Mitchell Feinberg © Cartier. **P. 208:** Archives Cartier © Cartier. **P. 209:** © Photo Cecil Beaton, courtesy Sotheby's London. **P. 210:** Courtesy Christie's, photo Christie's. Collection Cartier, photo Nick Welsh © Cartier. **P. 211:** Photo Katel Riou © Cartier. **P. 212:** Archives Cartier © Cartier. **P. 213:** Courtesy Elizabeth Arden © Cartier. **P. 214-215:** Archives Cartier © Cartier. **P. 216:** Photo Time Life Picture / Getty Images. **P. 217:** © *Time* Magazine / Getty Images. **P. 218:** Photo Katel Riou © Cartier. **P. 219:** From top to bottom: Courtesy Sotheby's, photo Sotheby's. Photo P. Lippmann © Cartier. **P. 220:** Photo Katel Riou © Cartier. **P. 221:** Collection Cartier, photo Nick Welsh © Cartier. **P. 222:** Photo Katel Riou © Cartier. **P. 223:** Photo M. Feinberg © Cartier. **P. 224:** From top to bottom: © Cartier. Photo Katel Riou © Cartier. **P. 225:** Photo Katel Riou © Cartier. **P. 226:** Courtesy Sotheby's, photo Sotheby's. **P. 227:** Photo Michel Feinberg © Cartier. **P. 228:** Photo Michel Feinberg © Cartier. **P. 229:** © Cartier. **P. 230-231:** Photo Patricia Canino © Éditions du Regard. **P. 232:** Photo Katel Riou © Cartier. **P. 233:** Collection Cartier, photo Nick Welsh © Cartier. **P. 234:** From top to bottom: Archives Cartier © *Paris-Match*. © Cartier. **P. 235:** Photo H. P. Horst. **P. 236:** Private collection. Photo Tino Hammid / GIA. **P. 237:** © Cartier. **P. 238:** From top to bottom: Courtesy Pierre Bergé & Associés, photo Philippe Sebert. Photo Roger Viollet. **P. 239:** Collection Cartier, photo Patricia Canino © Éditions du Regard. **P. 240:** Bert Stern, © *Vogue* / Condé Nast Publications Inc., Courtesy *Vogue US*. **P. 241:** Courtesy Sotheby's, photo Sotheby's. **P. 242:** Photo Katel Riou © Cartier. **P. 243:** Photo Michael Baumgarten © Cartier. **P. 244:** Private collection. © Cartier. **P. 245:** Courtesy Sotheby's, photo Sotheby's. Courtesy Artcurial, photo Philippe Sebert. Courtesy Artcurial, photo Philippe Sebert. **P. 246:** Collection Cartier, photo Nick Welsh © Cartier. **P. 247:** © *L'Officiel de la couture et de la mode.* **P. 248:** Courtesy Christie's, photo Christie's. **P. 249:** Collection Cartier, photo Nick Welsh © Cartier.

Acknowledgments

The publisher would like to thank Nadine Coleno for writing the text and Isabelle d'Hauteville for researching the illustrations for this book.

The publisher is also grateful to Bernard Fornas, Pierre Rainero, Michel Aliaga, Christine Borgoltz, Pascale Milhaud, Betty Jais, Bernhard Berger, and Véronique Sacuto.

Grateful acknowledgment to all those who contributed to this publication: Carl Adams; Antiquorum, Karin Tasso; Artcurial, Marie Saint Jalmes; Bénédicte Audiau; Christopher Banks; Charlotte Batchelor; Françoise Benoist; Pierre Bergé & Associés, Eric Marquand Gairard; Gregory Bishop; Nicole Bondino; Bonhams, Kirsten Everts; Thierry Bousquet; Odile Buruil; Brigitte Chabbert; Marie Claudel; Michèle Claudel; Christie's, Claire de Truchis Lauriston; Christie's Image Ltd., Angela Minshull; Conde Nast New York, Florence Palomo; Gwenael Connan; Céline Daudin-Bolliger; Jacques Diltoer; Éditions Jalou, Marie-Josée Susskind Jalou, Michèle Blaustein, Département du Patrimoine Gérald Chevalier, Nathalie Ifrah; Etude Eric Beaussant & Pierre-Yves Lefèvre, Soizic Michelin; Étude Olivier Couteau Begarie; Étude Tajan, Gabrielle Moral, Romain Monteaux Sarmiento; Fondation Pierre Cartier; Xavier Gargat; Monique Gay; Marie-Claire Jacobs; Jacqueline Karachi; Karry'O, Karine Ohana; Régine de Kerchove; Dominique Laffont; Mathilde Laurent; Karen Miller; Violette Petit; Phillips de Pury & Company, Cécile Demtchenko; Primavera Gallery, Audrey Friedman; Saint Louis University, Randy McGuire; Pauline Schaefer; Philippe Serret; Sotheby's New York, Jaclyn A. Carr, Carol P. Elkins, Valérie Vlasaty; Suzanne Tennenbaum. With special thanks to: Sotheby's Paris, Marie-Anne Bouet, Gabriella Mantegani.

Photographers
Agence Roger Viollet, Michael Baumgarten, Cecil Beaton, Jacques Boulay, Patricia Canino, Condé Nast Publications, Corbis, Frank Dieleman, Dorvyne, Tony Duquette Estate, Eyedea / Keystone, Mitchell Feinberg, Luc Fournol, Getty Images, Tino Hammid, Florian Kleinefenn, Peter Lippmann, Philippe Massard, Helmut Newton, *L'Officiel de la couture et de la mode*, André Ostier, Daniel Podva, Katel Riou, RMN Agence photographique, Rue des Archives, E. Sauvage, A. Savitch, Philippe Sebert, Ettore Sottsass, Jean-Michel Tardy, Louis Tirilly.

*

Design and Typesetting: Olivier Canaveso
Copyediting: Kate Clark
Proofreading: Chrisoula Petridis
Color Separation: L'Arte, Vitoria

Distributed in North America by Rizzoli International Publications, Inc.

Originally published in French as *Cartier Etourdissant*
© Éditions du Regard, Paris, 2008

This English-language edition
© Flammarion, Paris, 2009

All rights reserved.

No part of this publication may be reproduced in any form or by any means, electronic, photocopy, information retrieval system, or otherwise, without written permission from

Flammarion
87, quai Panhard et Levassor
75647 Paris Cedex 13

www.editions.flammarion.com

09 10 11   3 2 1

ISBN: 978-2-08-030098-0

Dépôt légal: 04/2009

Printed in Spain by Castuera SA